AF291290

# The Colour
# Bible

For Rufus *(ˈruːfəs)* my little 'red head'.

# The
# Colour
# Bible

The definitive guide to
colour in art and design
**Laura Perryman**

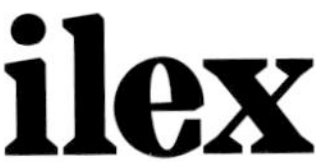

An Hachette UK Company
www.hachette.co.uk

First published in the United Kingdom in 2021
by ILEX, an imprint of Octopus Publishing Group Ltd,
Carmelite House, 50 Victoria Embankment,
London EC4Y 0DZ
www.octopusbooks.co.uk



While every effort has been made to trace the owners
of copyright material, to secure permissions and give
correct accreditation, the publishers would like to
apologise for any omissions and errors and will be
pleased to incorporate any missing information in
future editions of this book.

Publisher: Alison Starling
Commissioning Editor: Ellie Corbett
Managing Editor: Rachel Silverlight
Editorial Assistant: Ellen Sandford O'Neill
Art Director: Ben Gardiner
Design: She Was Only
Picture Research: Giulia Hetherington
Senior Production Manager: Katherine Hockley



ISBN 978-1-78157-784-4

A CIP catalogue record for this book is available
from the British Library

Printed and bound in China

10 9 8 7 6 5 4

## The Colours

# Preface

Colour is intrinsic to the human experience. It guides us with subconscious visual cues throughout our lives. Get it right in your design or art and you can enhance mood and atmosphere, and create a desired psychological or even physiological effect. Finding success in colour requires a level of nuance in approach, context, form and use, and that's where dedicated study of colour comes into play.

*The Colour Bible* is a contemporary handbook for navigating the fascinating world of colour. Inside you will find 100 significant colours and explore their importance or role in the world around us, from milestone industrial processes to social media sensations. Every colour profile starts from the colour's origin then tracks its evolution, historical use and where it lands today – the then and the now. Each entry finishes with a suggestion for the modern utility of the colour. It is vital that we look to the present: as contemporary designers and arbiters of choice, style and ethical practice, we each have a role to play in selecting colour that has real value and meaning behind it, with the wellbeing of humans and of the planet at the forefront of our minds.

This edit includes only a fraction of the colours we see and experience, and the selection is based on my own research, associations and informed preferences. The shades were chosen by observing the physical materials used in art and design as well as the resulting outcomes. Each chapter also reveals much about my own background and working methods as a design trend forecaster. I'm naturally drawn to sourcing visual cues, ordering and connecting ideas, and that is reflected in these pages. Colour has many facets, and this isn't a list of colours from a paint chart; colours represent much more than physical pigment – they are digital, material and even little pieces of cultural narrative.

This book is not just about singular colours; it's also about how to create successful palettes, and that is where context and colour relationships come into play, as the context reveals other supportive tones and hues in which successful palettes can be observed and then formed. Colour choice can be daunting, but with practice anyone can learn to create colour combinations by eye in an instinctual way by exploring simple principles such as opposing cool and warm colours, and learning to recognize harmonious and dynamic colour pairings.

The book aims to be an inspirational resource for your journey with colour; to help you make informed decisions in your work and art. Colour is complex, a sum of many parts and approaches, and it's critical to understand the core ideas before searching for new ones. Colour is useful beyond pure aesthetic appeal: it can aid, guide and connect objects, services, people and communities. Look to the work of ink-makers, pigment-producers, artists, designers, architects, manufacturers, scientists and even bioengineers to unlock this medium's true potential.

'Colour choice can be daunting, but with practice anyone can learn to create colour combinations by eye in an instinctual way.'

# Colour & Light

In the most basic sense, we see different colours because different objects absorb or reflect different wavelengths of light depending on their physicality or matter. When the wavelengths they reflect reach our eyes, light receptors transmit messages to the brain via the optic nerve. The brain then interprets these messages as colour. Humans are trichromats, meaning that our eyes have three cones that interpret colour – one for red wavelengths, one for blue and one for green – with the potential to distinguish a million distinct colours.

The colour spectrum was first identified by Isaac Newton in 1666. By splitting a ray of white light through a prism, he cast a rainbow on his wall and divided the spectrum into seven observable zones: red, orange, yellow, green, blue, indigo and violet. We are now able to identify the wavelengths that make up Newton's spectrum, which are measured in nanometers, and we know that the visible section only makes up a part of the broader electromagnetic spectrum of light. Our eyes find it harder to interpret colours at the edges of the colour spectrum, namely red and violet, and are more able to read yellow, green and blue tones in the middle. The fringes of infrared and ultraviolet are in fact invisible to the human eye. At one end, violet (380–450nm) has the shortest wavelength and therefore the highest frequency and energy, and at the other, red (620–750nm) has the longest wavelength and therefore the shortest frequency and lowest energy.

'Colours and light...stand in the most intimate relation to each other.'
– Johann Wolfgang von Goethe

These delineated colour zones bleed into one another: greens range from grassy yellow tones to watery teals as they begin to encroach upon the blues. It's hard to say precisely where we can locate the perfect shade of shimmering emerald, but it sits somewhere just before green tips into the blues. Half the allure of colour is the hunt for the perfect shade, to reproduce what we've witnessed in nature or even to invent a new hue that might exist only in the mind's eye, or not at all before its creation. The advancement of colour has always been a balance between happy accidents and focused pursuit, but throughout its history, colour has repeatedly shown its capacity to surprise us, to fascinate us and often to help us in unexpected ways.

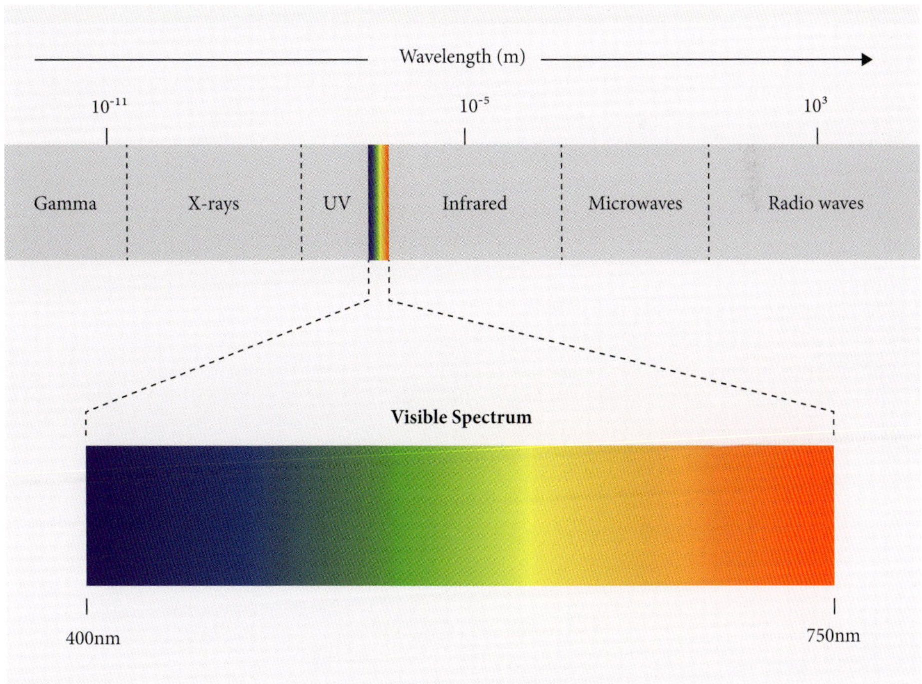

# Addition & Subtraction: Material & Immaterial Colour

The interplay of primary colours is fundamental to how we craft colour for use in art and design, both in print and on screen, but there are different models of primaries depending on the nature of our medium. First, it depends on whether we are working with immaterial colour, or light, which entails an *additive* system, or material colour, such as paint and ink, which is known as *subtractive*.

Artists and designers who work with light as a medium rely on additive colour theory. Light has three primary colours from which the other spectral colours can be made: red, green and blue (RGB). An overlap of pure red and green light makes yellow; green and blue make cyan; and red and blue create magenta. If all three overlap in one spot, they make white light – hence the term additive, because adding colour adds light. RGB is the colour system used for digital displays such as computer and phone screens.

The subtractive colour method that applies to physical colour takes yellow, cyan and magenta as its primaries (CMY), while red, blue and green are secondary shades. Colour mixing in this system subtracts the amount of reflective light: adding more different colours gives a darker result. Fully coalesced, CMY creates a murky mud colour, hence the need for a pure black to be added to the trio to complete the CMYK four-colour process that was developed specifically for the print industry. The unspoken letter in this system would be W for white – the base colour of the paper that designers learn to work with instinctively.

Subtractive colour also includes the red, yellow and blue primary model (RYB), developed for painters as a tool to explain colour relationships, and the system most commonly used in school art classes. In most fields today, this has been largely replaced by the RGB/CMY models that offer a gamut of colours more relevant to modern uses.



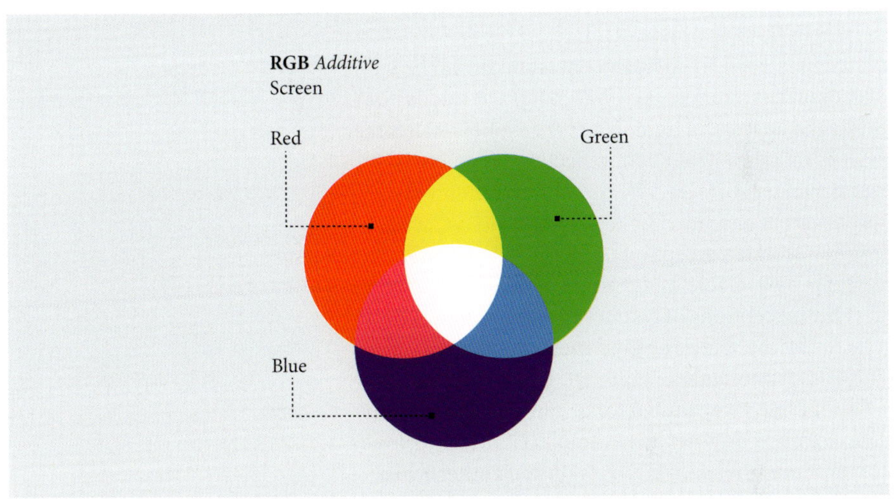


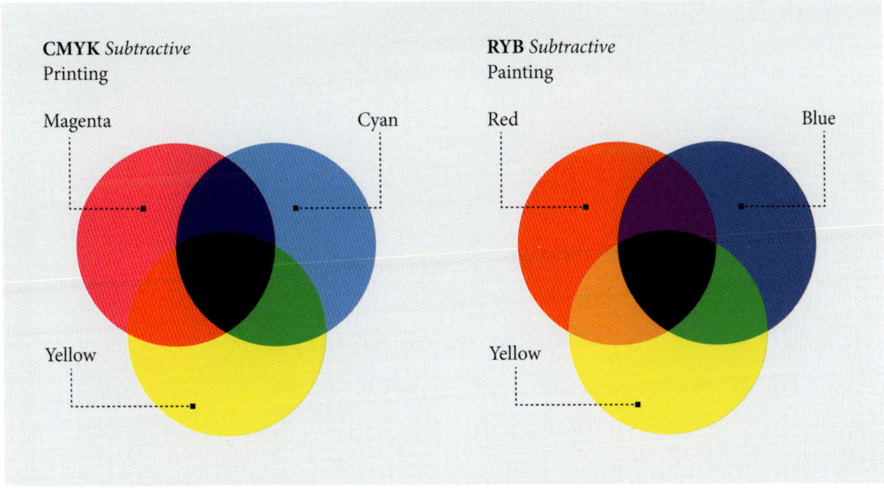

 # Colour & Visual Perception

Bias or debate around precise shades is a natural human response. As artist Josef Albers reflected, 'If one says "red" – the name of a color – and there are 50 people listening, it can be expected that there will be 50 reds in their minds."* One reason is that reflective light depends on its environment: sunlight in the late afternoon has a different colour to light at midday or at dusk. The amount of light in a space makes a difference, as does influence from light reflecting off coloured walls or other surfaces. The use of LEDs, fluorescent, incandescent and other artificial lights do no favours for the accurate perception of physical colour if the full gamut is only visible under white, 'daylight' conditions.

Our perceptions of colours and tones are also affected by the shades around them, a phenomenon known as 'simultaneous contrast'. Placing a saturated colour beside more muted tones can make the bright colour appear brighter, for example. Contrasting tones can produce unexpected effects on each other when closely placed, for instance what appears a vibrant red in isolation can take on an orange hue when placed next to blue, as our eyes try to balance the contrast.

We should aim to see these subtle variances, as

'The sensation of colour is a reverberation of light, originating on a surface of an object, which then absorbs, reflects and resonates and finally evolves into a tangible material phenomenon.' – Hella Jongerius

* Albers, Josef *The Interaction of Color*, 50th Anniversary Edition, New Haven and London: Yale University Press, 2013

many artists have done in the past, as opportunities. Hella Jongerius is a contemporary designer who studies the evolution of light throughout the day through materials. The textured forms of her vessels break the changing light into patterns of tone and colour, revealing the interplay between light, colour and form.

Colour systems tend to be printed on brilliant white paper stock, but the reality is that very little is genuinely white in the world. The consistency, texture and tonality of the base material – onto which the colour will be added or which comprises the colour itself (a pigment, for example) – can drastically affect how the colour is perceived. (See also Colour & Material, page 30.)

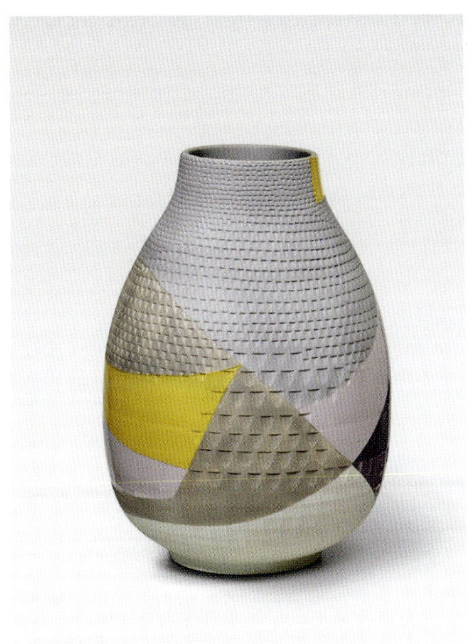
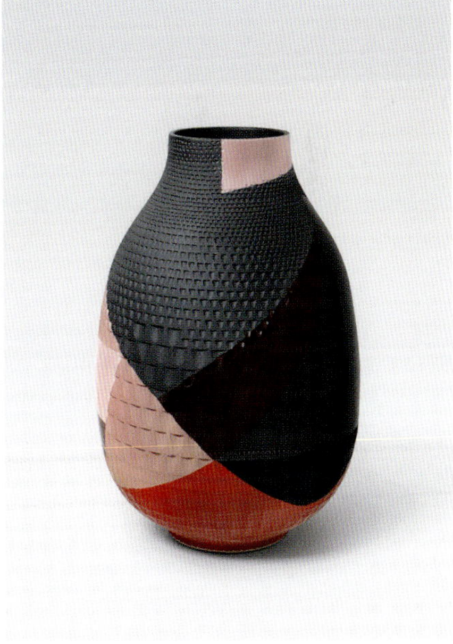

Diamond vase, Day and Diamond vase, Night by Hella Jongerius, 2019. Limited Edition Galerie kreo

# Colour Theory

You might remember being taught the basics of colour theory at school by mixing pots of primary red, yellow and blue paints. Basic colour principles can help us use colour more effectively, and ensure you pick the right type of palette for your projects. The following timeline highlights ideas that have transformed our understanding of colour.

**A brief history of colour theory**

**Aristotle (384–322 BCE):**
Aristotle developed what is generally thought of as the first linear colour scale, from white at midday to black at midnight. He also proposed that all hues came from light/white and black/no light.

**Isaac Newton (1642–1727):**
Newton's work established the relationship between colour and wavelengths of light, identifying seven distinct colours in the visible light spectrum. A new interest in colour theory took off from this point.

**Jacob Christoph le Blon (1667–1741):**
Le Blon invented the system of three- and four-colour printing, using an RYB-K colour model similar to the modern CMYK system. Using the mezzotint method, he proved you can create a wide range of colours by layering these simple primaries in different densities.

**Moses Harris (1730–1787):**
An entomologist and engraver by trade, Harris's 1766 *The Natural System of Colours* presented a comprehensive colour system, with two colour wheels that broke colours down into 18 'prismatic' hues based on RYB primaries, and 18 compounds based on the 'mediates'.

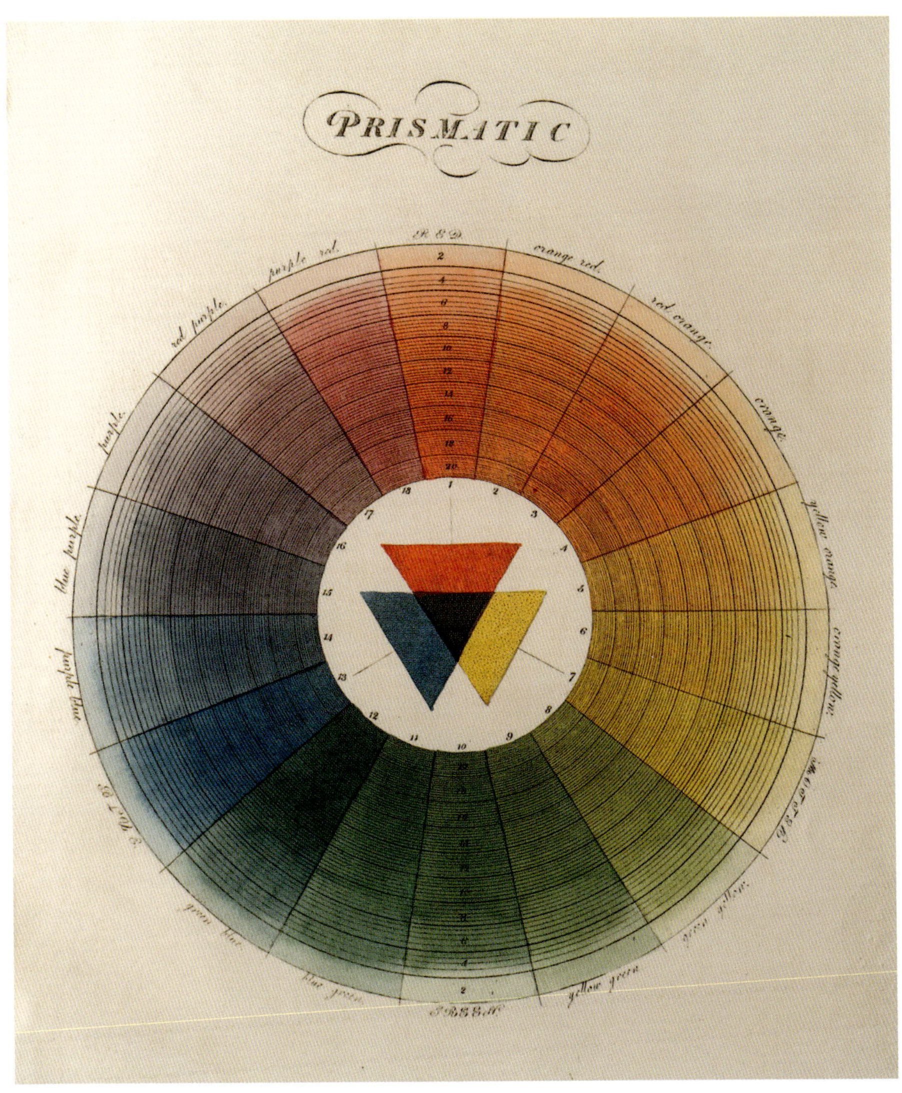


Prismatic Color Wheel by Moses Harris, 1766

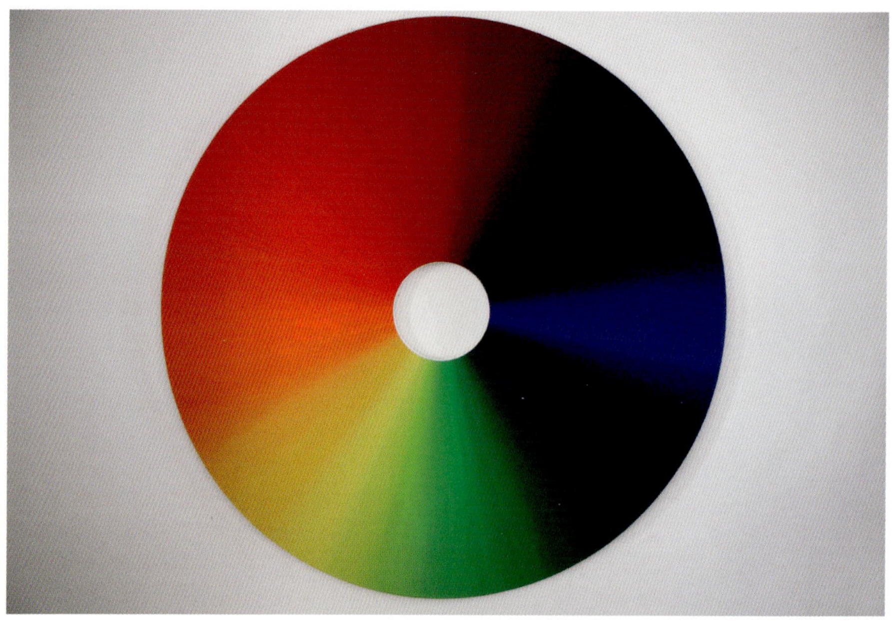

*Colour experiment No. 10*, by Olafur Eliasson, 2010

**Michel Eugène Chevreul (1786–1889):**
Chevreul's *Laws of Simultaneous Contrast* (1839)
demonstrates his influential theory that it is not the
material aspect of a colour that is most important but
how it is perceived by the viewer. He coined the idea of
'contrast', describing the optical mixing that happens
when colours are affected by those around them.

**Albert Munsell (1858–1918):**
Munsell created the first functional and universal colour-
matching tool, allowing for the accurate reproduction of
colours. Explaining colour through numerical systems
of hue, value and chroma, his work gave birth to a
standardization of colour still widely used by industry
today, laying the foundation for ordered colour libraries
such as Pantone, NCS and RAL (see Colour Systems,
page 42).

**The Bauhaus (1919–1933):**
The combined teachings of Johannes Itten, Wassily
Kandinsky, Paul Klee and Josef Albers contributed
to what we know today as applied colour theory. The
movement developed the idea of colour's synaesthetic
qualities – relating colour to shape and form, as well as
music – and built on Chevreul's work on simultaneous
contrast to outline key contrast effects and properties.
Albers went on to write his seminal *Interaction of
Color* (1963) that helped train artists and designers to
interpret colour through examples of colour harmony,
juxtaposition and simultaneous contrast.

**Olafur Eliasson (1967–):**
In an ongoing project that began in 2009, Eliasson
worked with a chemist to create a model representing
an exact pigment match for every nanometre of the
visible spectrum. He went on to use this palette to create
painted works on circular canvases, known collectively
as the *Colour Experiment Paintings*. By transforming
what we perceive in light (RGB) into physical pigment,
the model represents a single, cohesive colour theory.

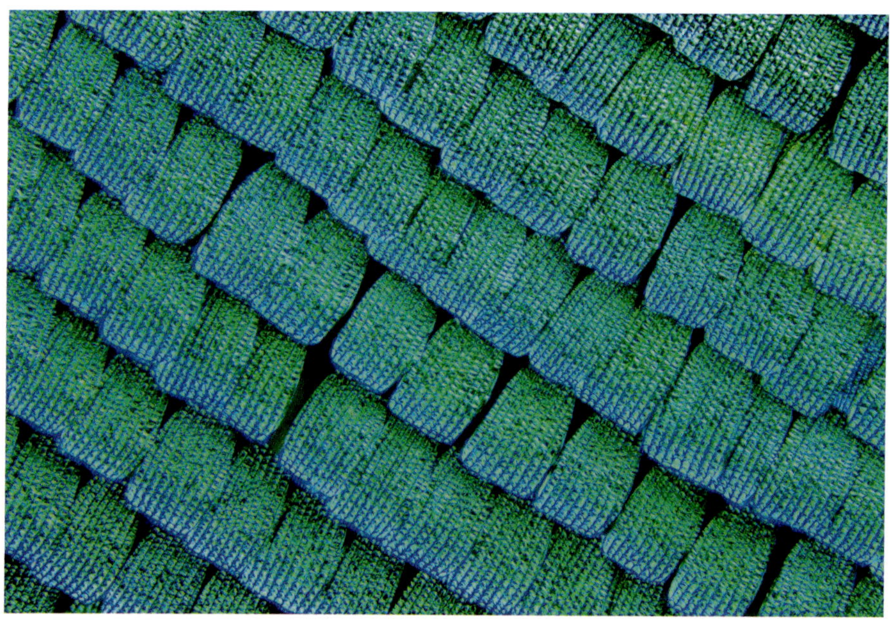

Photonic crystals in the wing scales of some butterfly species enable them to shine

**Colour into the 21st Century**

Today, leaps in science and technology, and knowledge of the way colour is embedded in materials, have profoundly changed how we see, feel and relate to colour. Carriers such as liquid-suspended pigments, glossy plastics, plied weft fibres and layered computerized dots have indeed led to dimension and nuance. The Structural Colour Studio, a research platform at Finland's Aalto University, has proven that non-pigmented photonic crystals (found in nature), which assume shades through their contact with light alone, can be engineered to surfaces. The result is a shimmering polychromic spectrum rather than just one flat hue.

As we continue to develop our understanding of what colour is – and what it can do – materiality may well be key to the future of colour theory. Almost all the colour chapters in this book include at least one colour or pigment that pushes the boundaries of our traditional ideas about colour, from the plant-derived pigments with extraordinary qualities to the engineered substances with untold possibilities.

 # The Colour Wheel

First visualized in the 17th century, today, the colour wheel is one of the most useful tools for understanding colour relationships. Unlike most colour wheels, which are based on the subtractive RYB model, the wheel opposite is based on the RGB/additive CMY/ subtractive models, whose primary colours form each other's secondaries, with tertiaries in between.

Although the wheel neatly divides colour into distinctive colours, the full spectrum contains a plethora of nuanced shades in between each distinct hue. Its basic circular form shows us that colour is connected while also allowing us to see at a glance how distinct primary, secondary and tertiary colours relate to each other. It also indicates how the spectrum can also be graded into values of lightness and darkness, helping us to grasp a sense of the full dimension of colour.

Over the follow pages you will find some key colour relationships, and how they relate to the colour wheel. It will be useful to familiarize yourself with some of the key terms used to describe colour and colour relationships, which will pop up throughout this book.

**RGB/CMY Colour Wheel**

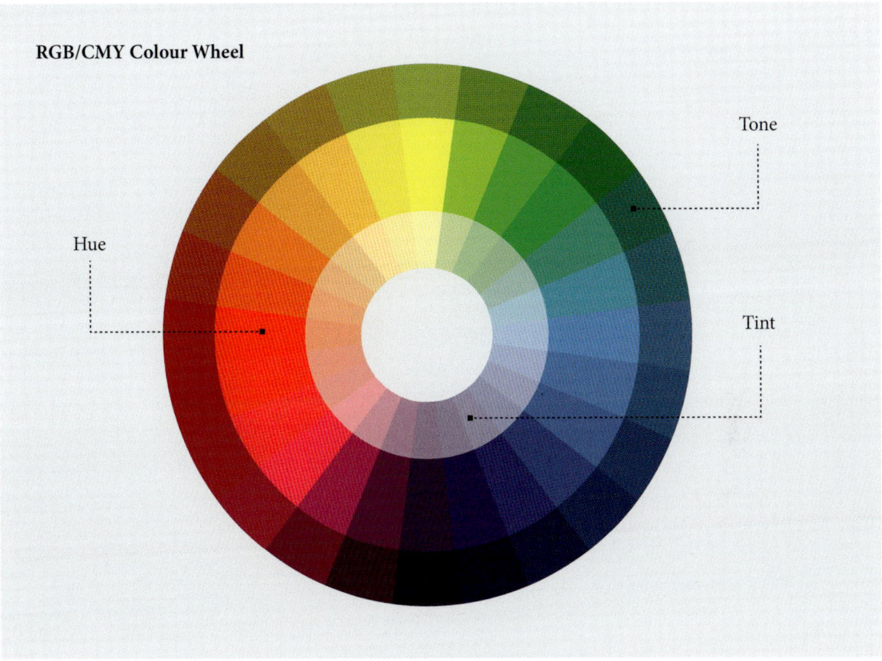



## Key Terms

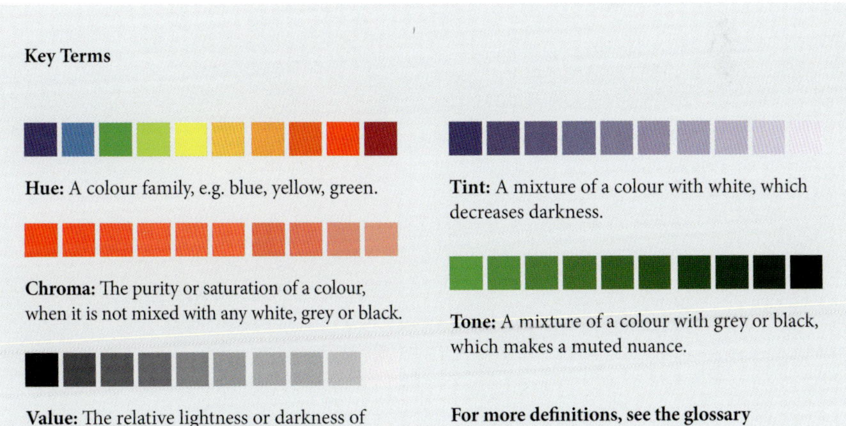

**Hue:** A colour family, e.g. blue, yellow, green.

**Chroma:** The purity or saturation of a colour, when it is not mixed with any white, grey or black.

**Value:** The relative lightness or darkness of a colour.

**Tint:** A mixture of a colour with white, which decreases darkness.

**Tone:** A mixture of a colour with grey or black, which makes a muted nuance.

**For more definitions, see the glossary on page 46.**

**Primary Colours**

The main hues that can be mixed to achieve other all other colours. They cannot be made from any other colours and are therefore considered to be 'pure'. Primary colours vary according to different colour models; the one illustrated below is the familiar model based on RYB primaries.

**Secondary Colours**

Colours that can be made from mixing two primary colours. For example, in RYB models, red and yellow create orange. Secondary hues are often easier to look at and use as pure chromas than primaries.

**Tertiary Colours**

Intermediate colours on the colour wheel, made from mixing one primary and one secondary colour; for example, blue and green make blue-green (teal). Tertiary colours can also be created by mixing two secondaries – for example, green-orange (citron) – and in theory, the more you mix, the more nuanced the colour becomes: mix citron with russet (an orange-purple) and you'll get shades of buff or taupe.

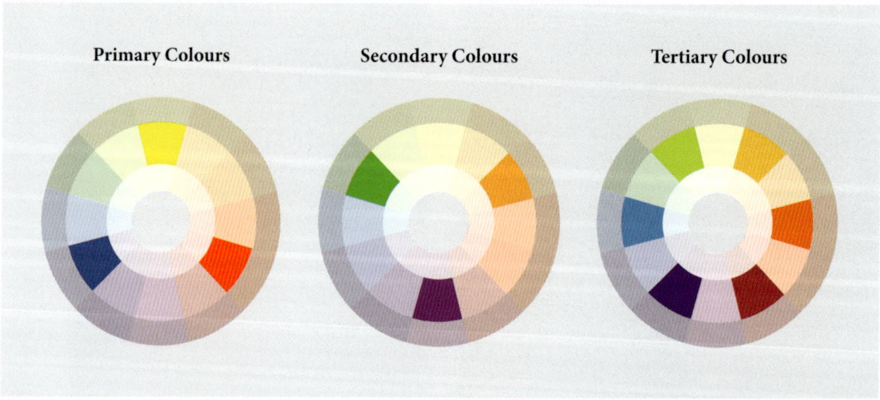

**Monochromatic**

A colour scheme based on one hue that may be varied with tones or tints. The visual effect is simple and sophisticated, streamlining forms and minimizing distractions. Example approaches appear in *Carmine (page 64), Indigo (page 168), Violet (page 210), and Charcoal (page 278).*

**Analogous**

Colours that are neighbours on the colour wheel, such as green-yellow, yellow and yellow-orange. Analogous designs are harmonious by nature and can be used to evoke specific moods such as tranquility or warmth. *See Madder (page 70), Yellow-Red (page 86) and Bottle Green (page 148).*

**Complementary**

Opposites attract, and it's no different with colours directly opposite each other on the colour wheel, such as blue and orange. Used together, these pairings create visual energy and interest. You can play with proportions to create different effects, and you can create calmer combinations by making one colour lighter and the opposite darker. *See Tangerine (page 92), High-Vis Orange (page 102), Glaucous (page 142) and Teal (page 188).*

**Split Complementary/Compound**

A three-colour palette based on complementary principles, but it uses the two colours on either side of a colour's opposite number rather than the opposite itself. Split-complementary designs still have strong contrast but feel a bit more balanced than straightforward complementary pairs. *See Emerald Green (page 146), Pale Pink (page 232) and Burnt Sienna (page 298).*

**Dyad**

Two colours that are two spaces apart on the colour
wheel, such as blue-violet and blue-green. The closeness
of the colours lends a dyadic pair natural harmony
while the degree of separation creates visual interest.
This approach can include lighter tints as well as darker
tonal combinations. *See Faded Sunflower (page 120) and
Prussian Blue (page 178).*

**Triad**

Three colours evenly spaced on the colour wheel e.g.,
violet, orange and green. This is a vibrant combination
that often works best with one dominant colour and two
accent colours within a palette. *See Blood Red (page
72), Coral (page 100) and Heliotrope (page 214) .*

**Tetrad**

Four colours spaced evenly on the wheel – or two sets of
complementary opposites. A trick often used in fashion,
tetradic groupings result in bold designs that offer both
contrast and harmony, with the success of a combination
highly dependent on the proportions used. *See Lemon
Yellow (page 112) and Wheat (page 122).*

**Cool & Warm Colours**

Colours associated with heat and fire (yellows, oranges
and reds) are considered to be warm in temperature;
colours we associate with cool things such as ice and
water (mainly blues) are cool in temperature. Greens
and purples have qualities of both. Temperature is
relevant to all hue families – a yellow may be cooler
than another if it has more green present, for instance.
*See Electric Lime (page 160).*

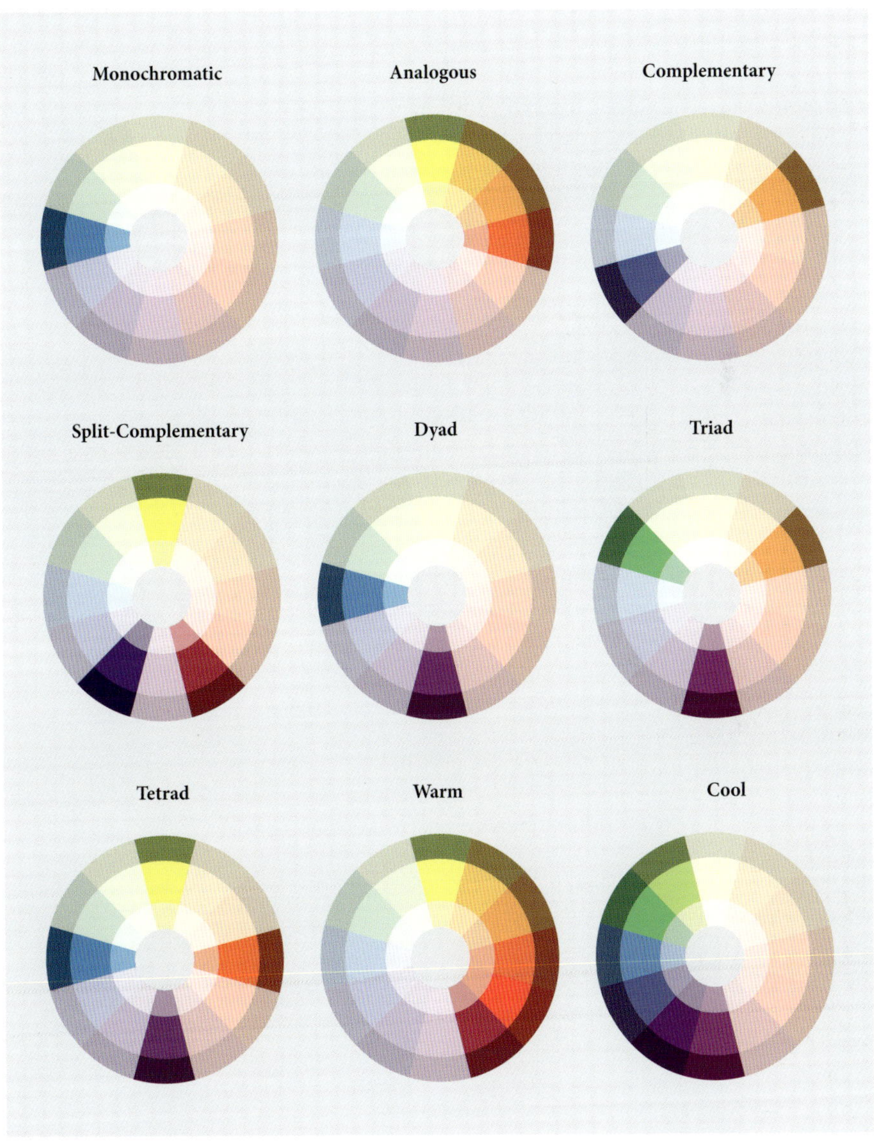

Monochromatic
Analogous
Complementary
Split-Complementary
Dyad
Triad
Tetrad
Warm
Cool

 # Colour Proportions

Knowledge of colour behaviours and attributes in different combinations and contexts is essential to achieving good colour proportions. The total number of colours chosen for a palette affects the outcome, as does the quantities in which they are used, and many other factors besides. Josef Albers' *Homage to the Square* series is a 26-year experiment in which everything in the composition of the paintings stays the same except the palette, allowing the artist to explore the effects of colour interactions. The possible combinations are infinite, so the below just offers a starting point; in addition to the contrasts outlined here, the colour relationships described over the previous pages will always factor in.

**Contrast of Quantity:**
Using two or three colours in different quantities forms a simple dynamic between the dominant and supporting colours.

**Contrast of Saturation:**
Combinations of pure, chromatic colours with more muted or low-chroma tints or tones from the same hue range can draw the eye to critical details and create supportive backgrounds.

**Contrast of Value:**
Tonal contrasts can influence mood and atmosphere. Strong tonal contrasts across a large space can be dramatic and energizing or provide structure. Try framing a light area between two areas of darkness to create a strong visual focus – a technique known as chiaroscuro in painting. Schemes with little tonal contrast can offer a soothing environment.

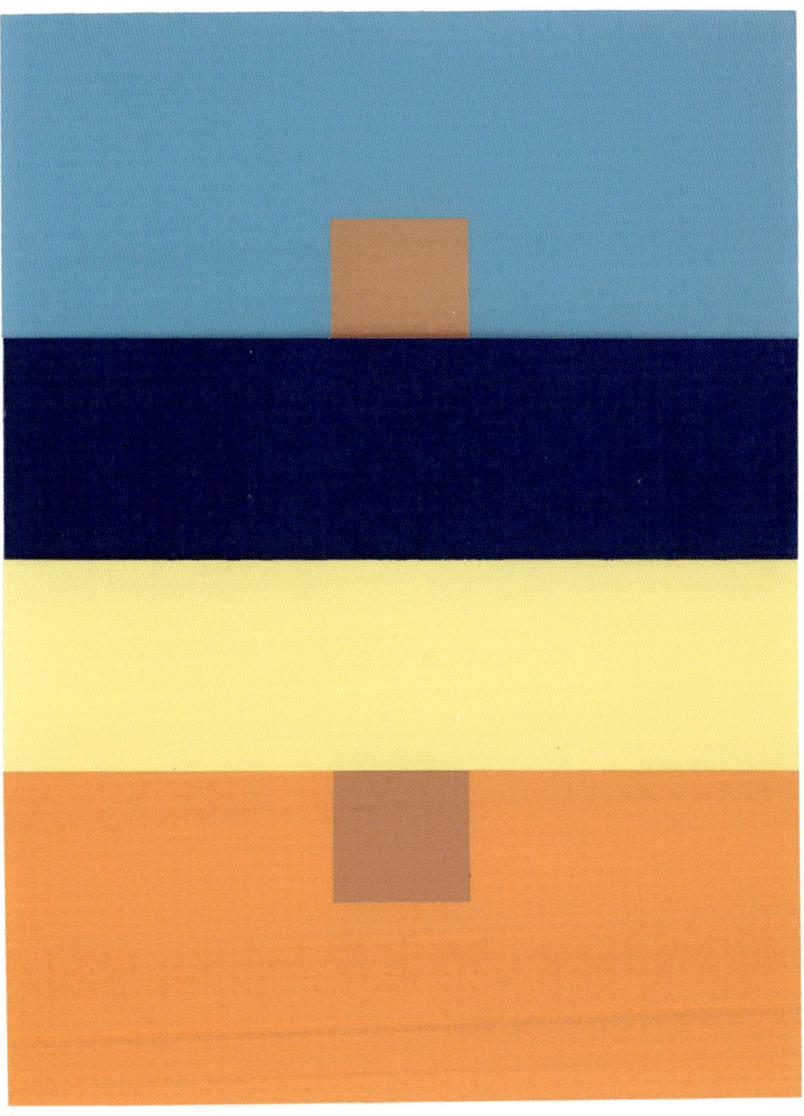

Josef Albers, *Interaction of Colour*, Plate IV-1b, 1973

**Contrasts of Quantity** *(Bottle Green, page 149)*

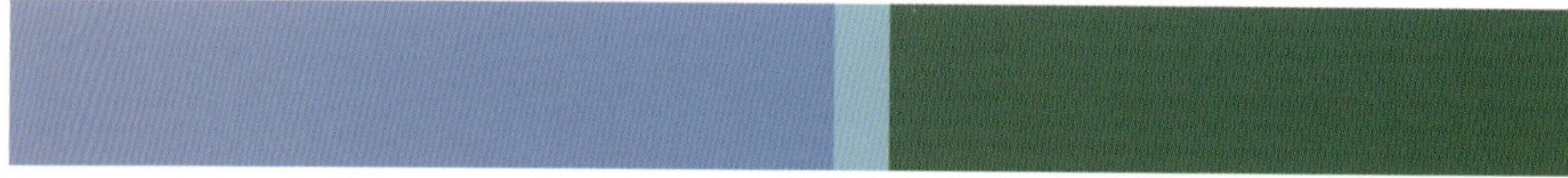

**Contrasts of Saturation** *(Indigo page 171)*

**Contrasts of Value** *(Van Dyke Brown page 293)*

**Contrasts of Chroma** *(Factory Yellow page 116)*

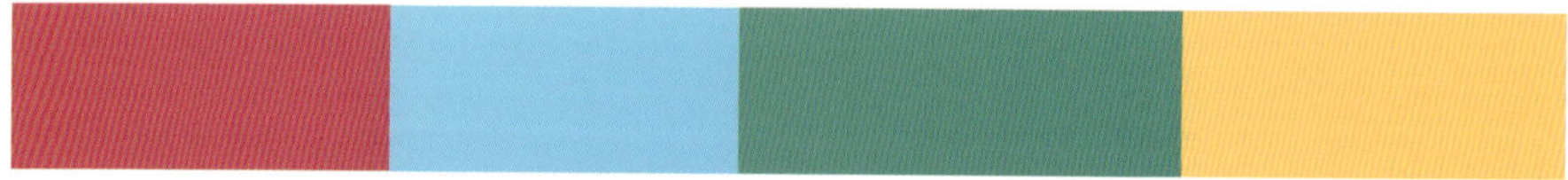

**Contrasts of Neutral & Chroma** *(Vital Green page 156)*

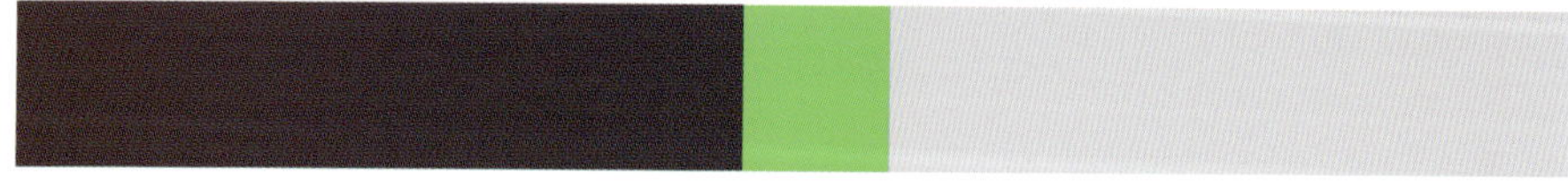

**Contrasts of Temperature** *(Scarlet page 63)*

**Contrasts of Chroma:**
Combinations of hues with chromas that are the same level of intensity can create a vibrant, cohesive harmony. If you want to create impact, try out three or four matching high-chroma colours together, but be mindful that they must really match: if they are only similar, they will cause visual tension.

**Contrasts of Neutral & Chroma:**
A slice of a saturated hue among a predominantly neutral scheme can enliven the more subtle shades and will immediately draw the eye to a key function or detail. Conversely, achromatic black and white can be used to temper or frame strong chroma hues.

**Contrasts of Temperature:**
A simple yet key combination of the fundamental complementary shades, warm and cool. Place warm oranges on a background of blues and your eye will be immediately drawn through the composition to the warmth. Also useful with low-chroma combinations to encourage engagement without tiring out the eyes.

'[C]olor, as the most relative medium in art, has innumerable faces or appearances. To study them in their respective interactions, in their interdependence, will enrich our "seeing," our world – and ourselves.'
– Josef Albers

# Colour & Material

From the precious stones used to make pigments that captured many artists' imaginations to the rise of material literacy in art and design in the later part of the 20th century and into the 21st – understanding material is the key to understanding the genesis and history of colour.

The first pigments were made by hand. Until the 20th century, washing, thinning, smelting, crushing, grinding and mixing with chalk, oils, animal fats or egg to give different effects was still common practice. Plants provided deep yellows; reds such as scarlet came from insects; prized purples came from sea snails. Shades were often available only to the regions where the base materials could be found or the techniques for their production known. When it comes to creating new colours, science, technology, art and design have played equal and symbiotic roles. The modern dye industry was devised and cultivated by the demand for colour: Van Dyke's quest for all-encompassing shadows saw him devise a pigment from soil, while Yves Klein applied chemistry to create a new vibrant and arresting blue.

**Raw Material**

In some cases, a material's inherent colour has been celebrated and exploited to create tone and shade. Many modern artists such as Max Lamb and Donald Judd have worked with raw materials as a primal aesthetic expression, either leaving them unprocessed or enhancing their surfaces with heat and chemicals, creating serendipitous outcomes. *See Copper (page 98), Smalt (page 180) Silver (page 266) and Aluminium (page 268).*

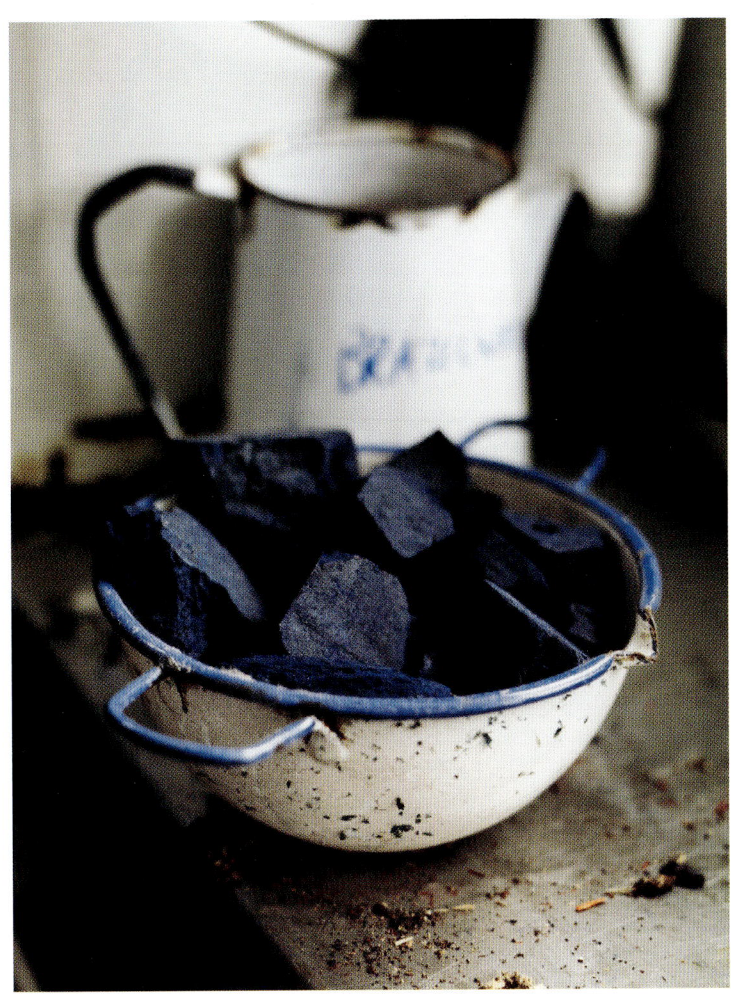

Blocks of indigo pigment

**Light as a Medium**

Shimmering light always catches the human eye. Artists such as Jan van Eyck mastered the replication of light in paint form by using gems and jewels in his pigment concoctions. Contemporary artists have even used coloured light instead of pigment; for example, James Turrell's incandescent art mimics the changing conditions of night and day. New disciplines such as 3D visualization and digital arts are changing our perception of colour all over again. *See Reactive Red (page 80), Vital Green (page 154), Neon Pink (page 226) and Lunar White (page 254).*

**Scientific Colour**

Modern science links colour to material and performance to take colour beyond aesthetics. The photosynthetic qualities of natural pigments such as chlorophyll can be harnessed to generate energy, while the blackest nanotubes repel detection. Meanwhile, new colour technology can limit production waste, with colour biofabricated directly into material surfaces. *See Chlorophyll (page 162), YInMn Blue (page 198), Living Lilac (page 238) and Vantablack (page 286).*

**Waste Colour**

Colour derived from post-consumer, industrial or agricultural waste is being harnessed by designers in order to curb landfill, resulting in recycled hues that are unusual and diverse. Common examples include vegetable dyes derived from agricultural waste and metal-tinted glazes from post-industrial waste. *See Red Ochre, (page 54), Beetroot (page 236) and Slag (page 276).*

**Base Material**



Material is also important insofar as it refers to the base that a pigment is applied to. Generally, the colour of a base material will contribute some of its colour to the mixture of pigments applied; for example, a silvery aluminium plate will never render a true neutral black as there is too much yellow in the substrate. If a piece of fabric is already blue, it will never turn yellow with transparent dyes alone.

There are some industry tricks to get around this, however: in CMYK printing, it is possible to print a spot white before the colour goes on top, to eliminate any colour contamination. But these controlled approaches are not necessarily appropriate in every situation. In a world choked by waste-generating processes, it might be worth abiding or even celebrating the unexpected effects we get when our material's inherent colour speaks for itself.

'When it comes to creating new colours, science, technology, art and design have played equal and symbiotic roles.'

 # Psychology of Colour

Colour psychology is a relatively new area of research that works on the principle that the impact colours have on us goes beyond aesthetics. Psychologist Angela Wright highlights the effect colours can have on our mood when she describes the way coloured light wavelengths are transmitted via the eyes to the brain and 'eventually to the hypothalamus, which governs the endocrine glands, which in turn produce and secrete our hormones. In simple terms, each colour (wavelength) focuses on a particular part of the body, evoking a specific physiological response, which in turn produces a psychological reaction.'*

'Soon it got dusk, a grapy dusk, a purple dusk over tangerine groves and long melon fields; the sun the colour of pressed grapes, slashed with burgundy red, the fields the colour of love and Spanish mysteries.'
– Jack Kerouac, *On the Road*

* Sevenic, Kurt and Kelechi Kingsley, Osueke, 'The Effects of Color on the Moods of College Students', Sage Journals, 2014
*https://journals.sagepub.com/doi/full/10.1177/2158244014525423*

Colour psychology proposes that different colours have distinct effects that influence sensory, emotional and physical responses. Colours like Reactive Red (see page 80) can produce a physiological effect, increasing our heart rates as our brain interprets danger, while other colours, such as a Baker-Miller Pink (see page 224), have been developed specifically to soothe. The term 'sensorial association' is used to describe the mental connection we might have with a particular shade. It can be personal and meaningful for individuals or collectively applied to certain brands or experiences. Colour perception is also affected by cultural associations; deeply embedded connotations often linked to religion, tradition and even propaganda. Specific colours may have coded symbolism in certain cultures, such as white, which signifies purity and death in China, or marigold yellow, which signals rebirth in Mexico. Finally, our associations are affected by the contemporary zeitgeist: how we feel about ourselves in our individual tribes and as part of a wider culture; how we see colour used in different contexts; the myriad ideas and influences we are exposed to in our daily lives that directly or indirectly alter our perceptions.

Overleaf you will find some of the psychological effects or associations we might expect certain shades to produce. Different times, cultures and contexts all interpret colours differently, so this should be seen as a jumping-off point for initial inspiration and perhaps further research.

**Passionate, Adored, Powerful**
The hottest and most dynamic
primary hue, red, is activating,
stimulating and expanding. In
full saturation, it draws attention
and excites.

**Energizing, Responsive, Vital**
Gentler than red and yellow, orange
is friendly, warming and genuine.
A flexible secondary hue, it's perfect
for communicating vital information.

**Happy, Hopeful, Utopic**
If optimism were a hue, it would
be yellow. Visually stimulating
and refreshing to contemplate, it
combines with other colours to
create a variety of moods.

**Fresh, Abundant, Soothing**
Calming, balancing and rejuvenating, green is the most restful colour to look at. Pale shades pacify while darker shades create a contemplative mood.

**Calm, Divine, Meditative**
Deeply connected with the natural world, blue is easy on the eye and mind. Lighter tints are expansive and serene while darker shades are perceived as reliable and trustworthy.

**Royal, Creative, Spiritual**
A shade associated with spiritual connection, purple speaks of awareness and reflection. Light colours evoke play and creativity while deeper shades have a distinctive, mysterious allure.

**Calm, Youthful, Modern**
A soft and appealing shade with
a powerful, rebellious side. Low
chroma pinks express empathy and
lower heart rates, while powerful
magentas burst with energy.

**Human, Elegant, Gentle**
The family of pales ranges the whole
gamut of subtle hues. Softened and
muted, pale neutrals invite us to
perceive the nuances, encouraging
calm and mindful attitudes.

**Pure, Clean, Minimal**
Pure white is often a starting
point. We perceive it to be
clean, but when used in too
great a proportion it can be
sterile and off-putting.

**Moody, Conservative, Universal**
Although perhaps dull and conservative at first glance, greys communicate serene neutrality and appear tranquil to our eyes. Less intense than darker neutrals, they have become a modern default in an often complicated world.

**Mysterious, Elegant, Innovative**
Night-dark shades can seem as deep and full as brilliant whites appear stark and empty. Physiologically, they offer a safe place to hide or be concealed, and they can be deeply meditative.

**Natural, Wholesome, Regenerative**
The colour of the earth, shades of brown represent nature and its cyclicity. Dependable and grounding, humble brown can help us feel calm and secure.

# Key Names in Colour Psychology

**Johann Wolfgang Goethe (1749–1832):**
The German author and polymath devised principles
using experiments to demonstrate not only the optical
effects of colours but also their emotional effects. His
subjective colour system was theoretically woolly but
highly influential for later artists and thinkers.

**Carl Jung (1857–1961):**
The Swiss psychoanalyst defined the link between
colour perception and association. His idea of
'individual preference' – that we are personally
influenced by learned, suppressed and inherited
experience – is integral to colour perception.

**Johannes Itten (1888–1967):**
The artist and Bauhaus teacher aimed to free colour
from its shackling associations with form by devising
a subjective system based on psychoanalysis and
analogous associations. His gridded visual experiments
reference nature and the seasons to explore theories of
colour harmony.

**Angela Wright (1934–):**
Wright's Colour Affects System applied scientific
methodology to the psychological effects of colour
for the first time. Her findings established that
different personality types can be linked with specific
colour groups, and that each hue produces particular
psychological responses.

**Karen Haller (1961–):**
Working with applied psychology in a commercial, industrial context, Haller's practice is rooted in the belief that colour selection can influence consumer/user behaviour across all design fields.

**Bevil Conway (1974–):**
Neuroaesthetics is a new and burgeoning field of study mixing psychological and neural research with aesthetics. By mapping the brain, Conway has been able to show in studies how individual colours elicit unique patterns of emotion. Brands including Google and IKEA are starting to use these techniques to track consumer preferences.

'He who wishes to become a master of colour must see, feel and experience each individual colour in its endless combinations with all other colours.'
– Johannes Itten

 # Colour Systems

Finding the best or most useful arrangement of the colour spectrum is a task that has preoccupied thinkers since Aristotle first presented it as a day-to-night continuum in the 4th century BCE. More modern systems have aimed to develop a common language of colour: entomologist Moses Harris developed his colour system to fulfil the need for accurate and consistent identification or description of colours seen in nature; Charles Darwin took a copy of *Werner's Nomenclature of Colours* – a 19th-century catalogue of colours with their flora, fauna and mineral equivalents – on his voyage on the *Beagle* for the same reason; and it is no different today. One Pantone 7652 C will be the same as another Pantone 7652 C, no matter where you are in the world.

Today, we live with colour system idioms such as 'hex code' and 'CMYK' in our everyday lives. Trending colours like 'Living Coral 16-1546' and 'Cool Gray 9' have been celebrated on mugs and T-shirts. By learning how to read these codes like geographic coordinates, we can learn to identify and use colours up and down the chromatic spectrum. The colours included in this book come with their own set of references to various colour systems including CMYK and RGB.

**Munsell Colour System**
In 1905, Albert Munsell developed the first truly three-dimensional system of colour. In his model, or 'colour space', which is still used by some industries today, Munsell arranged colour by three criteria: *hue, value* and *chroma*.

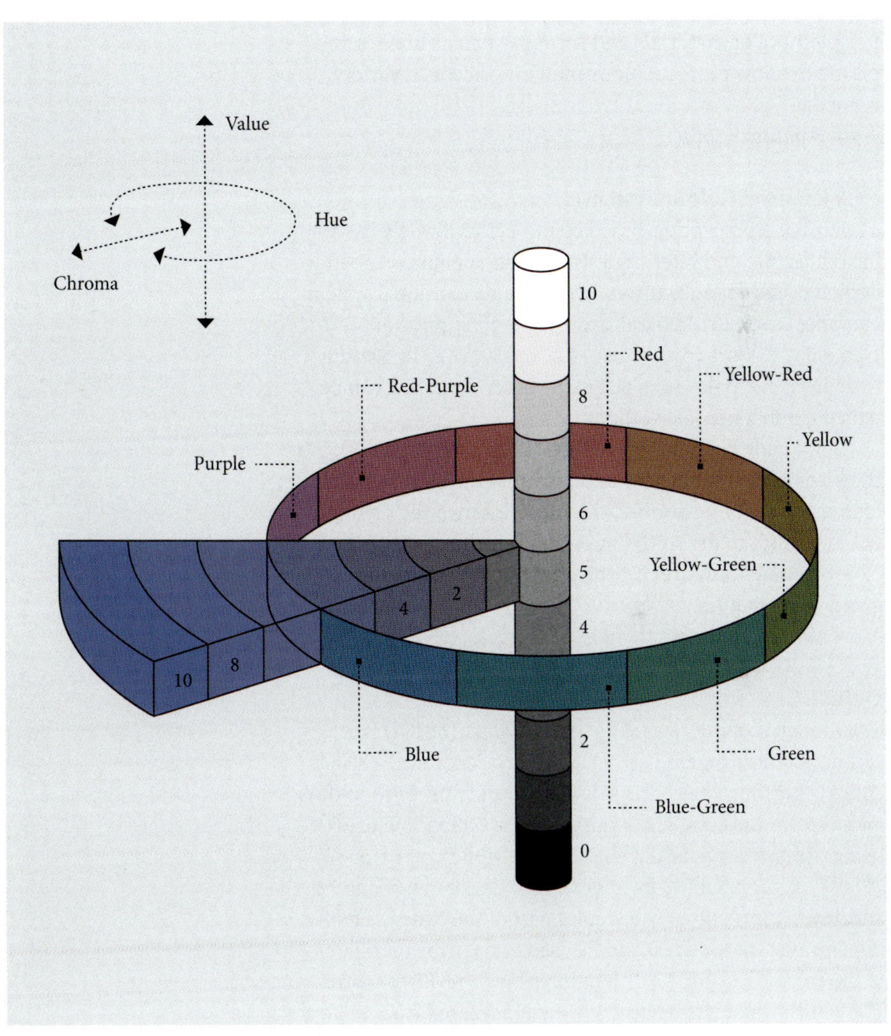


The Munsell Colour System

**Pantone Colour System®**

Pantone's colour chips are recognized worldwide and an industry standard in many high-end productions. Established in 1963, the numerical colour-matching system originated in graphics and print but has since expanded to a plethora of materials and formats such as textiles and plastic to allow perfect colour matching across a variety of media.

→ *www.pantone.com*

**NCS (Natural Colour System)**

The NCS is a perception-based colour system widely used in architecture and interior design to align colour between designers and manufacturers. The three-dimensional system comprises a spectrum based around the four 'pure' or 'elemental' colours (red, green, blue and yellow), lightening to white at one pole and black at the other. Each hue can be pulled out in a triangle section.

For a code such as '3055-B10G' (Teal, see page 188), the blackness is set at 30% and chromaticness at 55%; the higher the second number, the more intense the colour will be. B10G refers to the hue: the 10 indicates that it is closer to blue than green, whereas 'B90G' would appear green to most eyes.

→ *www.ncscolour.com*

**Dulux/ICI**

The monarch of interior paint charts, Dulux (or ICI) is a colour notation system used for interior decoration. Their codes begin with the chroma, based around four pure colours and four secondaries, each with a scale of 00 to 99, with 50 being the purest version of each family. In the case of '60YY-73/497' (Lemon Yellow, page 112), the hue is indicated to be an almost pure yellow. The second part of the code is a two-digit number between 00 and 99 used to describe the value of the colour: 73 shows that lemon yellow is relatively light. The remaining digits relate to chroma measured from neutral (000) to the most intense (999). The measure '497' shows that Lemon Yellow is a moderate chroma shade.

→ *www.icipaints.co.uk/colours/duluxtrade/palette/notation.jsp*

### Hex (hexadecimal) Codes



This digital coding system defines web-safe colour and has gained popularity due to growth in digital design areas such as web and UX/UI app design. Colours may be specified as an RGB triplet or in hexadecimal format (a hex triplet). There are lots of useful hex tools; here is just one: → *www.colorhexa.com*

### RAL Colour

RAL is a colour system used to standardize colour reference across industrial coatings, such as powder-coated colours. → *www.ralcolorchart.com*

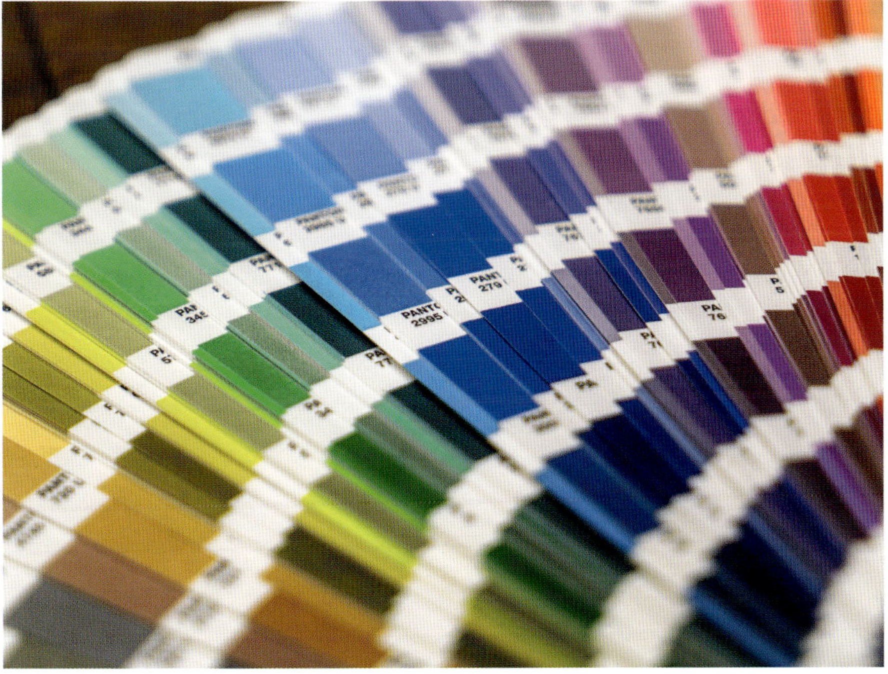

A Pantone® fan deck, representing a fraction of the full colour system

 # Glossary

**Achromatic**
Hues that are considered colourless, i.e. only using only blacks, whites and greys. Achromatic colours have no chroma and are only in neutral hue.

**Biological Dye**
A living substance from a biosource, such as bacteria or algae, which imparts its pigment colour onto a material. *See Living Lilac (page 238).*

**Chroma**
Chroma is the purity of a colour. Chroma shades are pure and have no grey. They can be fully saturated or light but are always pure and clear.

**Chromatic Dark**
Made famous by the impressionist art movement, chromatic darks are colours mixed to be dark using many different hues instead of pure black. For example, a chromatic dark such as obsidian (page 284) is composed from the dark shades of red, blue and green.

**Contrast**
A visual clash or vibration between two colours, normally generated by hues that are direct opposites on the colour wheel or the maximum distance apart. However, the more/less colour space separating two colours, the greater/lesser the contrast.

**Desaturation**
A descriptor used by artists to articulate the dullness of a hue.

**Duotone**
A palette of only two shades of the same colour. Originating from printed duotypes or duographs.

**Dye**
A soluble molecule of colour that absorbs into the material it is applied to.

**Earth Colours**
Colours derived from naturally occurring clays or soils within the earth, often including iron oxide. *See Red Ochre (page 54) and Burnt Sienna (page 296).*

**Fastness**

Fastness indicates how well-bonded a dye pigment is to the material, to withstand fading and running.

**Fugative**

Fugitive pigments lack permanence, altering over time, due to exposure to various environmental factors or their chemical composition. The effect can be seen in historical artworks *(see Faded Sunflower, page 120)*.

**Glaze**

A ceramic medium that is used to modify how a colour is presented through a transparent or a thin, semi-transparent layer. *See Tenmoku (page 296)*.

**Greyscale**

A limited scale of shade from black to white.

**Harmony**

Defines colours that fit together well or create a serene visual aesthetic. Normally they are close together on the colour wheel in hue or shade or are chromatically similar. Analogous and split-complementary groupings make successful harmonies.

**Hiding Power**

Indicates a colour or pigment's opacity – how well it hides the surfaces it covers. (See also *Opacity*, overleaf.)

**Hue**

A term to also define a colour family; e.g. blue, yellow and green are all hues. Often compounded or connected adjectives to further define a nuance; e.g. 'yellow-green', 'soft yellow' and 'acid yellow'.

**Ink**

A coloured solution comprised of particles and molecules suspended in liquid, mainly used for writing and printing.

**Inorganic Pigment**

An insoluble pigment that comes from a mineral or metal-based source.

**Iridescence**

A natural effect caused by differential light diffraction on surfaces such as certain feathers, pearls and oils. (See also *Structural Colour*, overleaf.)

**Lake Pigment**

A pigment created through combining organic dye with a mordant (an inert, usually metal, compound).

**Lightness**
Relates to how much light is reflected
into our eyes. A pale colour will reflect
more light and appear lighter. The
less pigment in a physical colour, the
lighter the colour will appear.

**Luminescence**
An effect caused by a colour's
molecular ability to reflect back more
light than it absorbs.

**Metallic Colour**
A coating that has a shine or lustre
created by the electron configuration of
metals and their interaction with light.

**Monochromatic**
Colour combinations that feature
exclusively the same hue but may
vary other colour qualities, such as
tint and shade.

**Muted or Greyed-off**
A colour with some level of grey added.

**Nuance**
A slight or delicate variation in tone,
colour or sense.

**Opacity**
A descriptor for how solid a colour or
material is. An opaque coating would
cover a surface completely and not
allow colour or light through.

**Organic Pigment**
An insoluble pigment from a vegetable,
plant or animal source, or from a
natural carbon-based compound.

**Pale**
Hues that are mostly composed of
white with little saturation.

**Pigment**
A small particle of insoluble coloured
material. Mixed with a carrier, such
as oil, it sits on top of the surface it's
applied too.

**Polychromic**
A surface showing a variety or a
change of colours, also known as
multicoloured. It can also refer to
a surface that has more than one
wavelength of light.

**Richness**
Describes a colour that is both intense
but also dark and deep in shade. A
chromatic dark brown, for example,
would be classed as a rich colour.

**Saturation**
The highest possible brilliance or intensity of a hue.

**Shade**
A mixture of a colour with black or its complementary opposite on the colour wheel, which increases darkness. Often used interchangeably with *Hue*.

**Structural Colour**
Colour that's created through light interacting with nanostructures. These structures originate in nature, such as in feathers and insect wings, and can be replicated through biomimicry. *See Pearl (page 260).*

**Substrate**
A surface of a material in which a pigment or dye is received and deposited.

**Synthetic**
A medium fabricated from two or more chemicals or biochemicals. Synthetic colour can also refer to tones that have an artificial appearance.

**Tint**
A mixture of a colour with white, which decreases darkness.

**Tone**
A mixture of a colour with grey, making a muted nuance.

**Translucency**
A descriptor for how semi-opaque a colour or material is. A translucent material would be cloudy but also could have a colour tint.

**Transparency**
A descriptor for how see-through a colour or material is. A transparent coating would be completely clear but could have a colour tint.

**Undertone**
A hue quality that is present but not clear or obvious; for example, a dark botanic green looks cold when opaque, but when diluted reveals a warmer yellow undertone.

**Value**
The relative lightness or darkness of a colour.

**Waste Colour**
Colour created from substances considered 'waste' or a redundant byproduct, such as industrial waste and food waste. *See Slag (page 276) and Red Ochre (page 54).*

# The Colours

 # Red

Humanity has a long history with red. Easily accessible as a pigment, it was the first true colour to be adopted into our palettes alongside black and white when we began daubing cave walls with the figures of animals and humans. Red has remained important to us ever since and has garnered so many associations it's become almost cliché: blood, passion, danger, anger, love, sanctity, war… the list goes on.

Opposite on the colour wheel to soothing green, red is an 'active' colour: it grabs the eye, demanding attention, popping out at us where other colours recede and making hearts race – perhaps even literally. It has been hypothesized that sports teams and competitors who wear red have an advantage; a 2013 study showed that the colour was 'associated with higher heart rate and strength'.[*] Since the predominant colour in nature is green, reds in nature have often evolved either to warn potential predators of foul taste or toxins, or to attract mates or pollinators, so it is no wonder this colour stands out to us.

While red may most immediately be pictured as a bombastic shade we should not overlook its subtler side: earthy clay tones and the deep, dusky hues of some tree barks such as rosewood, for example. Cherry hues and earthy reds have had symbolic significance for many Asian cultures since ancient times. In Japan, deep reds were derived from plants such as Rubia akane (Asian madder) and minerals such as cinnabar, which had deep mystical importance in connection with the fiery life force of the world, being formed from volcanic activity. Red pigments have been used in clothing and makeup, and as lacquer for earthenware and jewellery since the earliest days. Today, drapes of cinnabar red still protect the gates of Shinto shrines.

* Dreiskemper *et al*, 2013, quoted in 'Seeing Red at the Olympics', Oxford Psychology Team, 1 September 2016

In Christian times, red came to symbolize the blood of Christ; from the 13th century, cardinals in the Catholic church wore a red hat to denote their holy status. The tide turned against the shade during the Protestant Reformation, however, when it came to be seen as the colour of sin, in particular that of lust, and was connected with promiscuity.

Nevertheless, bright reds have remained in vogue, worn by emperors and royalty, and more recently seen on the carpets walked by stars, as well as on the underside of the seductive Louboutin shoes that often tread them. Traditional earthy reds, meanwhile, should not be overlooked. Stabilizing and grounded, these tones remain vital and bring a balanced energy to today's palettes.

## Colours in this chapter:

# Red Ochre

**Then**

A pigment used by humans since the dawn of civilization, red ochre is derived from iron oxide formations. In prehistoric times, we used it to decorate burial sites, tan hides and make cave paintings. These Late Stone Age paintings are found all over the world; a testament to the universal instinct to colour – and the stability of this ancient pigment.

Red ochre enjoyed a long life in the hands of artists. A chalk form was used by Michelangelo and Rembrandt and it was popular until the 19th century, when synthetic colours began to be produced. As the consistency of natural earth pigments varies from one location to another and according to methods of production, synthetic versions offered more vibrant and repeatable shades. Synthetic iron oxide pigments were manufactured in shades that are still available today, including Mars red, Indian red and Venetian and English reds.

**Now**

This deep red is enjoying a revival, becoming popular in contemporary interiors and architecture due to its primal associations with the land. In 2016, architects Ateliers O-S selected rusted steel and shuttered concrete dyed with local iron oxide for a new educational building in Lugrin, France, creating a material dialogue with the village's roofs in red and brown hues.

Iron oxide pigments are also frequently created as a byproduct in the aluminium-making process, left unused in waste pits, from where they filter into streams. By making clay bodies, slips and glazes out of this waste, designer Agnė Kučerenkaitė unearths the value of secondary materials in a world of finite resources.

**Colour Values**
Hex code: #963522
RGB: 59, 21, 13
CMYK: 0, 65, 77, 41
HSB: 10°, 77%, 59%

**Also Known As**
- Red Earth
- Red Oxide
- Red Soil

**Common Connotations**
- Primal
- Natural
- Grounded

**Red Ochre in Art, Design & Culture**
- *Exposed Painting Paynes Grey/Yellow Oxide/Red Oxide on White* by Callum Innes, *painting,* 1999
- 'Tessera Earthscape' collection by Forbo Flooring, *flooring,* 2019
- 'Red Mud' project by Studio ThusThat, *ceramics,* 2020

Ignorance is Bliss by Agnė Kučerenkaitė, 2016

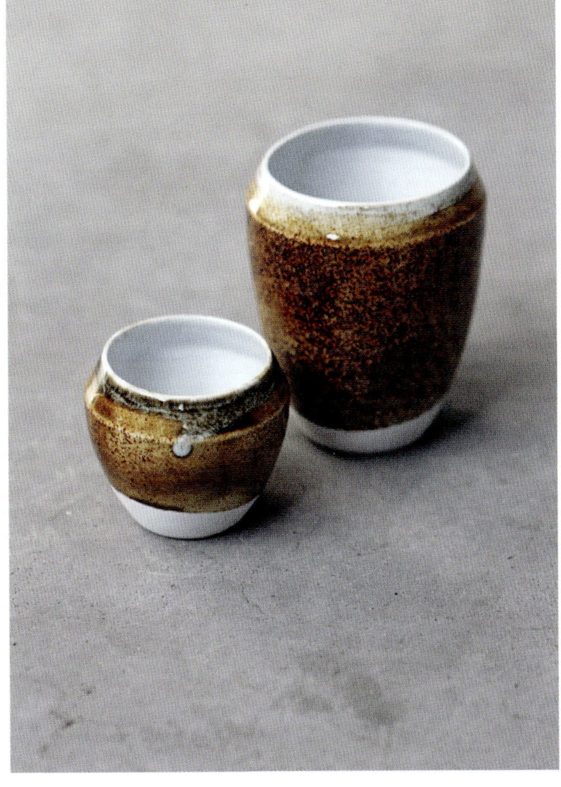

## Use
Explore the beauty and variation of this earthy red. Combine a balanced palette of warm tones, including soft honey, bronze and roasted rust shades; ideal for interiors or objects where a sense of grounded comfort is essential.

'This deep red is
enjoying a revival,
becoming popular
in contemporary
interiors and
architecture
due to its primal
associations with
the land.'

Lugrin School, Lake Geneva,
by Ateliers O-S, 2016

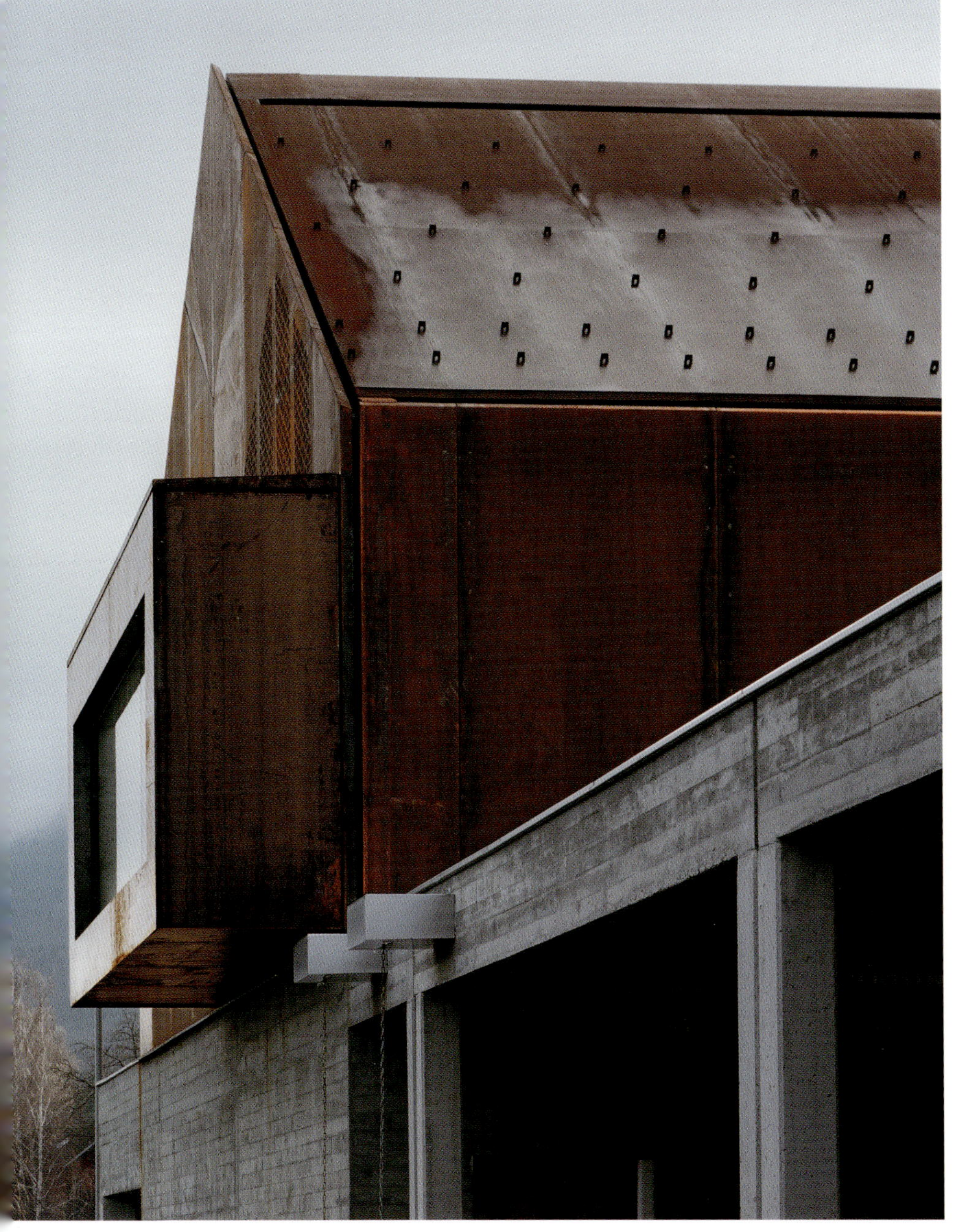

# Safflower

**Then**

Safflower is an ancient plant. It was cultivated in Mesopotamia as long ago as 2500 BCE, and in ancient Egypt, where the red and yellow dyes its petals produced were used to colour textiles: 4,000-year-old mummies have been found with garlands of safflower. As safflower made its way into Asia and eventually Europe via the Silk Road, the cherry-red carthamin pigment found wider use, including in cosmetics, carpet weaving and as a food dye.

Known in Japan as *beni*, safflower pigment was used in the iconic red lip paint worn by geishas. The best *beni* cosmetics had a natural green iridescence until dissolved in water, at which point they turned vivid red, and when applied to the lips, the hue could vary from orange to pink depending on the wearer.

**Now**

Like many plant-based dyes, carthamin red is not lightfast, and it fell out of widespread use in the 19th century with the advent of synthetic pigments such as magenta. However, it has made something of a comeback with the contemporary resurgence of natural dyes. Sachio Yoshioka was the fifth-generation head of the Somenotsukasa Yoshioka dye workshop in Fushimi, Kyoto, whose work celebrated the beauty of plant-based dyes and traditional pigments, including *beni* red.

While traditional *beni* cosmetics have all but died out – they continue to be produced in Japan's single remaining *beni* shop, Isehan Honten, first established in 1825 – the concept of colour-changing lipstick has lived on. Charlotte Tilbury's limited edition Glowgasm lipsticks come in two personalized shades that alter according to the wearer's natural complexion, as well as warmth, moisture and pH level.

**Colour Values**

Hex code: #b7454d
RGB: 183, 69, 77
CMYK: 0, 62, 58, 28
HSB: 356º, 62%, 72%

**Also Known As**

- Carthamin Red
- Cherry Red
- Beni Red
- Geisha Red

**Common Connotations**

- Beauty
- Passion
- Ceremony

**Safflower in Art, Design & Culture**

- *Maple Leaves* from the series *Flowers of Edo* by Kitagawa Utamaro, *print*, c.1803
- *A Japanese Woman* Józef Pankiewicz, *painting*, 1908
- *Job Parilux: Skin* by Li Edelkoort & Anthon Beeke, *book*, 1997

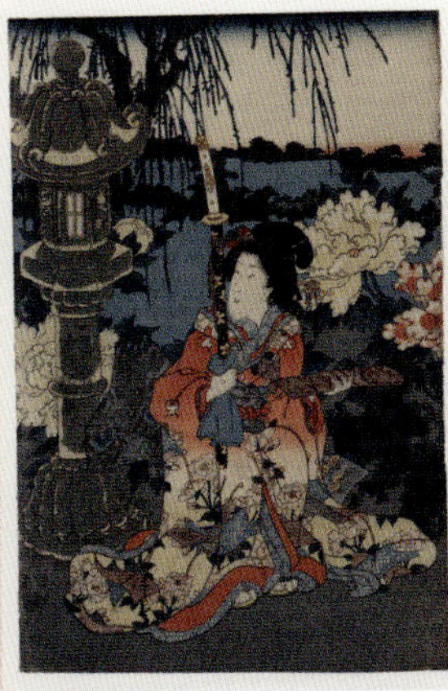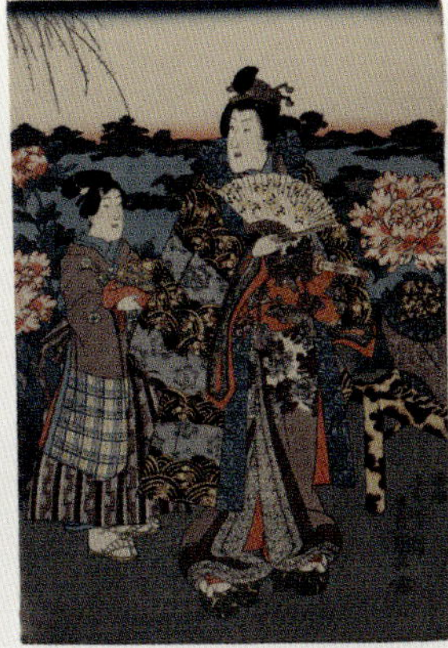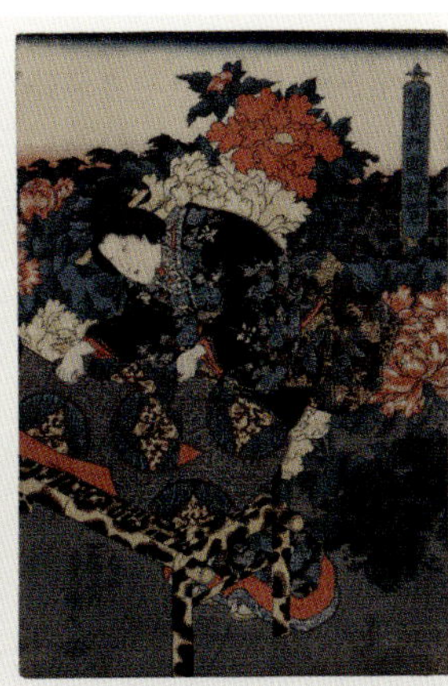

*Enjoying a Garden of Peonies* by Utagawa Kunisada, 1849–52

## Use

Borrow from history and use this alluring red as an eye-catching accent to bring warmth and energy to contrast cooler-toned backdrops. Consider adopting several different tints of the shade to honour its colour-shifting properties and pay homage to the historical Japanese fashion of layering colours.

# Scarlet

**Then**

A bombastic flame-red, scarlet arrives with a host of associations – most of them attached to female sexual activity. But throughout its history, including today, scarlet has been a much sought-after shade that speaks most strongly of power and strength.

'Scarlet' is a relatively new term for a very old colour. As first used in the 13th century, the term did not even refer to a colour, but to expensive, brightly coloured fabric in general. The older name is crimson, deriving like the colour itself from Kermes, a genus of scale insects. Pigment made from the dried bodies of female Kermes was known to ancient Mesopotamians, and prized by Ancient Egyptians, Greeks and Romans, remaining the known world's number-one red right up until the 16th century with the discovery of the New World (see Carmine, page 64).

Although scarlet pigments were used in painting, the shade was not lightfast, so the bright hues originally seen in paintings by the likes of J.W.M. Turner and Pierre-Auguste Renoir have faded.

**Colour Values**

Hex code: #d62220
RGB: 214, 34, 32
CMYK: 0, 97, 85, 0
HSB: 1°, 85%, 84%

**Also Known As**

- Crimson

**Common Connotations**

- Power
- Confidence
- Desire

**Scarlet in Art, Design & Culture**

- *Red Canna* by Georgia O'Keeffe, *painting*, 1924
- Dior Cosmetics campaign by Guy Bourdin, *photography/design*, 1972
- The 'Mini-Crini' collection by Vivienne Westwood, *fashion*, S/S 1985

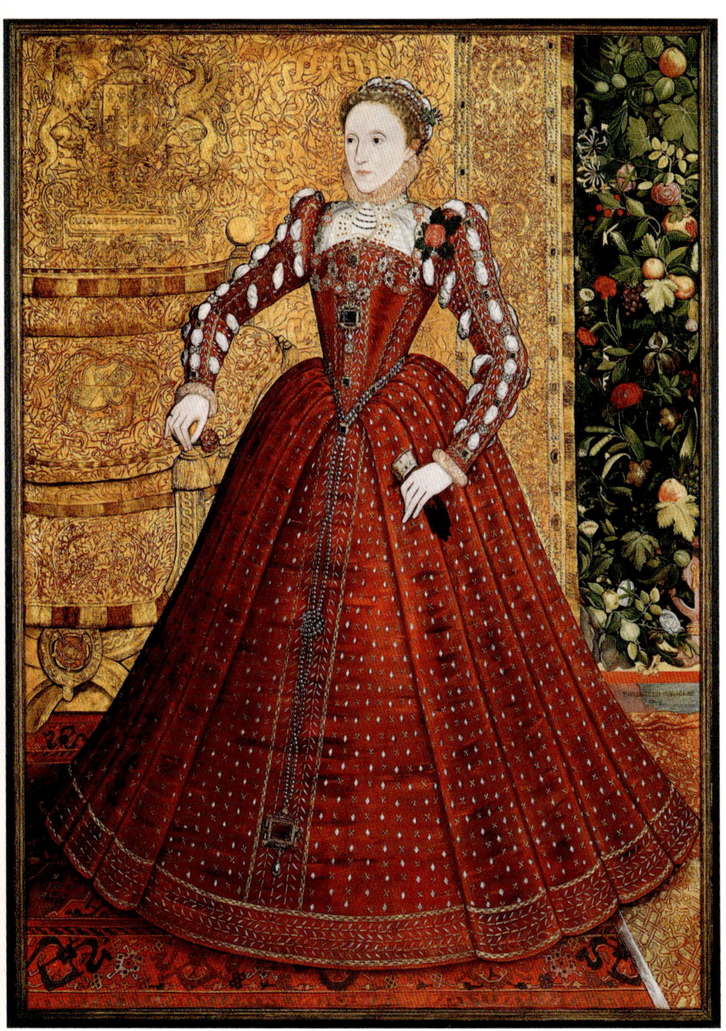

*Portrait of Elizabeth I* by Steven van der Meulen, 1563

**Now**

In the 19th century, synthetic pigments such as alizarin crimson were invented and eagerly pounced upon by artists. By the turn of the 20th century, artificial dyes had also replaced expensive cochineal production. But the shade itself lived on, perhaps peaking in modern expression in the 1980s with the iconic flame-red Ferrari and Guy Bourdin's provocative advertising campaigns for Dior.

As the world has changed, so has the way this powerful shade has been deployed: in Shepard Fairey's *Hope* poster to support Barack Obama's 2008 election campaign, scarlet underscores the optimistic message. Back on the catwalks, designers such as Vivienne Westwood, Chanel and newcomers Chromat have used the tone to signal female empowerment. Chromat's brightest moments of their S/S 2020 collection used scarlet as an energizing tour de force.

**Use**

Liberate the heritage of dress codes by pairing this hot tone with cool slices of sky blue for a more multicoloured and sensational pairing that oozes modernity.

'As the world has changed, so has the way this powerful shade has been deployed.'

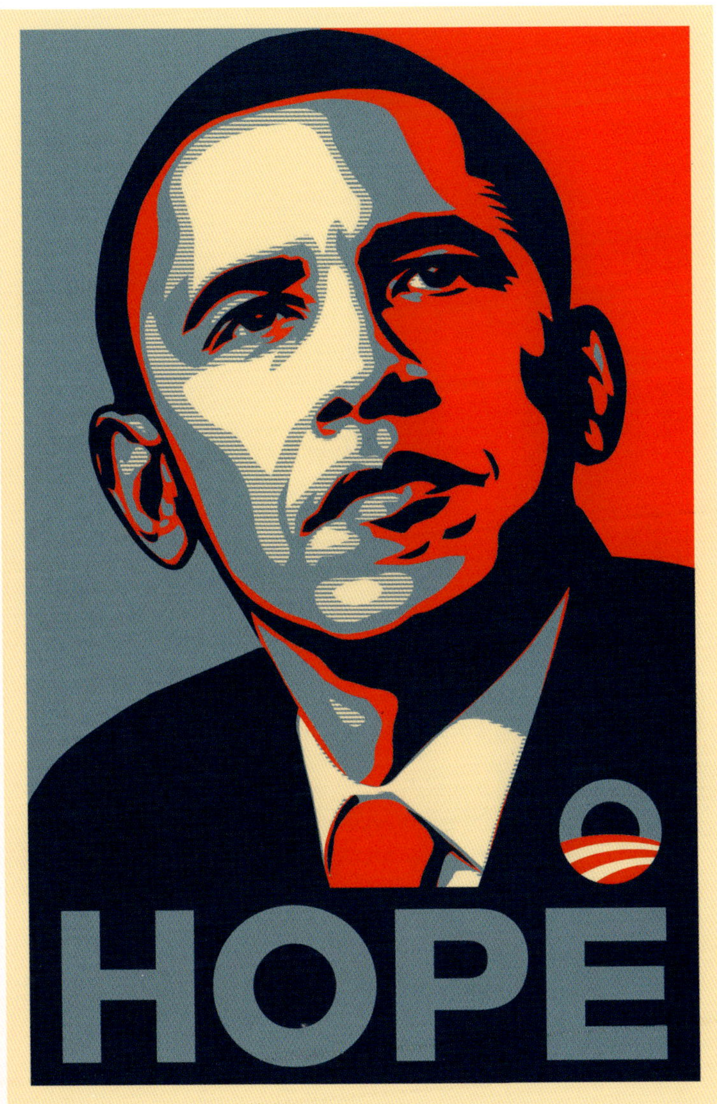



*Hope* by Shepard Fairey, 2008

# Carmine

**Then**

In Europe, the most vibrant red pigments were rare and expensive to obtain, but in the Americas, a scale insect called cochineal, similar to the European Kermes, had been cultivated by Mesoamerican cultures since at least the 3rd century BCE to make vivid red dyes, which were liberally used. When the Spanish conquistadors arrived in the 16th century, they were amazed by the Aztecs' scarlet, and after their conquest of the new territory, they began shipping the insects back to Europe.

Cochineal red was cheaper to produce than Kermes (though it still required 70,000 insects to make a pound of dye), more dazzling in intensity and more versatile in hue, as well as being lightfast. The brilliant new pigment was an instant hit, worn by royalty, the noble elite and officers of the British Empire.

**Now**

Largely replaced by modern chemical colourants, today cochineal red is known as carmine and mainly used as a food colouring. However, the hue has attained a new relevance in a world where environmentalism is on the agenda and traditional dyes like carmine are celebrated for their natural qualities. Danish artist Julie Lænkholm highlights the value of organic colours, using historical methods to treat materials such as wool and silk with natural dyes, including carmine.

**Use**

Cochineal dye was originally celebrated for the scarlet reds it produced, but it was capable of creating a much wider range of reddish hues. Try out a monochromatic palette to explore the tonal depth that natural reds can provide, along with a gentler quality not always associated with the colour group.

**Colour Values**

Hex code: #841422
RGB: 132, 20, 34
CMYK: 30, 100, 79, 37
HSB: 353°, 85%, 52%

**Also Known As**
- Cochineal
- Crimson Lake

**Common Connotations**
- Prestige
- Abundance
- Natural

**Carmine in Art, Design & Culture**
- *The Incredulity of Saint Thomas* by Caravaggio, *painting*, c.1601–2
- Ready-to-Wear collection by Clover Canyon, *fashion*, A/W 2016
- *Untitled* by Julie Lænkholm, *textile artwork*, 2018

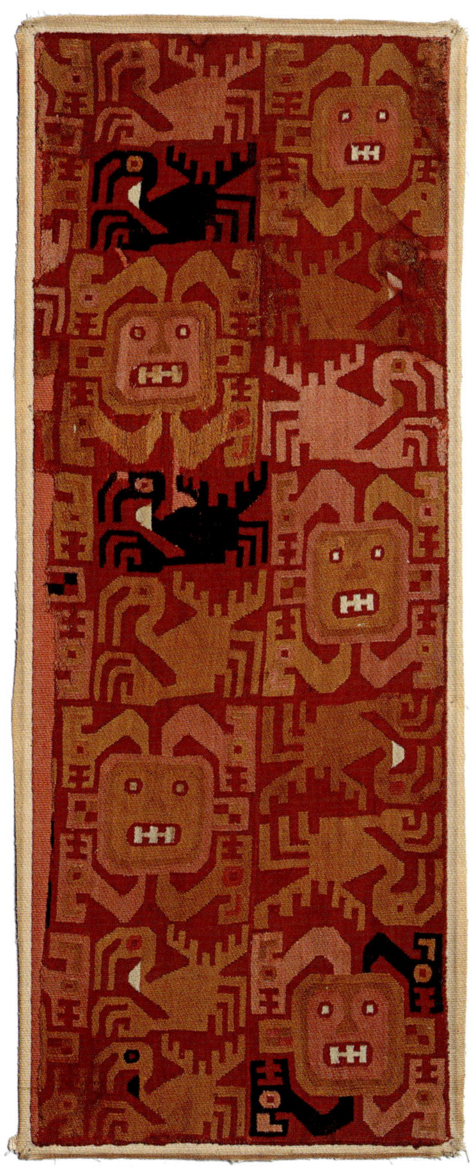



Textile fragment, Recuay culture, Peru, 4th–6th century CE

# Vermillion

**Then**

A bright red derived from the oxidized mercury ore cinnabar, vermillion has had strong symbolic associations in many cultures throughout its long and widespread use. In ancient Rome, vermillion was associated with blood and war – victorious generals painted their faces with it for triumphal processions – but it was used in many other forms of decoration, including frescos and cosmetics. The name comes from the Latin *vermis*, meaning 'worm', linking it with the reds made from insects such as the Kermes that yielded scarlet (see page 60).

In China, the readily available pigment was celebrated in a variety of forms including calligraphic ink and cosmetics, but most notably in the lacquer known as Chinese red used on beautifully detailed boxes and other objects. In ancient Indian practice, a husband would mark his new wife's forehead with a spot of the vermillion dye, called *sindoor*, on their wedding day as a sign of her devotion to him. Still in use today, though now made from less harmful ingredients, the dye has become increasingly linked with misogyny and patriarchal control.

**Now**

One of the first pigments to be synthesized when ancient China learned how to make it from mercury and sulphur, today vermillion has been replaced by modern synthetic pigments such as cadmium red (see page 66). Even so, the colour is still making history, thanks to Christian Louboutin's legal battle to trademark the Chinese red soles of its shoes. The colour (Pantone 18-1663TP), inspired by the distinctive Chinese lacquerware, joins a handful of others – including Tiffany's blue and UPS's brown – to gain this protected status.

**Colour Values**
Hex code: #d6441b
RGB: 214, 68, 27
CMYK: 10, 84, 97, 2
HSB: 13º, 87%, 84%

**Also Known As**
- Sindoor
- Cinnabar
- Chinese Red

**Common Connotations**
- Strength
- Devotion
- Luxury

**Vermillion in Art, Design & Culture**

- *Battre les Blancs avec le Coin Rouge* by El Lissitzky, *lithograph*, 1919
- *Graphics Standards Manual* by New York City Transit Authority, *book/ graphic design*, 1970
- *My Moon II* by Hayoon Jay Lee, *mixed-media artwork*, 2016

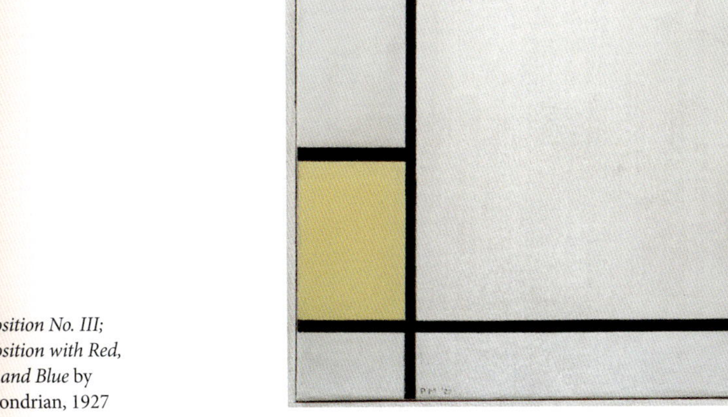

*Composition No. III; Composition with Red, Yellow and Blue* by Piet Mondrian, 1927

## Use
Ideal for striking graphics and wayfinding signage. Used with black and white, vermillion still has a place in the modern world in creating striking high-contrast combinations.

# Iro-Urushi

**Then**

*Iro-urushi* is a type of art lacquer used for millennia in Japan, China, Korea and other South Asian countries. By carefully processing the sap of Toxicodendron vernicifluum – commonly known as the Chinese lacquer tree, or *urushi* in Japan – and adding pigments, a limited palette was created. While not a colour in itself (*iro-urushi* simply means 'colour lacquer'), the most significant shades were red and black, which could be used in combination to striking effect.

Japanese artisans layered black and red-tinged, semi-transparent lacquers, sometimes up to 60 coats, each one meticulously dried and polished before the next was begun. The effect is not only decorative but has preservative properties as well: 9,000-year-old objects have been found with evidence of the lacquer still present.

**Now**

The long history of lacquer and the skilful coatings of *iro-urushi* have been crucial to developments in materials and design. The process laid the foundations for the development of enamelling and lacquering processes that are still used today to create lustrous colours. Contemporary *urushi* artist Genta Ishizuka explores the technique's surface qualities and mesmerizing depth effects in his totemic moiré red-to-black sculptures.

**Use**

Layer semi-transparent dark red shades with glossy, textured black accents to evoke a traditional aesthetic that speaks of an age-old quality. Ideal for timeless branding and lithography techniques.

**Colour Values**
Hex code: #330909
RGB: 51, 9, 9
CMYK: 0, 82, 82, 80
HSB: 0º, 82%, 20%

**Common Connotations**
- Depth
- Timeless
- Quality

**Iro-Urushi in Art, Design & Culture**
- Two red lacquer Mingei-style bowls by Kado Isaburo, *lacquerware*, 1989
- *Screen* by Anish Kapoor, *sculpture*, 2008

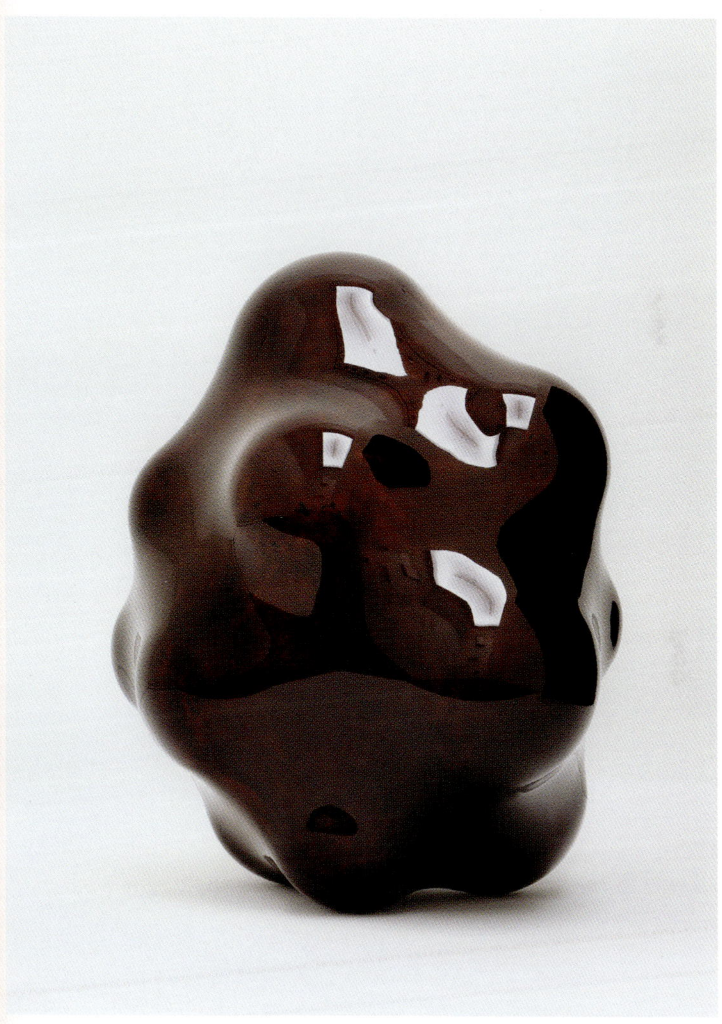

*Surface Tactility #12* by Genta Ishizuka, 2019

# Madder

**Then**

The climbing herb known as the madder plant was first encountered by early civilizations in Asia and the Middle East. More than 3,500 years ago, people were boiling the ruddy madder roots to extract purpurin and alizarin, natural plant dyes used to colour fabrics, paint walls and make art.

From the 13th century, madder was cultivated for use in dyes in Europe, but the often-muddy reds that faded in light were less revered than expensive alternatives such as the scarlet produced from the Kermes insect (see page 60). When a new madder dye known as Turkish red – confusingly, it was originally developed in India – began to be imported from the Ottoman Empire in the 18th century, European dyers were desperate to reproduce the rich colour, but they were never able to discover the secrets of its production.

**Now**

The synthetization of the colour was driven by the vast quantity of roots required to produce the colour, as demand increased along with population and wealth. The chemical form, still available today, is known as alizarin crimson. Recently however, a growing awareness of environmental issues within the dye industry, such as water pollution and the finitude of resources, have led to sustainable methods of dyeing and colouring being widely investigated again. The result is a revival in the use of many traditional, plant-based dyes including madder.

**Use**

Dip into the colour's natural variations towards orange and rose, or pair with an energizing accent of yolk yellow as a vibrant signal of innovation.

**Colour Values**
Hex code: #a34836
RGB: 163, 72, 54
CMYK: 0, 56, 67, 36
HSB: 10°, 67%, 64%

**Also Known As**
- Turkish/Turkey Red
- Rose Madder
- Purpurin
- Alizarin

**Common Connotations**
- Humble
- Traditional
- Ecological

**Madder in Art, Design & Culture**
- Casa Della Venere, Pompeii, *fresco*, c. 79 CE
- 'Woman in a sari with peacock and floral border' by Archibald Orr Ewing and Co. *block-printed textile*, c.1870s
- 'Strawberry Thief' by William Morris for Morris & Co. *printed furnishing textile*, 1883

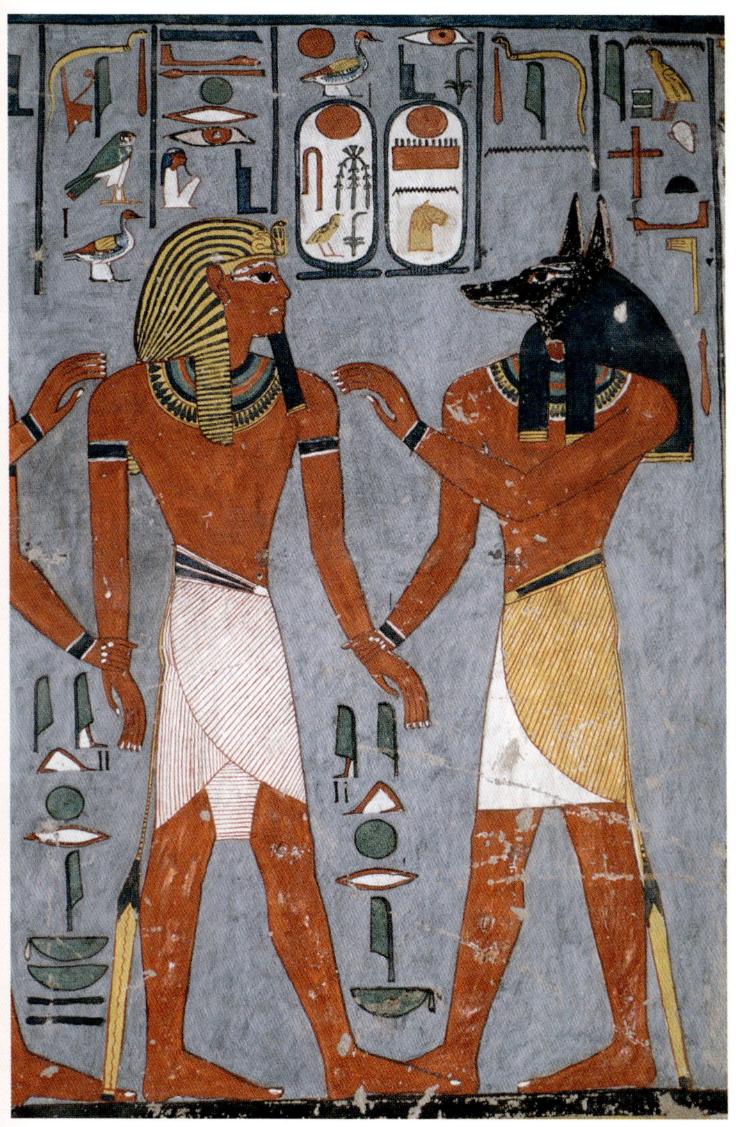

Pharoah Ramses I with the god Anubis, Valley of the Kings, Luxor, Egypt, 19th dynasty

# Blood Red

## Then

Sacrifice, violence, courage, pain: blood red's history is a visceral and symbolic one. Animal blood was even occasionally used as an actual source of colour in medieval European art. Symbolic blood reds – those used for colouring the fires of hell, the Devil's sanguine form and the coats or feathers of infernal creatures – were more often than not painted with the same pigment commonly called 'dragon's blood', which was brought to Europe via the Incense Route in ancient times.

In the Middle Ages, the colour was sometimes believed to come from actual dragons – or at least elephants. The red pigment of cinnabar was also occasionally referred to as 'dragon's blood' on account of its volcanic origins. But 'true' dragon's blood is extracted from the resin of trees of the Dracaena genus, native to Africa and southern Asia.

## Now

Scientific research has shown that red speeds up our heart rate, blood flow and body temperature; no wonder it's closely associated with passionate forms of expression. Mexican artist Frida Kahlo was preoccupied with the symbolic properties of colour. Blood red frequently punctuates her paintings, from the embroidery on her blouse to the gushing of blood from the veins of her severed heart in *Self-Portrait; Memory AKA the Heart*, a pictorial expression of the anguish felt after learning that her husband had had an affair.

## Use

Create a symbolic palette with blood red by pairing it with other essential life-affirming shades such as sea green and grass green in a split-complementary palette.

**Colour Values**
Hex code: #78001b
RGB: 120, 0, 27
CMYK: 31, 100, 79, 45
HSB: 347°, 100%, 47%

**Also Known As**
- Dragons Blood

**Common Connotations**
- Sacrifice
- Passion
- Mortality

**Blood Red in Art, Design & Culture**
- *The Last Judgement* by Hieronymus Bosch, *painting*, c.1482
- Hermès flagship store, London, UK by Studio Toogood, *interior design*, 2013
- Womenswear collection by Antonio Berardi, *fashion*, S/S 2015

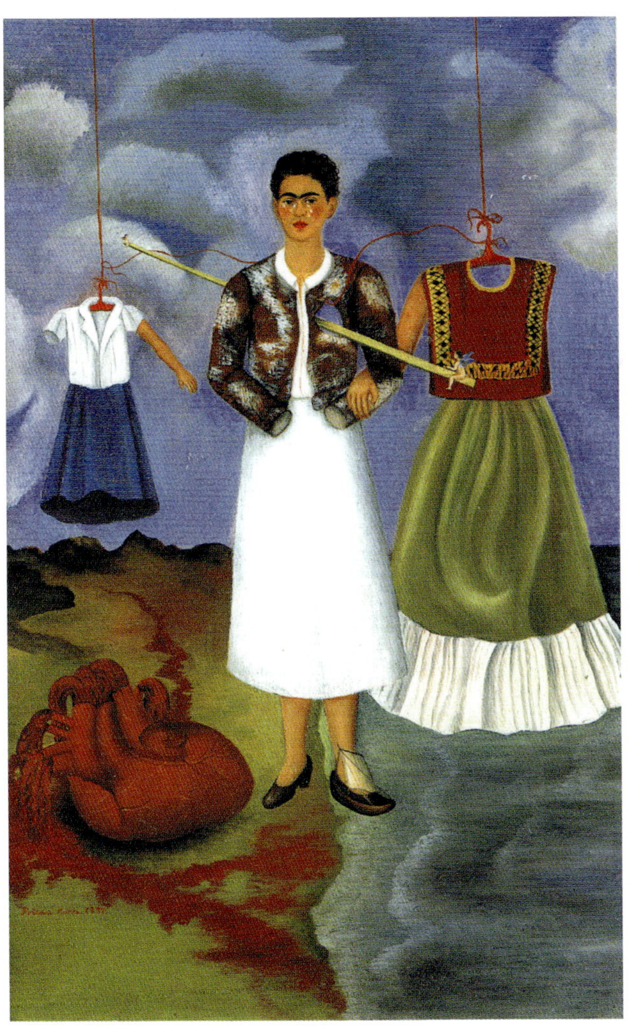

*Self-Portrait; Memory AKA the Heart* by Frida Kahlo, 1937

# Hot Tomato

**Then**

The quest to produce the colour of choice – whether a bright, lasting red or a mesmerizing sky blue – has driven chemists to invent an ever-widening palette of pigments. In the 18th century a glut of synthetic pigments was produced, including the cadmium family, which created a warm family of shades from yellow through to red. Cadmium red was produced commercially from 1919 – replacing the older, toxic vermillion (see page 66) – and enjoyed by artists for its opacity, brightness and lightfast nature.

The vibrant tone was used by designers of the 1960s and '70s to add impact and a sensational 'hot' appeal; orange-red pigment became a playmate of epoxy resin and polyurethane. Italian manufacturers such as Vitra, B&B Italia and Kartell brought the shade to mainstream high-end interiors, and as advances in plastic moulding took off, industrial designer Joe Colombo took tomato red to new levels in modern lighting and seating designs. Graphic designer Lance Wyman deployed a celebratory palette of hot tomato, lavender and grass green for his Mexico City 1968 Olympic logo and brand designs.

**Now**

The enormous applications in industrial processes are particularly significant for cadmium red. The colour was one of the first mass-manufactured and accepted consumer colours, perhaps an early indicator of the coming world of 'fast-moving consumer goods' (FMCG). This modern hue is now well-established on the palettes of artists. Bridget Riley's dazzling colour works frequently involve the use of contrasting tones to induce movement and playful shifts, with hot colours like tomato red taking an active role.

**Colour Values**
Hex code: #ff6844
RGB: 255, 104, 68
CMYK: 0, 70, 71, 0
HSB: 12°, 73%, 100%

**Also Known As**
- Tomato Red
- Cadmium Red

**Common Connotations**
- Confidence
- Celebratory
- Playful

**Hot Tomato in Art, Design & Culture**
- Mexico City 1968 Olympics design concept by Lance Wyman, *graphic design*, 1968
- *Untitled (Cadmium)* Jean-Michel Basquiat, *painting*, 1984
- *Carnival* by Bridget Riley, *painting*, 2000
- Halo chair by Michael Sodeau, *furniture*, 2014

## Use

Tomato is at home among other joyful colours. Take cues from Wyman's bright palette to create appealing, almost mouth-watering prints and graphics.

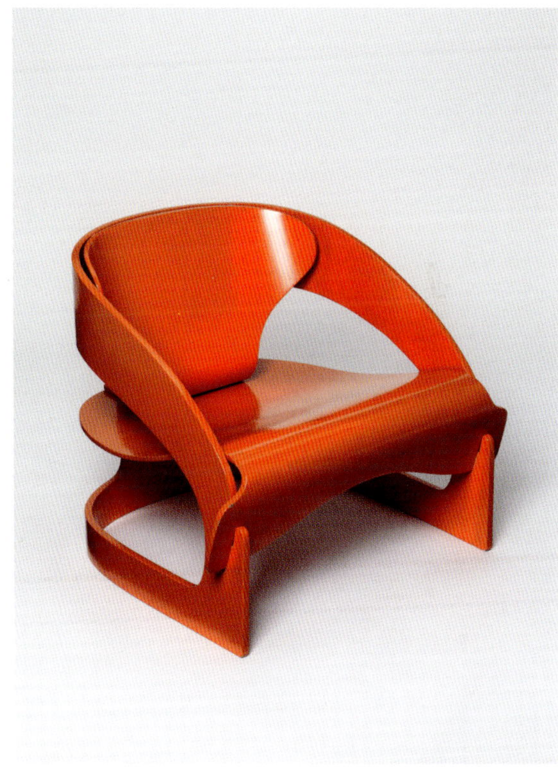

Model 4801 armchair, lacquered and bent plywood, by Joe Colombo for Kartell, 1964

'When I eat a tomato, I look at it the way anyone else would.

But when I paint a tomato,
then I see it differently.'
– Henri Matisse

# Rosewood

**Then**

The use of the ruddy hardwoods collectively known as rosewood can be traced back to the elaborately grain-matched cabinet pieces from the Ming period in China, but it was its common use in the mid-century modern design palette that ensures its relevance in interior design today.

Mid-century designers such as Knoll and Herman Miller incorporated luxurious, attractive materials such as marble, thick glass, teak and rosewood to underscore status in office design. The wood-clad lounge chair and ottoman designed by Charles Eames in the late 1950s became a standout symbol of achievement, especially in the ambitious offices of corporate America.

**Now**

Unfortunately, the popularity of rosewood has led to disastrous logging in the forests of Madagascar and Brazil. According to the United Nations Office on Drugs and Crime, rosewood, now a protected species, is currently the most trafficked form of flora or fauna in the world. Alternatives are available by treating ethically sourced wood with plant-based stains such as that from alkanet, whose red roots produce a vibrant hue.

Inspired by the diverse patterns and structures that can be found in the timber from a single tree, Dutch craftsman Ward Wijnant combines different grains with colour to create new products that are mindful of wasting this precious resource.

**Use**

A modern palette of rosewood stain, dove grey and cream will bring a sense of warmth and accomplishment to professional spaces.

**Colour Values**

Hex code: #b83a3e
RGB: 184, 58, 62
CMYK: 20, 87, 70, 11
HSB: 358°, 69%, 72%

**Common Connotations**

- Luxury
- Status
- Competence

**Rosewood in Art, Design & Culture**

- Lounge Chair and Ottoman by Charles Eames, *furniture*, 1956
- Rosewood Cabinet series for Herman Miller by George Nelson, *furniture*, 1956
- The Nest, Warsaw by Beza Projekt, *interior design*, 2018

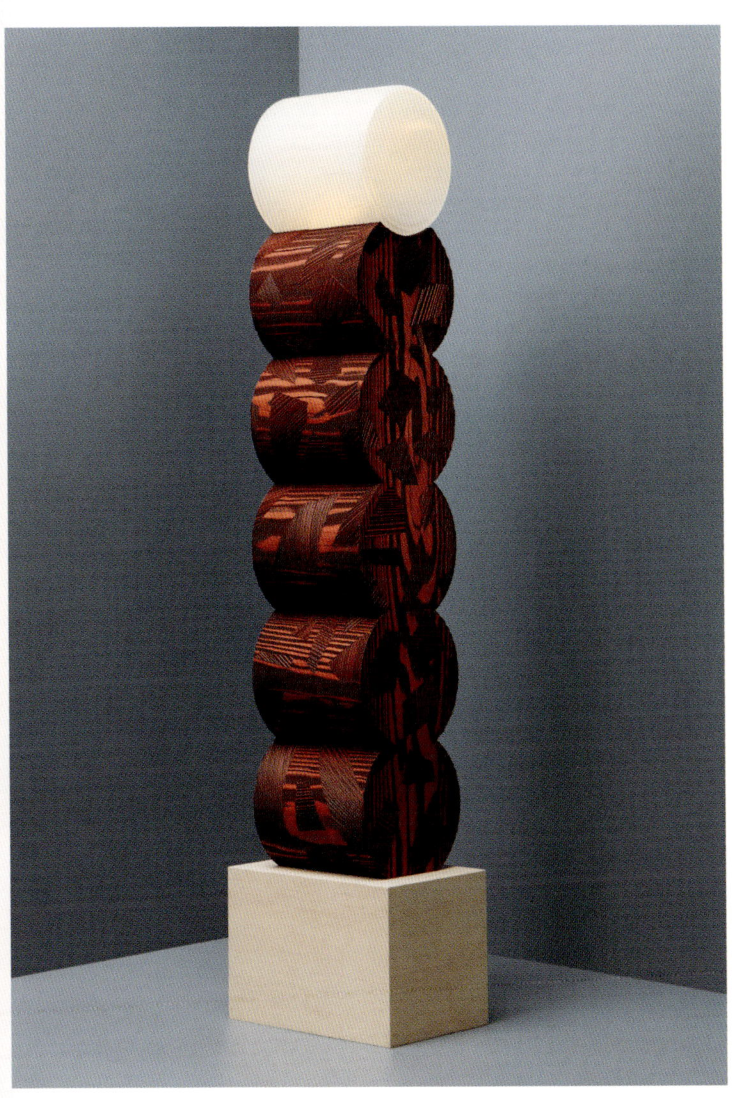

From the BLEND project by Ward Wijnant, 2018

# Reactive Red

**Then**

Red gives a strong signal, creating a reaction in both the natural and human world: a fully saturated red commands us to pay attention and watch out. Biological theory suggests red has evolved as nature's warning in plants and animals because it stands out most vividly against green foliage.

In 20th-century America, the increased production of personal automobiles demanded increased safety measures, so in 1913, engineer James Hoge tapped into the electricity that ran through the trolley lines of streetcars and rigged up bright red stoplights, with an opposite green light for 'go'. Since then, these colourful cues have become ubiquitous symbols. In branding and advertising, red ink was initially adopted for emphasis or the easy identification of information, and science backs the logic up: the receptors for red colours in human eyes are clustered near the centre, where the sharpest images are formed.

**Now**

Artist, singer and environmentalist Beatie Wolfe's recent work *From Green to Red* is a protest piece created for the 2020 London Biennale (rescheduled to 2021 due to Covid-19). Harnessing 800,000 years' worth of data, gathered by NASA, the audio-visual installation tracks human impact on the planet through time by visualizing $CO_2$ concentrations. As visitors approach, the visual timeline evolves from living green to vivid red.

**Use**

Use graded intensities of this searing hue to indicate the level of urgency or significance of critical information.

**Colour Values**
Hex code: #ff323b
RGB: 255, 50, 59
CMYK: 0, 88, 69, 0
HSB: 357°, 80%, 100%

**Also Known As**
- Signal Red

**Common Connotations**
- Danger
- Warning
- Urgency

**Reactive Red in Art, Design & Culture**
- *Exit* by Doug Aitken, *artwork*, 2014
- React Element 55 by Nike, *footwear*, 2018

Right: *From Green to Red* by Beatie Wolfe, 2018

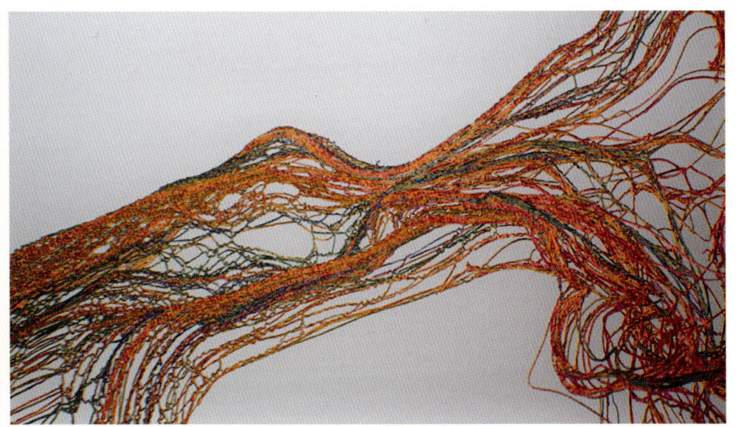

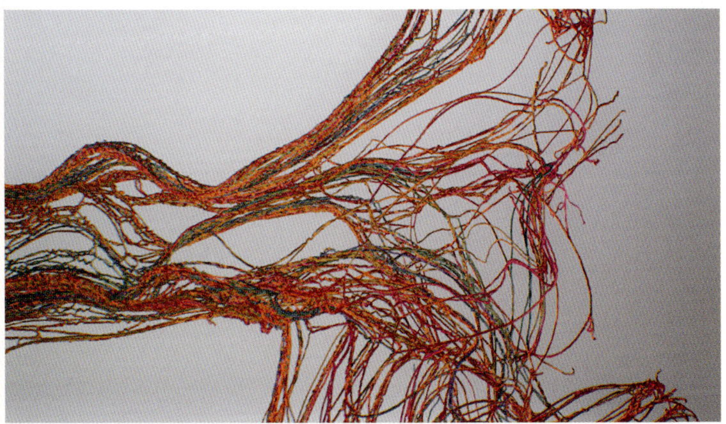

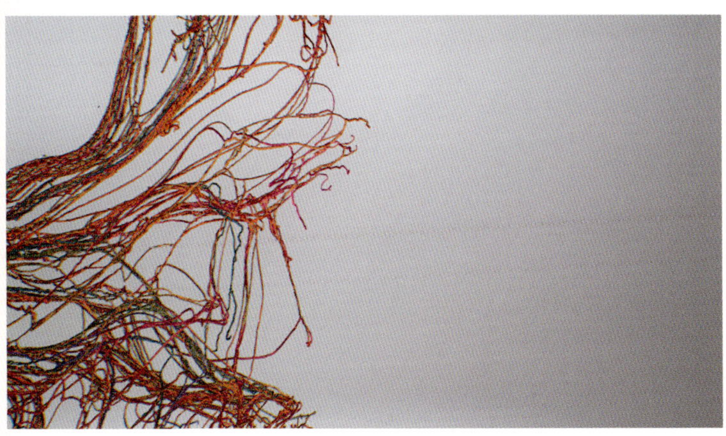

# Radiant Red



**Then**

It is known that blue light – emitted from devices like mobile phones – can disrupt our sleep cycles, but can red light help us get a better night's sleep? Recent studies suggest that exposing ourselves to red LED light before bedtime may help us wake up feeling more refreshed.

In 1876, Augustus Pleasonton published *The Influence of the Blue Ray of the Sunlight and of the Blue Colour of the Sky*. The idea of using coloured light to treat physiological conditions dates back thousands of years. In Ayurvedic practice, colours are linked to the seven sacred chakras which, when they become unbalanced, are believed to cause bodily disfunction. His work on coloured light led to modern day 'chromotherapy' – dismissed by most as a pseudoscience. In 1893, however, Danish scientist Niels Finsen devoted himself to photobiology, studying how coloured light could be used to treat skin diseases. In 1903, he was awarded a Nobel Prize for his work.

**Colour Values**
Hex code: #ff3403
RGB: 255, 52, 3
CMYK: 0, 86, 93, 0
HSB: 12°, 99%, 100%

**Also Known As**
- Red Light
- LED Red

**Common Connotations**
- Warmth
- Healing
- Relaxation

**Radiant Red in Art,
Design & Culture**
• Living Colours by Philips,
  *lighting design*, 1990s

Halo Edition by
Mandalaki Studio.
Model: Halo ONE

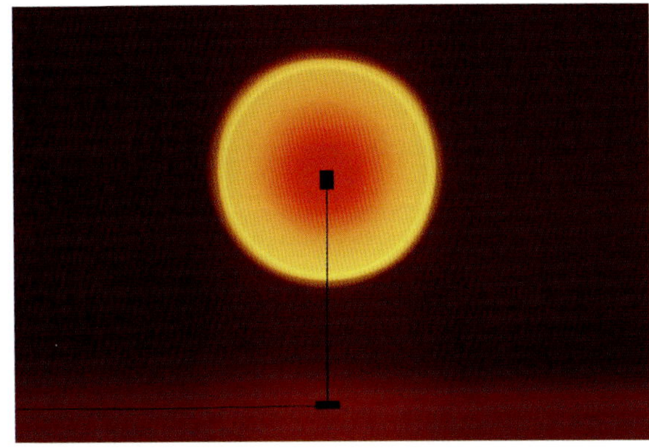

## Now

In 1993, Quantum Devices, inc. developed a light-emitting
diode (LED) for NASA. The project demonstrated that
red LED wavelengths could boost plant growth, but it
was noted that scientists' skin lesions began to heal faster
as well. NASA subsequently began to study the use of
LEDs to increase the metabolism of human cells and
stem the loss of bone and muscle in astronauts.

In the design world, red light is being harnessed in
more evocative ways. In 2019, Mandalaki Design Studio
produced a stunning circular projection in a sunset-red
colour, cutting out white light wavelengths to produce
extraordinarily saturated colours.

## Use

Explore radiant red's warmth and intensity by combining
it with an equally vibrant yellow; beneficial for
environments where people need an energizing pause.

 # Orange

A secondary colour that sits between high-energy red and cheerful yellow, orange is the ultimate warm colour with no cool undertones, making it a fantastic counterbalance shade for colour harmonies and contrast alike. From emotive peach to activating tangerine and iconic copper, orange has a truly diverse modern appeal.

The colour orange had no specific name in English until the 16th century. There is evidence of the use of *geoluhread* (yellow-red) in Old English, and early medieval records reference the sun, marigold and the colour of King Herod's hair. Orange dyes were for centuries extremely difficult to produce, as a 17th-century account suggests: 'Take two ounces of orleans yellow, put it overnight in water together with one ounce of post ashes: boil it up, add to it, after it has boil'd half an hour, one ounce of powdered cuccumi, stir it with a stick.' In Europe, orange only really began to take off as a separate colour family after the introduction of the eponymous exotic fruits, which were brought to European shores by early traders in the 16th century. These first oranges weren't always edible and were used as medicinal cleaners, fashion statements and even invisible ink.

The colour really came into its own with the invention of stable and synthesized orange pigments such as cadmium and chrome orange. Its high visibility makes it a popular choice in the modern world for lifeboats and safety equipment, and it is also widely worn by cyclists, road workers and even crew members of the International Space Station.

Scientific studies have shown that exposure to bright orange light can improve cognition and alertness, positively influencing the human circadian rhythm. Exposure to a less chromatic amber light in the evenings can trigger melatonin production to encourage relaxation.

Orange is also responsible for one of the most potent contrasts in the colour spectrum: without orange, there would be no counter to blue. From impressionism to abstraction, artists have played with this vibrating colour combination to frame compositions and trigger an immediate response. Contemporary filmmakers regularly tint frames in orange or peach to spark emotional reactions in audiences, and the ubiquitous blue/orange contrast is a design trope that can be seen on film posters from *Avatar* to *Dunkirk*.

* Smith, Godfrey, The Laboratory; or, School of Arts, printed for Stanley Crowder, No. 12, in Paternoster-Row, and B. Collins, in Salisbury, 1770

**Colours in this chapter:**

# Yellow-Red

## Then

Yellow-red is a hue comprising equal measures of its two constituent colours. Until the 16th century – when the orange fruit started making its way from China into Europe – this range of colours didn't have a name in English or any European language, which all use names derived from the Sanskrit word for 'orange tree'. Until the fruit ushered in a new recognition of the colour, 'yellow-red', or variants of *geoluhread*, was common terminology in languages across Europe. Curiously, there is still no word in Chinese for the colour.

Conversely, Japanese, which has always had a more nuanced colour vocabulary than English, often links colour with visual associations and experiences. In Japanese, many names for orange also reference the fruit, but there is also *akebono-iro*, meaning 'dawn-colour', used to describe the bright yellow-red shade of sunlight, just as it emerges from the horizon in the morning.

## Now

The transforming nature of the sky at dawn and dusk, and the power of the sun's colour, has captivated artists and designers for millennia – and it's a sight we are still drawn to. Colour field painter Barnett Newman worked with expanses of modern yellow-red cadmium pigment, and contemporary American painter Robert Roth uses the same pigment with bright amber and soft rose in his semi-abstract horizon canvases. Today, yellow-red's legacy can still be seen in interior paint charts, with modern names such as 'Fiery Sunset' and 'Orange Aurora'.

**Colour Values**
Hex code: #dd5114
RGB: 221, 81, 20
CMYK: 7, 78, 100, 1
HSB: 18°, 91%, 87%

**Common Connotations**
- Enlivening
- Hopeful
- Energizing

**Yellow-Red in Art, Design & Culture**
- *Monhegan, Maine* by Nicholas Roerich, *painting*, 1922
- *Sunrise over the Eastern Sea* by Fujishima Takeji, *painting*, 1932
- *Landscape 60* by Robert Roth, *painting*, 2013

*Who's Afraid of Red, Yellow and Blue III* by Barnett Newman, 1967–8

**Use**

Secondary yellow-red can create a memorable visual statement that is less harsh than its primary counterparts. Combine saturated yellow-red with pale peach and soft rose to make a creative combination that's easy on the eye.

# Dutch Orange

## Then

This deep hue has a special place in the national identity of the Netherlands. As Dutch folklore has it, farmers in the 16th century began to develop and cultivate orange varieties of carrot, previously purple, as a show of support for William of Orange, one of the leaders of the revolt against the ruling Habsburgs. While this national mythology is likely just that, the story shows the strength of the country's affinity with the colour. The Dutch royal family still wears it to this day, as does its national football team, and the national flag even began as orange, white and blue, and is only thought to have changed to red, white and blue due to a lack of available stable orange pigments.

## Now

Allegedly, the only paperboard available during the Second World War that French fashion house Hermès could make their boxes from was a faded orange. A makeshift symbol of elegance, the colour's links with luxury still stand firm today, with a more stable shade now firmly embedded as an icon of the brand.

## Use

Deeper oranges have an embedded sense of warmth and luxury that offer brands a distinguishable and memorable colour. Try pairing with the opposite tone, ice blue, and soft black for a brand identity that communicates tradition and excellence.

**Colour Values**
Hex code: #b15519
RGB: 177, 85, 25
CMYK: 23, 72, 99, 14
HSB: 24°, 86%, 69%

**Common Connotations**
- Royalty
- Luxury
- Warmth

**Dutch Orange in Art, Design & Culture**
- *Venus and the Lute Player* by Titian, *painting*, c.1565–70
- *Four Generations of the Princes of Orange* attributed to Pieter Nason, *painting*, c.1660–2
- *Apollo and Aurora* by Gerard de Lairesse, *painting*, 1671
- Hermès packaging, *branding*, since 1942

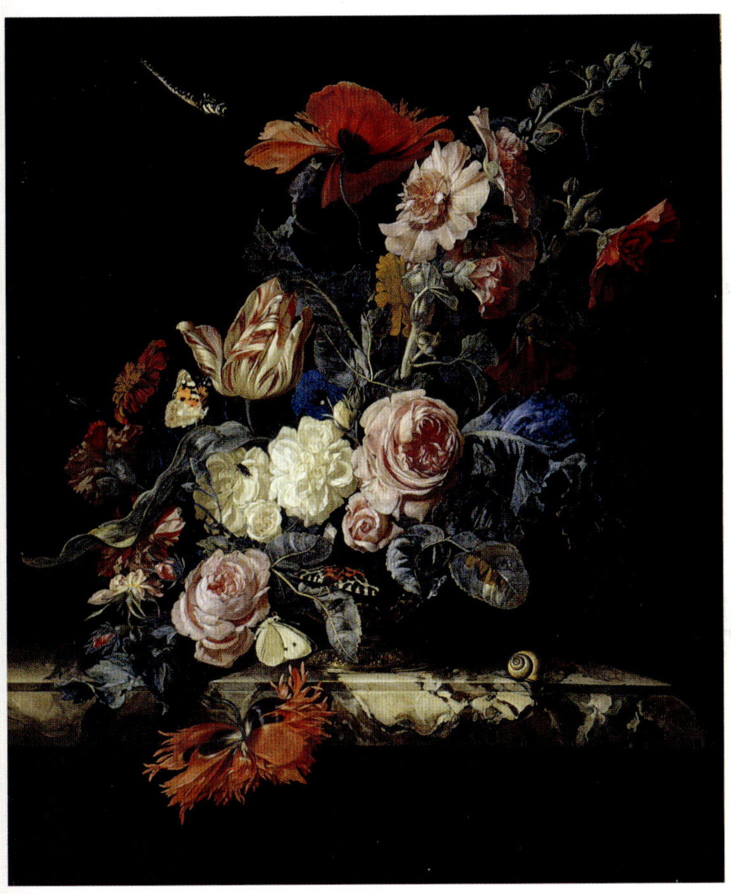

*A Vase of Flowers* by Willem Van Aelst, 1663

# Amber

### Then

Often found washed up on the Baltic shoreline – the original location of the vast conifer woodlands that produced the substance – the solidified tree gum known as amber was first believed to have originated in the sea. In Polish mythology, these washed-up pieces of amber are said to be remnants of the destroyed underwater palace of the sea goddess Jurata.

Perhaps the most famous use of the radiant orange material was the Amber Room, a chamber decorated in exquisite amber panelling, commissioned by Frederick William I of Prussia in the early 18th century as a gift to Peter the Great of Russia. The panels were dismantled and removed from Leningrad (now St Petersburg) by Nazi forces during the Second World War, and were subsequently lost.

### Now

In China, amber's significance as a good luck charm led to what has been described as a modern-day gold rush for amber in the early 21st century. In design, the colour's rarefied glow and warmth is ideal for lighting and interiors, and mid-century design classics have long paired the warming shade with brushed brass details.

### Use

Connect with the colour's symbolic links to the natural world and its ability to captivate and support. Combine the warm tone with soil browns, deep reds and comforting cream for an energizing, earthy palette ideal for ambient interior spaces.

**Colour Values**
Hex code: #c47114
RGB: 196, 113, 20
CMYK: 19, 60, 100, 8
HSB: 32°, 90%, 77%

**Common Connotations**
- Beauty
- Vitality
- Protection

**Amber in Art, Design & Culture**
- *Ruby Conical Intersection with Amber Sphere* by Harvey Littleton, *sculpture*, 1984
- Limited edition PH 3/2 Amber Coloured Glass Floor Lamp by Louis Poulsen, *lighting*, 2019
- Soda table by Yiannis Ghikas for Miniforms, *furniture*, 2020

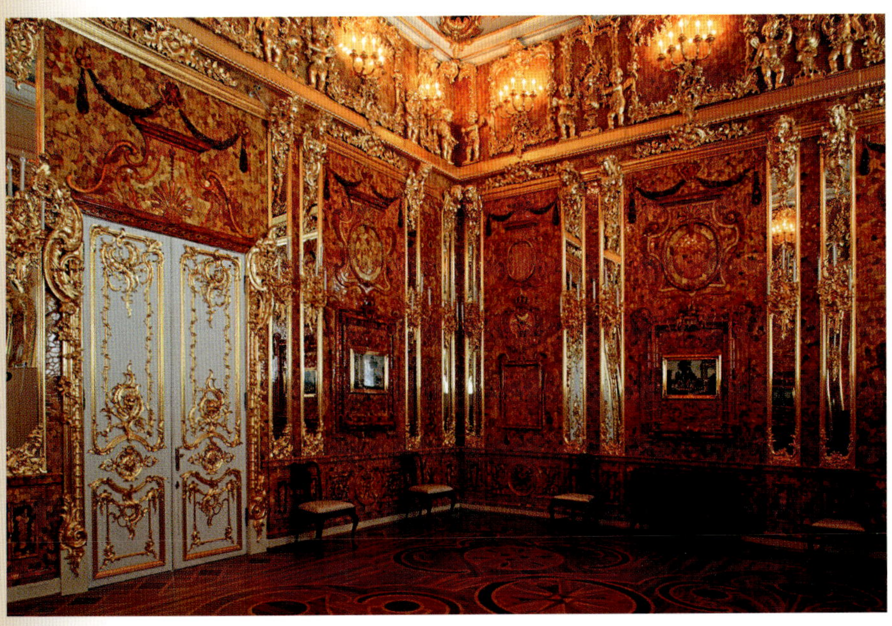

The Amber Room at Tsarskoye Selo, Russia

# Tangerine

## Then

Like a shot of vitamin C, tangerine has a bright and healthy feel about it. The colour name recalls the etymology of 'orange' itself, which came directly from the fruit tree after it was imported to Europe in the 16th century. Nonetheless, tangerine is a thoroughly modern colour, with an opaqueness not possible without high-performance synthetic pigments such as quinacridone orange.

Popular in interiors and product design in the 1960s and '70s, euphoric tangerine was part of a chromatic departure from sombre post-war conservatism. Robin Day's injection-moulded polypropylene school chairs added freshness to the classroom and underscored orange as a useful shade in educational environments. The bright synthetic tone went on to be used by brands such as Brionvega to replace an austere palette of greys. Furnishing company Heals created arresting abstract patterns for printed textiles in the colour, and other relics of the time – lava lamps, platform shoes and bulbous space-age sofas – became awash with the shade.

## Now

Despite its retro design past, tangerine has proven to be a colour with purpose and staying power in contemporary design. Recent studies suggest exposure to bright orange light increases mental activity, possibly indicating its true vocation in human- and learning-centred applications. British artist Sarah Morris uses chromatic opposites, including saturated cyan and tangerine, to create bombastic, hyperbolic effects on her canvases.

**Colour Values**
Hex code: #ff7e00
RGB: 255, 126, 0
CMYK: 0, 60, 94, 0
HSB: 30º, 100%, 100%

**Common Connotations**
- Refreshing
- Optimistic
- Active

**Tangerine in Art, Design & Culture**
- 'Volution' by Peter Hall for Heals, *printed furnishing textile*, 1969
- Camaleonda Sofa by Mario Bellini for B&B Italia, *furniture*, 1972
- *Pools – Ritz Carlton Coconut Grove [Miami]* by Sarah Morris, *painting*, 2002

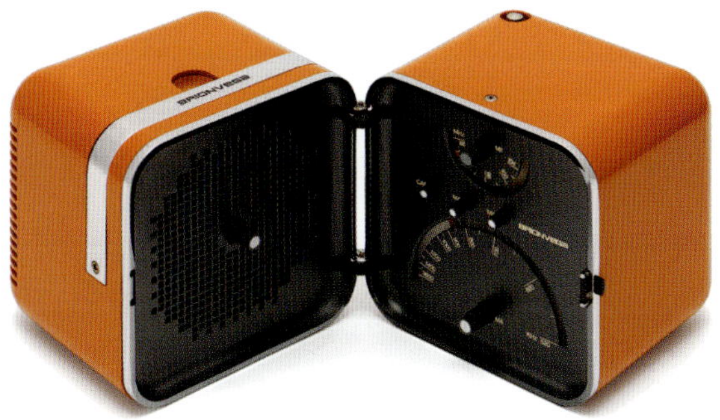

Foldable transistor radio
by Marco Zanuso for
Brionvega, 1964

## Use

Tangerine is a flexible and creative shade. Couple with muted oranges and soft pinks for a serene yet energizing interior design scheme. For contrast and clarity on digital interfaces, a stimulating union with chromatic cyan on a clean white background could help vital information stand out.

# Terracotta

**Then**

A brownish-orange shade with a soft pink undertone, this colour is named after the earthenware clay, the distinct shade of which comes from its iron content reacting with oxygen when heated. Early terracotta artefacts were left out to be baked by the sun, while in more modern techniques, the material is fired in kilns or open pits.

In 1974, a discovery beneath rural rice fields near Xi'an in China became an extraordinary testament to the material's ability to transcend time: entombed underground was an army of terracotta warriors from the 3rd century BCE. The life-size figures depicted over 8,000 soldiers, along with horses, chariots and non-military figures. As the ochre paints that originally covered them dried up and flaked off, the terracotta was returned to its raw state.

**Now**

Terracotta's utility means it has never really been out of style. Ornate Victorian-era facades stand as a monument to bygone craftsmanship. In modern architecture, it's still common for elements such as roof tiles and bricks to be left unglazed due to the material's natural durability and attractive colour. Today, many contemporary architects use the material to keep modern buildings cool, demonstrating that what's old is new when it comes to creating enduring features.

**Use**

Earthy terracotta brings natural warmth and comfort to environments and can enhance even the coolest of rooms or areas. Pair the shade with sandy neutrals and soft pinks.

**Colour Values**
Hex code: #c36d4c
RGB: 195, 109, 76
CMYK: 19, 63, 70, 8
HSB: 17°, 61%, 76%

**Common Connotations**
- Earthy
- Expressive
- Enduring

**Terracotta in Art, Design & Culture**
- *A River God* by Giambologna, *sculpture*, c.1575
- *Fields for the British Isles* by Anthony Gormley, *installation art*, 2019
- Aura Vases in Apricot by Schneid Studio, *ceramics*, 2020

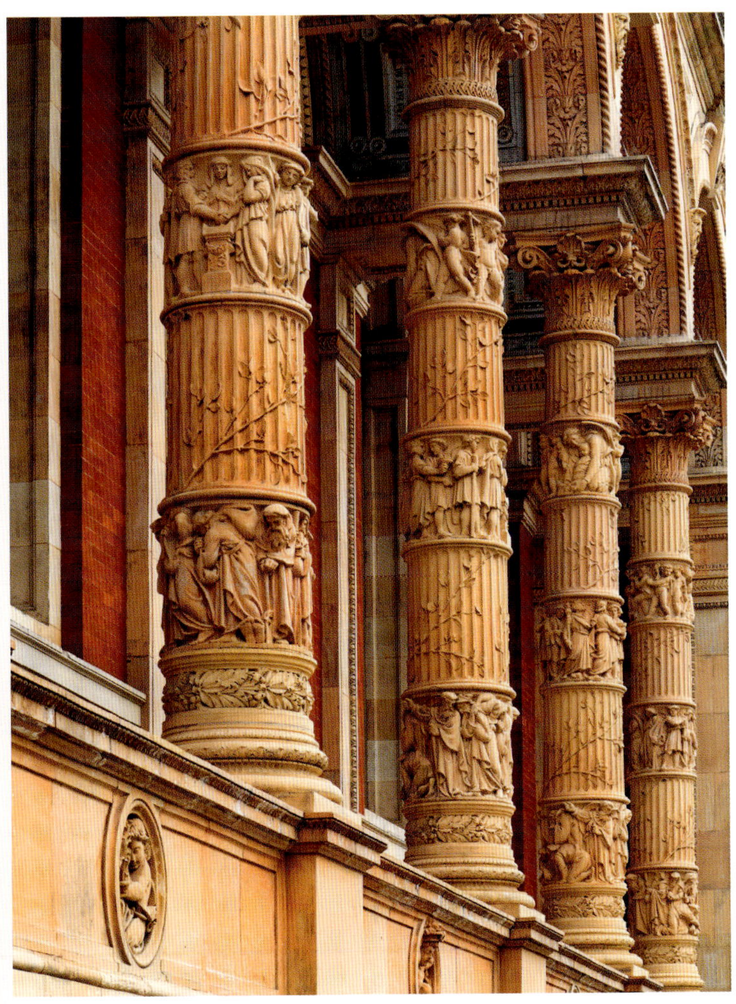

Ornate terracotta columns on the exterior of the Henry Cole Wing of
the Victoria & Albert Museum, South Kensington, London, 1871

 # Peach

## Then

A warm, fresh orange-pink, peach – another orange shade to be named after a fruit – is the ultimate symbol of indulgence and pleasure. Inextricable from its associations with the sweet and velvety fruit, peach has become linked with the aesthetics of all things romantic, and particularly with the Art Nouveau movement at the turn of the 20th century. Czech artist Alphonse Mucha deployed large expanses of peach, soft red and muted pink in his stylized theatrical posters that became icons of the movement. In works including *Au Quartier Latin*, he uses contrasting accents of subdued *eau de Nil* green to draw your eye around the composition and around the graceful detail of the female figure. When compositions use reduced contrasts, and colour qualities are constrained, our eyes may be better able to register subtle details in the image.

## Now

Today, this colour is still well-employed in film, often playing a supporting role where saturated colours take the lead in cinematic scenes. In Spike Jonze's 2013 film *Her*, the visual backdrops of urban sprawl are purposefully desaturated. Vibrant pinky-peach and warm red tones are used to draw attention to the main character, Theodore, and the amorous connection he has with Samantha, the intelligent computer system.

## Use

Nurturing peach has an organic and warm quality, which can be combined with soft browns to create a harmonious palette for modern products. Emphasis can be added with saturated rusty orange accents to convey a more human communicative function or quality.

**Colour Values**
Hex code: #fdd0ae
RGB: 253, 208, 174
CMYK: 0, 24, 33, 0
HSB: 26º, 31%, 99%

**Common Connotations**
- Indulgent
- Nurturing
- Romantic

**Peach in Art, Design & Culture**
- *Boy with a Basket of Fruit* by Caravaggio, *painting*, c.1593
- *The Rider (L'Ecuyère)* by Richard Ranft, *print*, 1898
- Gopuram table by Ettore Sottsass, *furniture*, 1986

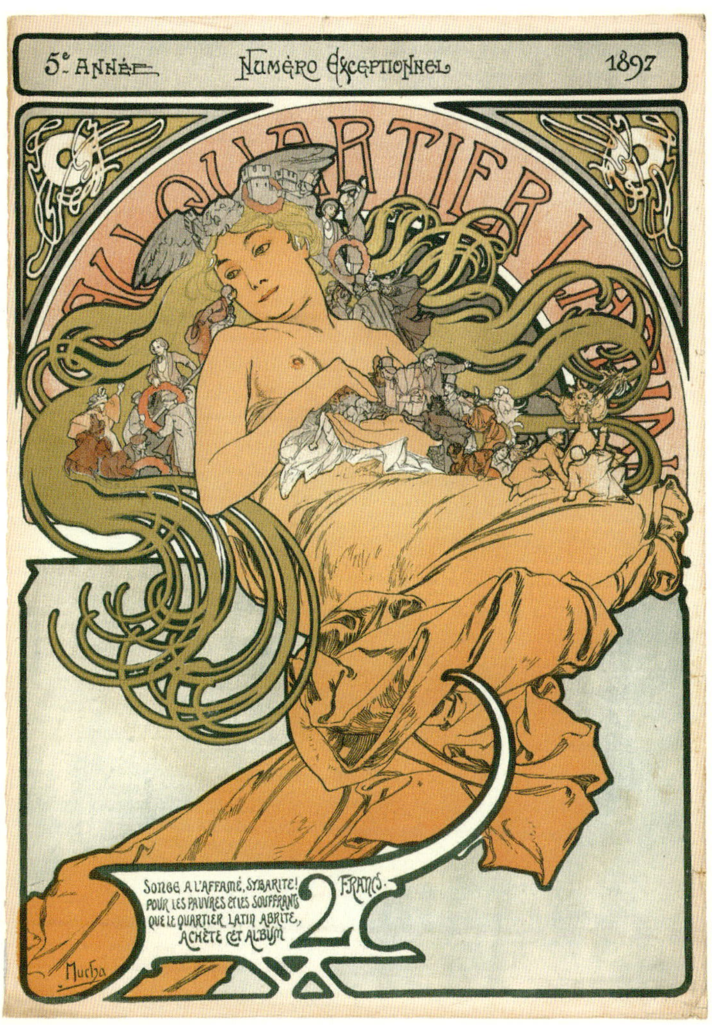


*Au Quartier Latin – Numéro Exceptionnel* by Alphonse Mucha, 1897

# Copper

**Then**

A rosy golden hue named after the naturally occurring metal element, copper can range from reddish to buttery in colour, due to the metal's reflective qualities. Copper has been known to and used by humanity since ancient times; it was employed by the Sumerian and Chaldean civilizations to make artworks, armour and various useful objects. And copper is an essential component of the harder alloy, bronze, which gives its name to the era of technological advancement that began in 3000 BCE.

The history of copper as a modern design feature really begins with the Industrial Revolution, which brought copper-piped hot water into homes and premises, and the naturally evolving patinated surface of the pipes from exposure to steam subsequently became a sought-after industrial aesthetic. Copper plumbing was itself nothing new, however, since the ancient Egyptians first created it long ago – some of which is still in good condition today.

**Now**

Today, copper appears on everything from plant stands to splashbacks. Industrial designer Tom Dixon exposed the graceful, highly polished and wonderfully malleable side of the colour, bringing copper's reflective glow to global interiors. In 2014, the brand's Design Research Studio kitted out the lobby of London's Mondrian hotel (now Sea Containers London) with an all-encompassing copper design, referencing the hull of a ship.

Ghanaian contemporary artist El Anatsui works primarily with recycled or found metal to create his 'assemblages'. In *Many Came Back* (2005), he wove copper wire together with flattened bottle tops to create a fabric-like tapestry, referencing the role of liquor trading in the transatlantic slave trade.

**Colour Values**
Hex code: #d78152
RGB: 215, 129, 82
CMYK: 13, 56, 70, 3
HSB: 21º, 62%, 84%

**Common Connotations**
- Captivating
- Advancement
- Warmth

Right: Mondrian Hotel, London, by Design Research Studio, 2014

**Copper in Art,
Design & Culture**
- 'Still' collection by
  Studio Formafantasma,
  *homeware*, 2014
- Chair, from Copper
  series by Max Lamb,
  *furniture*, 2015
- *Dans un verre* by Marie
  Lund, *sculpture*, 2017

**Use**

Patinated copper has a wealth of natural warmth and an inherently diverse palette. Experiment with metallic and non-metallic nuances of warm coppers with rusty red and charcoal black for an approachable look and feel.

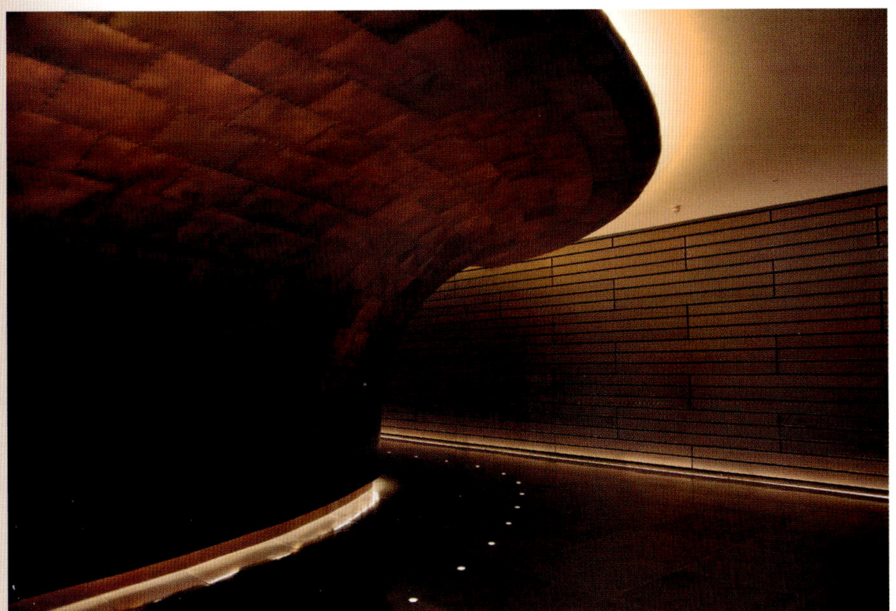

# Coral

### Then

The name of this mid-tone pinky orange has its origins in the colourful skeletons formed by reef-dwelling organisms. Early Mesopotamian civilizations are known to have dived to retrieve the glowing stems for use in jewellery, while ancient Romans believed that wearing coral gave one the ability to resist evil and temptation. This association persisted, with Italian masters such as Cecco di Pietro depicting baby Jesus wearing a coral amulet in the 14th century.

Coral as a material became hugely fashionable in Europe in the 19th century, coinciding with a period of extended colonial exploration (and exploitation) of areas of the world where coral was commonly found. By the 1960s and '70s, coral had taken a step away from high society to become a serviceable colour of public toilet tiles and retro cocktail chairs.

### Now

In design, the colour can offer a more approachable and versatile functionality than brighter oranges. Utilized by technology brands such as Google Nest and Jawbone, coral's friendly nature helps with the acceptance of digital information yet is vibrant enough to bring attention to important messages.

### Use

The amount of pink in the shade makes it easier on the eye than many other functional oranges. Used with a palette of complementary deep teal, pale wood and golden yellow, coral's natural warmth offers a thoroughly modern approach to support-focused interior environments or products.

**Colour Values**
Hex code: #ff8765
RGB: 255, 135, 101
CMYK: 0, 59, 58, 0
HSB: 13°, 60%, 100%

**Common Connotations**
- Wondrous
- Protection
- Approachable

**Coral in Art, Design & Culture**
- Wristband up24 by Yves Béhar for Jawbone, 2013
- Pantone 16-1546 'Living Coral' Pantone Colour of the Year, *design*, 2019
- Ready-to-Wear collection by Stella McCartney, *fashion*, S/S 2021

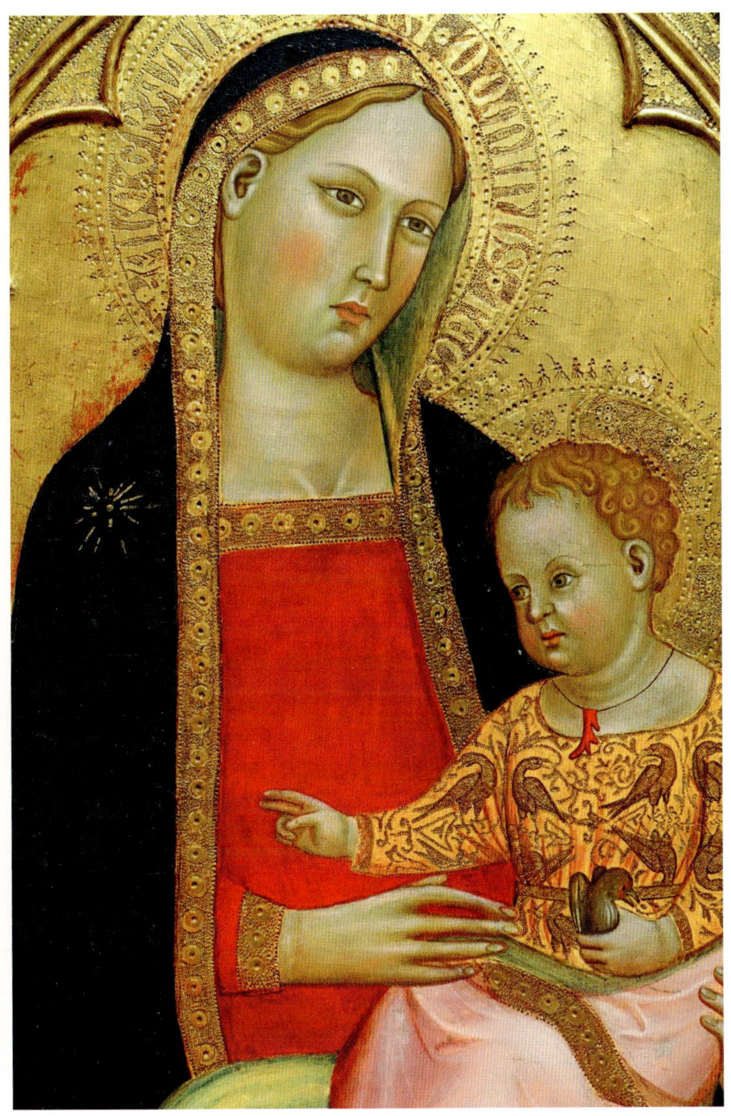

*Madonna and Child with Donors*, by Cecco di Pietro, detail, 1386

# High-Vis Orange

**Then**

A chromatic, glowing orange projects urgency and emergency, from lifeboats to aircraft black boxes (which are orange to increase their visibility after a disaster). Orange dayglow fabrics invented in the 1940s by the Switzer Brothers (see page 160) have found a raft of functional applications since Second World War, including high-contrast life jackets, parachutes and flotation devices.

The invention of intense cadmium, chrome and quinacridone pigments in the 19th century gave high-vis orange the opportunity to create vibrant colour contrasts with blue. Artist Francis Bacon used the visceral intensity of this contrast to highlight his figurative human forms, while in the 1980s Keith Haring produced screen-prints using the incandescent shade to bring public awareness to important social and public health issues.

**Colour Values**
Hex code: #ff9200
RGB: 255, 146, 0
CMYK: 0, 51, 93, 0
HSB: 34°, 100%, 100%

**Common Connotations**
- Vibrant
- Safety
- Functional

**High-Vis Orange in Art, Design & Culture**
- *Study from The Human Body* by Francis Bacon, *painting*, 1982
- *The Last Rainforest* by Keith Haring, *painting*, 1989
- 'Remade' collection by Raeburn, *fashion*, A/W 2018

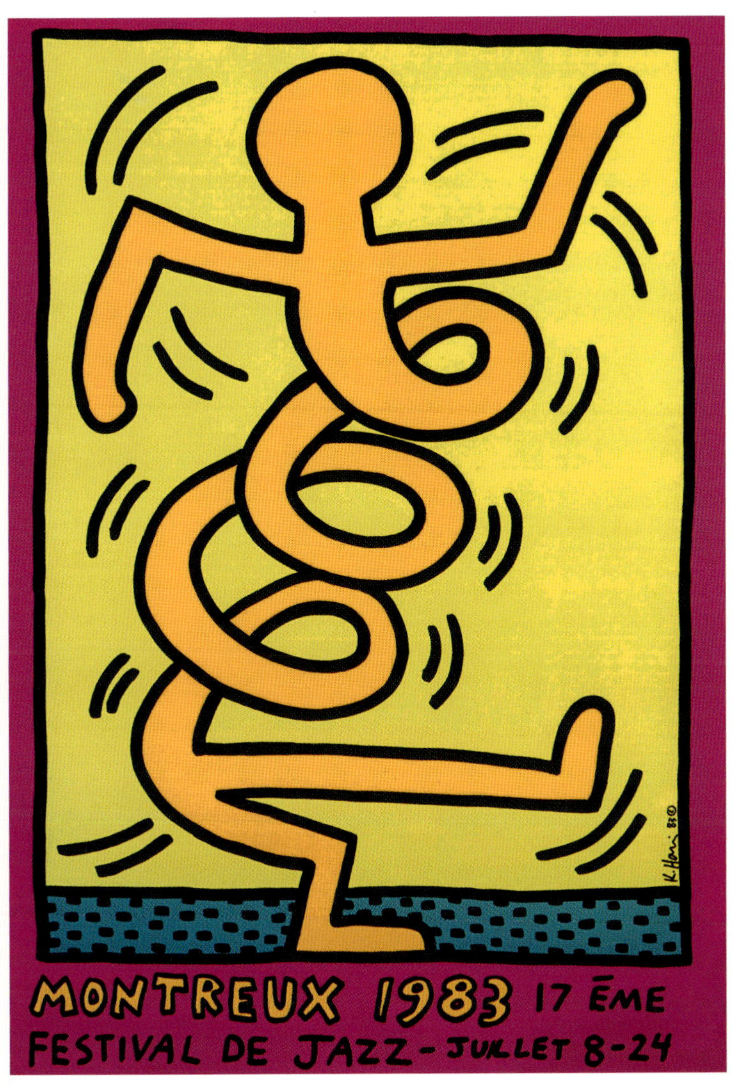


Serigraph Montreux Jazz Festival Poster by Keith Haring, 1983

**Now**

High-vis orange's capacity to draw attention to vital subject matters is still crucial today. A fashion brand known for its sustainable mindset, Raeburn creates cold-weather outfitting reusing original high-vis fabrics created during the Second World War. Glowing and perfectly functional, they highlight the need to reuse materials and avoid waste.

**Use**

High-vis orange does precisely what it says on the tin. Straightforward and powerful, pair with other vibrating opposites such as cyan and neon yellow for an ad campaign that commands full attention. Alternatively, a serious mood can be created by pairing the shade with achromatic colours for a timeless feel.

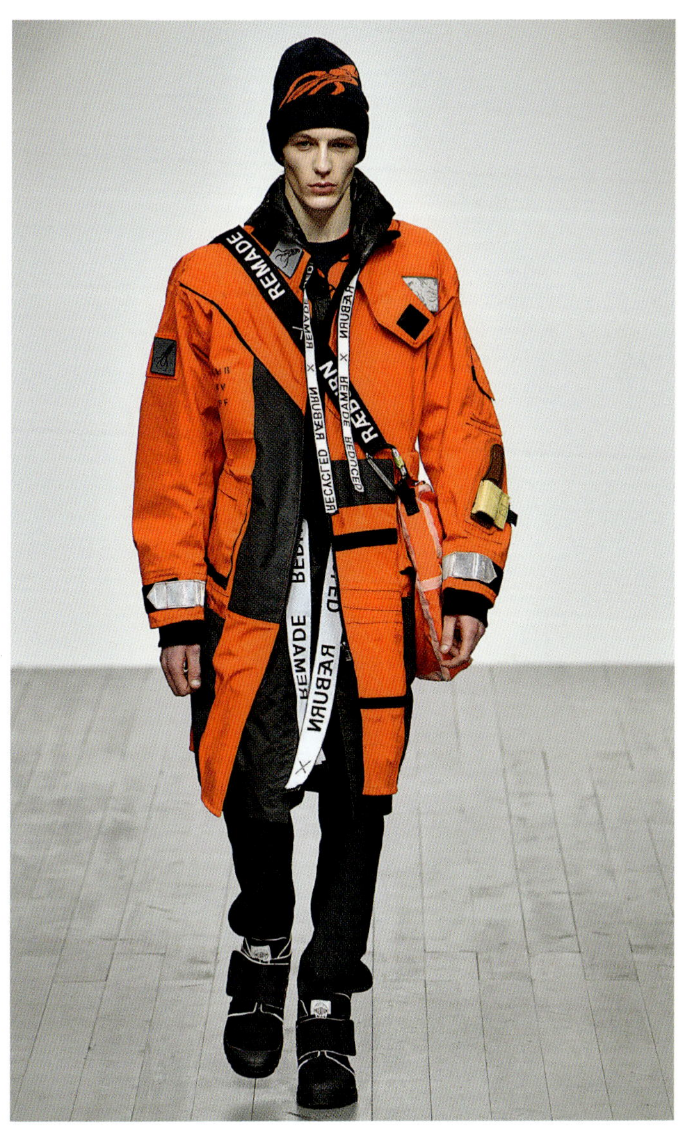

Christopher Raeburn, Fall/Winter 2018/2019, London

 # Yellow

Yellow is a feast for the eyes, and many of the shades in the family have a tactility and sensory appeal beyond their simple pigment. When we think of yellow, we might think of a freshly cut lemon, the spice and warmth of turmeric or the oozing yolk of a broken egg. We experience these colours at a deeper level through their texture and taste.

Pure yellow is a primary shade and a vital part of the CMYK printing technique. From zesty lemons and factory yellow to more buttery nuances, brown, green and orange all influence yellow tonality. While lighter shades tend not to be the most practical for certain material uses, yolky and muted mustards can take some wear and tear.

There were no completely stable yellow pigments until the 20th century. Lead, arsenic (orpiment), tree sap (gamboge) and even chemical-based chrome reacted and browned in the sunlight, and almost all had toxic side-effects. This frustration for artists and designers was solved with the creation of synthetic alizarin and azo pigments at the end of the 19th century, leading to a plethora of stable, transparent and clean dyes and pigments, including citrus-tinged hansa yellow and sunny cobalt yellow.

In the modern world, yellow is the colour of emojis, Post-its, taxi-cabs and signs that alert us to danger or caution. It's become industrialized and can be seen as tacky: too much bright yellow can overwhelm spaces. Nonetheless, it can still be used to great effect to create vibrant and attention-grabbing graphics. Inherently invigorating, studies have shown yellow can make us more alert and energized, boost our memory and encourage communication, giving it great purpose in learning environments.

Natural plant-based dyes are also back on the table; recipes for natural hues that have survived millennia offer a renewed sustainable purpose to waste products. These softer, faded yellows are a signifier of a more conscious consumerism. In our increasingly complex world, yellow still manages to cut through the noise, a shining beacon of optimism and play, inclusivity, calm and wellbeing.

## Colours in this chapter:

# Indian Yellow

## Then

Throughout history, new colours have been invented by accident or opportunity, and some have been actively pursued, but there are those whose origins remain mysterious.

We know that Indian yellow originated in 15th-century India and was imported to Europe in the 17th century, where the uniquely vibrant and lightfast yellow was much enjoyed by painters. But scant records from the 19th century reveal the mystery around the method of its making. Snake blood, camel urine and ox bile were all were suspected components, but one letter suggests that it came from cowherds (*gwalas*) feeding their cows exclusively mango leaves and collecting their urine. Even more strangely, the colour suddenly disappeared from the market. It was suspected that production had been banned in India due to issues of animal cruelty towards the cows – but no proof ever surfaced.

In India, yellow can symbolize spiritual attainment, and it is often used in holy ceremonies and religious clothing. In 15th-century Ragamala paintings that depict scenes from Hindu hymns, the striking compositions are dominated by yellow. When Indian yellow arrived on European shores, the imported (and rather pongy) dried balls of deep golden yellow were evocative of spices, sunshine, heat, flowers and dirt. The purified pellets created a beautiful sunny watercolour paint: J.M.W. Turner's extensive use of it in his watercolour palette was so influential, the colour sometimes took his name as 'Turner's yellow'.

## Now

After the original Indian yellow disappeared, it was synthesized in the 20th century with a shade mimicking the intense golden yellow of the original. Yellow is still a popular colour in Indian architecture and design today. In 2020, Sanjay Puri Architects completed a 100-acre development in Rajasthan with a vibrant and warm colour palette. The use of this sunny yellow on the exteriors gives the buildings a welcoming glow.

**Colour Values**
Hex code: #9c7a21
RGB: 156, 122, 33
CMYK: 31, 42, 95, 24
HSB: 43°, 79%, 61%

**Also Known As**
- Turner's Yellow

**Common Connotations**
- Welcoming
- Spiritual
- Uplifting

**Indian Yellow in Art, Design & Culture**
- *Krishna Plays his Enchanting Flute*, Lahore, Pakistan, c.1780
- *Abergavenny Bridge, Monmouthshire* by J.M.W. Turner, *painting*, 1798
- India Yellow, No.66 by Farrow & Ball, *paint*, 2020

## Use

Indian yellow conjures a rich identity when used as a prominent shade. The colour's natural saturation levels make it an energizing choice. Try balancing with deep, warm oranges and reds to create an inviting cosiness for interior spaces.

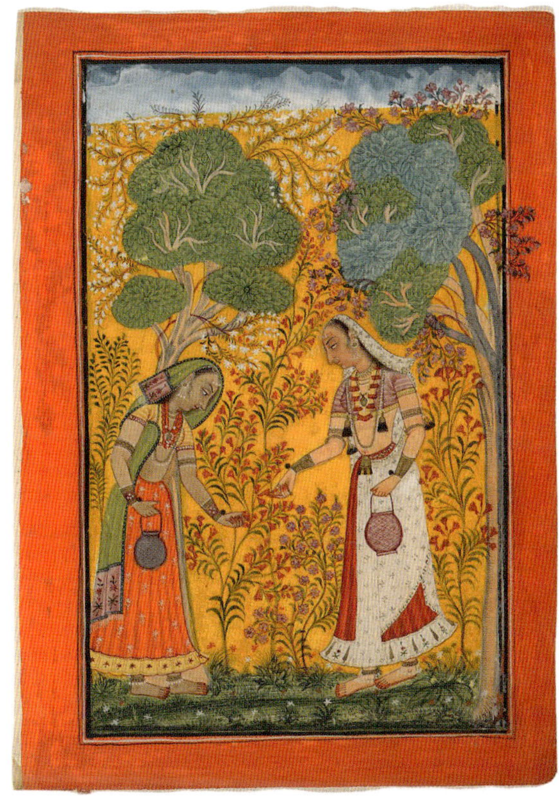

'Vasanti Ragini'; page from a Ragamala Series (*Garland of Musical Modes*), India, c.1710

 # Turmeric

**Then**

Turmeric (*Curcuma longa*) is part of the same plant family as ginger, and like ginger, its rhizomes have been valued in folk medicine and used as a preservative since ancient times. The rich orange-yellow powder, produced by finely grinding the rhizomes that have first been boiled and then dried in clay ovens, is a much-loved spice and an important dye throughout its native India and Southeast Asia, where it is also used as a body paste and a medicine, and is associated with religious iconography and literature.

Swaying between yellow and orange, turmeric is typically linked with the purity and spiritual attainment denoted by yellow as well as with protection and sunlight, signified by orange. Though not a lightfast dye, it has been used for centuries to colour the robes of Buddhist monks and women's saris. The 3,500-year-old sacred Hindu text, the Rig Veda, describes Lord Vishnu weaving the rays of the sun to make a garment for himself; he and Krishna can be found dressed in golden yellow in ancient miniatures and frescos.

**Now**

Although turmeric isn't one of the most lightfast dyes, it offers a natural alternative to chemical yellows, with less impact on the environment. In the work of contemporary maker Sophie Rowley, 10,000 threads are infused with turmeric to create graceful montages of frayed lines in the architectural textile pieces 'Khadi Frays'. The designer unpicks each thread, unravelling traditional weaving structures and creating new ones.

**Colour Values**

Hex code: #dcab1c
RGB: 220, 171, 28
CMYK: 14, 32, 94, 3
HSB: 45º, 87%, 86%

**Common Connotations**

- Sacred
- Sunny
- Authenticity

**Turmeric in Art,
Design & Culture**
- 'Kalamkari Hanging with Figures in an Architectural Setting', attributed to Deccan, India, *textiles*, c.1640–50
- *Study for Homage to the Square: Departing in Yellow* by Josef Albers, *painting*, 1964
- 'Khadi Frays' by Sophie Rowley, *woven textiles*, 2017

Fabric dyed by
Joanna Fowles, 2018

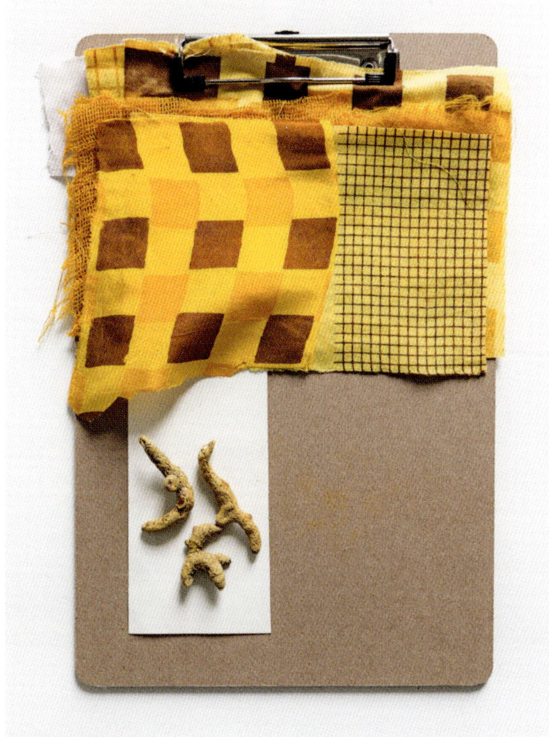

## Use

Yellow doesn't have to be eye-catching and bold all the time, and turmeric can give a muted, natural shade to cotton or linen. Team with soft bone-white and earthy soil shades for a palette that connects back to the colour's organic origins.

# Lemon Yellow

**Then**

Believed to have first been cultivated in India or China as a hybrid of the sour orange and citron fruit, the lemon was introduced to the Middle East around 600–400 BCE and was spread over the following centuries by Arab traders into other parts of Asia and Africa. In the 10th and 11th centuries the Moors occupied parts of southern Europe, bringing the lemon to places like Sicily and Andalusia, and in the late 1400s, Christopher Columbus took lemon seeds to the New World.

With the creation of new varieties since its exportation into Europe and the Americas, the lemon began to be adopted more in culinary use, but in most parts it remained a rare luxury, chiefly enjoyed for its older uses as a medicinal and decorative fruit. From the 15th century onwards, lemons became important symbolically for their vibrant hues, like bringing a ray of sunshine into dimly lit interiors, and were much depicted in Dutch art.

Despite its significance in painting, a stable lemon-yellow pigment wasn't invented until 1911, when German chemists developed the bright lemon yellow arylide lake pigment we now know as Hansa yellow. Previously artists used a mixture of plant-based concoctions including daffodils, watered down lead-tin yellow, to mimic citrus tones.

**Now**

In the 20th century, Henri Matisse picked up the baton from the Dutch and regularly featured lemons in his bright compositions. He made the most of their zesty colour in various colour combinations: with its complementary opposite lavender or pinks, neighbouring greens and oranges or in bold, primary-colour compositions. Design has also heeded these artists: a bowl of lemons is a contemporary kitchen cliché – but one that works, bringing a burst of positive colour to the environment, as well as being a healthy and delicious addition to many dishes and drinks.

**Colour Values**
Hex code: #ebed6f
RGB: 235, 237, 111
CMYK: 14, 0, 66, 0
HSB: 61°, 53%, 93%

**Also Known As**
Hansa Yellow
Arylide Yellow
Monoazo Yellow

**Common Connotations**
- Zesty
- Healthy
- Inviting

**Lemon Yellow in Art, Design & Culture**
- *Still Life with a Gilt Cup* by Willem Claesz. Heda, *painting*, 1635
- *Breton Woman in Prayer* by Paul Gauguin, *painting*, 1894

## Use

There is something innately appealing about lemon yellow. Clean and bright, it has a sharp, sophisticated edge; much like the flavour of the fruit itself. A joyful tetradic palette using turquoise, lavender, lemon yellow, and tomato red is ideal for outdoor eating and entertaining spaces.

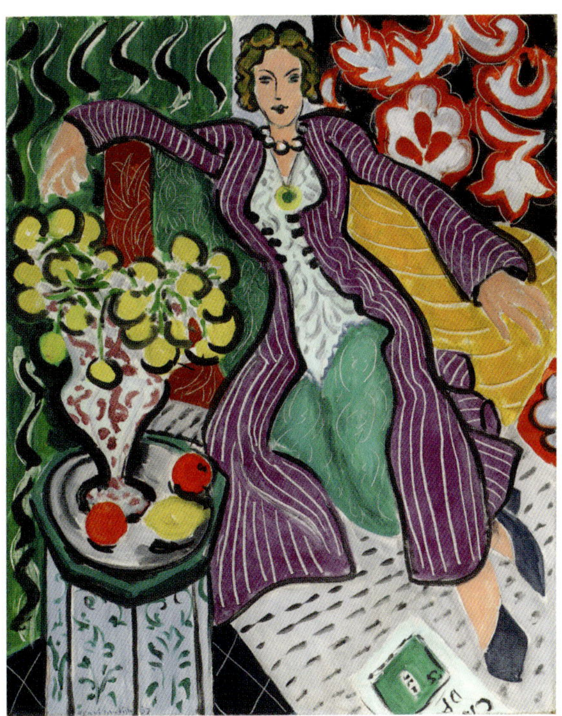

*Woman in a Purple Coat* by Henri Matisse, 1937

 # Factory Yellow

**Then**

This bold yellow takes its name from munitions factories. During the First World War, a group of women working in these factories in the UK obtained the nickname 'canary girls' because of exposure to TNT, which can turn the skin an orange-yellow colour. The shade was utilized in manufacturing environments to warn of toxic hazards.

To the human eye, a saturated yellow will always look as if it is slightly glowing, due to its enhanced ability to reflect light. The eye-catching nature of this synthetic hue has lent itself to use on enamel safety signs, emergency vehicles, taxis and powder-coated handrails. The company 3M trademarked the use of this signature yellow on Post-it Notes, helping them to stand out on creative walls around the world. A common choice for global brands, this bold hue is used by both IKEA and McDonald's, where it sits alongside other bright primaries to create maximum graphic impact.

**Now**

Inspired by his Nigerian heritage, designer Yinka Ilori used multicoloured batons, from factory yellow to magenta and sky blue, to create the Colour Palace with Pricegore architects at London's Dulwich Pavilion in 2019. In doing so, they created a piece of temporary architecture that encouraged playful interaction. In contemporary educational settings, the impact of this bold shade of yellow can be powerful in creating positive associations with learning. In an optimistic reinterpretation of the yellow school zone sign, Cottrell and Vermeulen Architecture used bright yellow to create an immediately recognizable and colourful identity for a London primary school in 2020.

**Colour Values**
Hex code: #f9dd00
RGB: 249, 221, 0
CMYK: 6, 8, 93, 0
HSB: 53°, 100%, 98%

**Also Known As**
- Canary Yellow

**Common Connotations**
- Playful
- Attention-grabbing
- Focusing

Right: Bellenden Primary School, Peckham, by Cottrell and Vermeulen Architecture, 2020

**Factory Yellow in Art, Design & Culture**
- Series 7 chair by Arne Jacobsen in 'True Yellow' from the 'A Sense of Colour' Series by Fritz Hansen, *furniture*, 2020

## Use
Thoughtful colour planning can stimulate and help facilitate learning, and yellow can provoke a feeling of optimism and creativity in educational settings. Apply this yellow around doorways and seating with natural wood tones to create a light, airy and inviting space for growing minds.

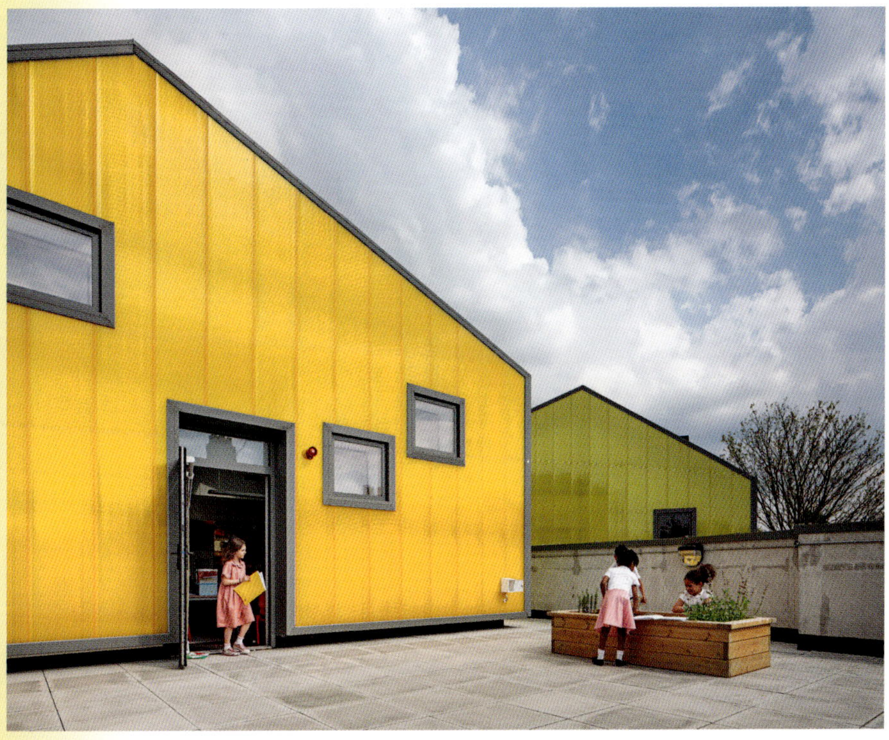

'To the human eye, a saturated yellow will always look as if it is slightly glowing.'

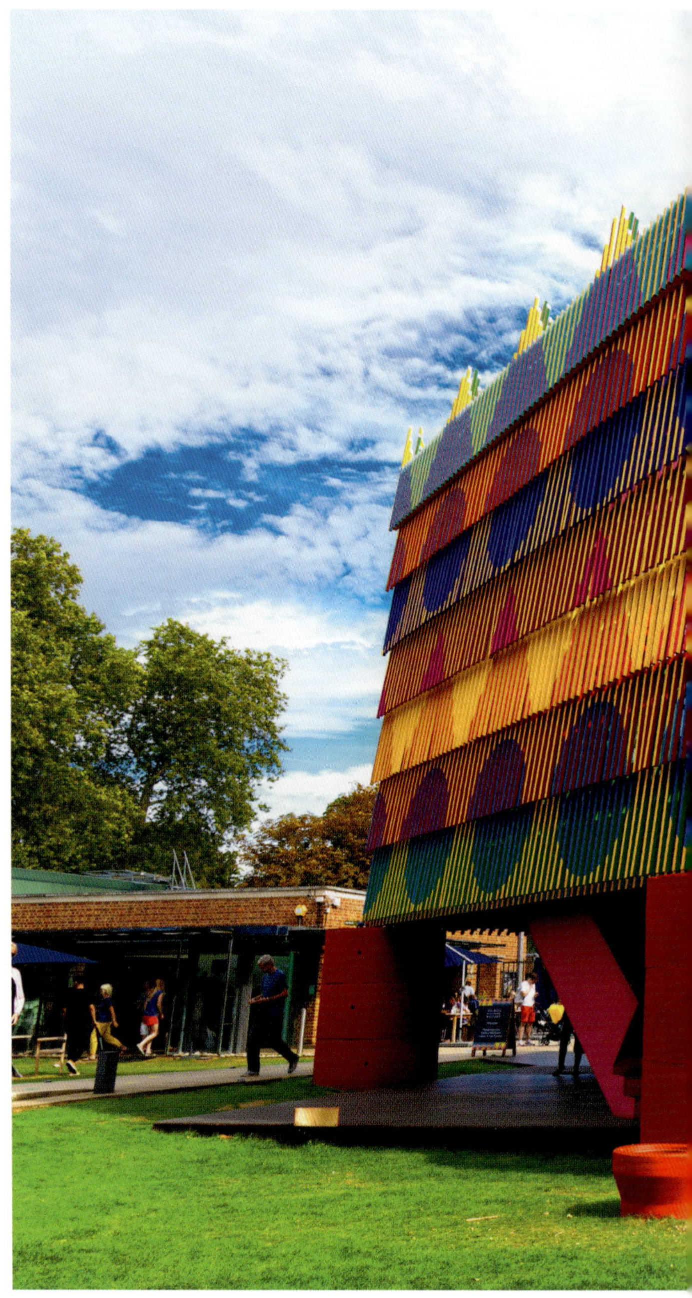

The Colour Palace for the Dulwich Picture Gallery, London by Yinka Ilori, 2019

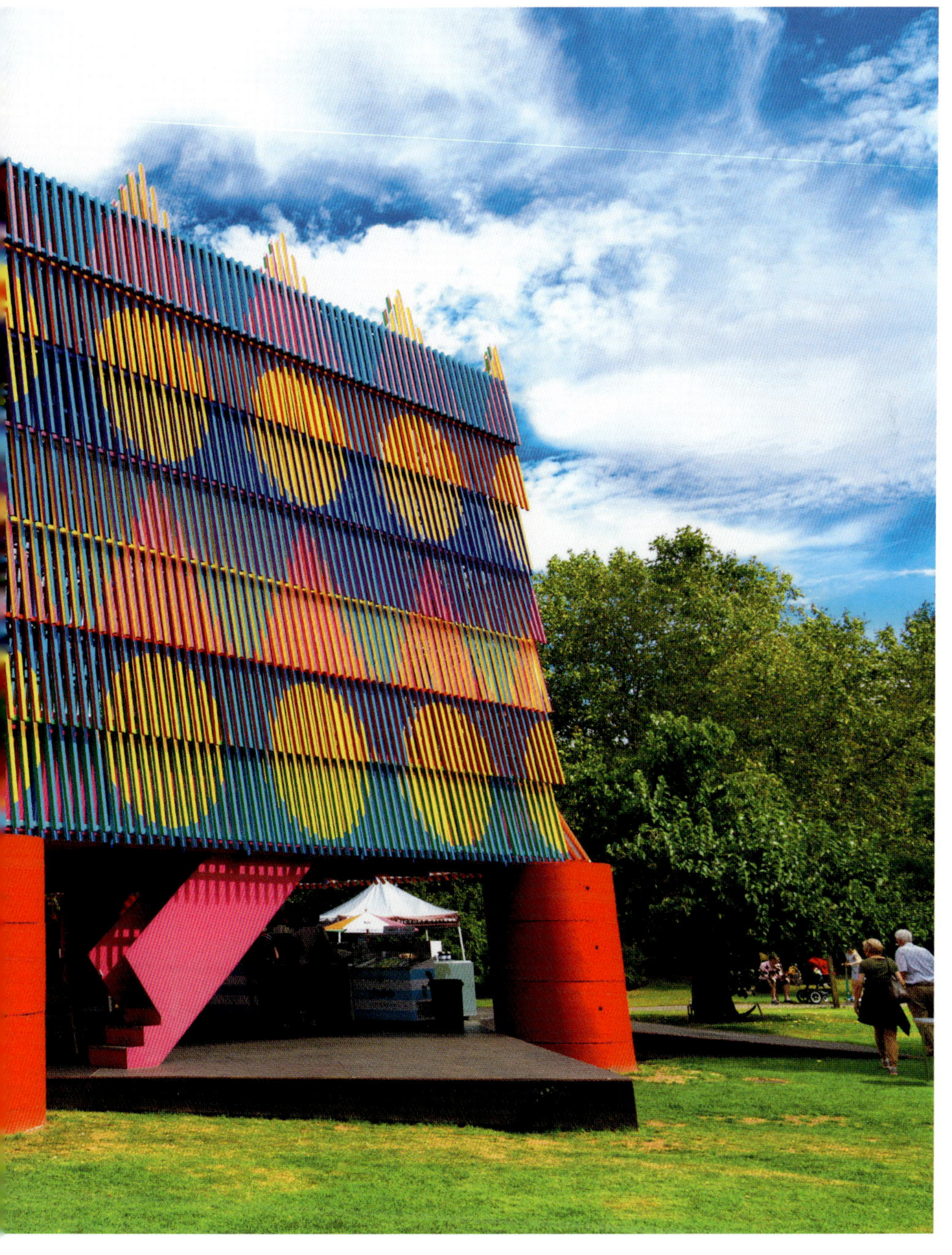

# Imperial Yellow



**Then**

The symbolism of imperial yellow has its origins in the regal robes worn by Chinese emperors. The earliest record of a certain shade of yellow being reserved for imperial use was under the rule of Emperor Gaozong of the Tang dynasty (618–907 CE). Records of palace inventories reveal the particular yellow used to dye royal robes was harvested from plants including native pagoda buds, and was then fixed with alum. Yellow, along with azure blue, red, white and blue-black, is part of the Five Elements Theory, an important concept in Chinese philosophy in which colour represents an equilibrium of interactions. In Europe, the 18th- and early-19th-century vogue for chinoiserie resulted in a renewed interest in this shade of yellow, which became a sophisticated and fashionable symbol of the upper classes.

**Now**

In a world where alternative power and energy sources are becoming increasingly important, this sunny yellow has been used to help support pioneering ideas and concepts. Automotive manufacturer Renault utilized the majestic shade in the interior of their all-electric, shape-shifting concept car in 2020. From the outside, glimpses of yellow helped to generate intrigue in the car's unique function and user experience.

**Use**

Imperial yellow can form an elemental and symbolic colour palette with ultramarine blue and traditional Chinese red (see Vermillion, page 66), suggesting a strong connection with an aristocratic heritage. Alternatively, a combination of pale gold, performance black and imperial yellow bestows status on innovative products and services.

**Colour Values**
Hex code: #f5cc5e
RGB: 245, 204, 94
CMYK: 0, 18, 70, 5
HSB: 44°, 62%, 96%

**Common Connotations**
- Sophistication
- Distinction
- Heritage

**Imperial Yellow in Art, Design & Culture**
- *Lady in Yellow (Eleanor Reeves)* by Susan Watkins, *painting*, 1902
- Renault Morphoz electric concept car, *automotive*, 2020

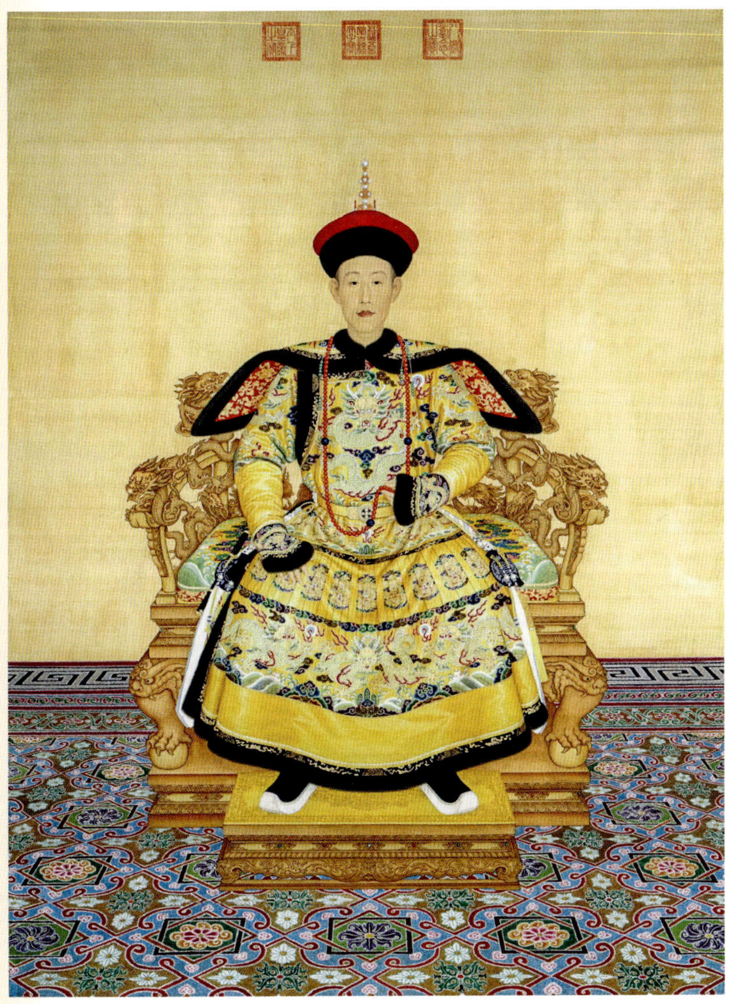

*The Qianlong Emperor in Court Dress* by Giuseppe Castiglione, 1736

# Faded Sunflower

**Then**

Evocative of warm days and happiness, sunflower yellow is a saturated hue with a long-lasting appeal. In 1887–8, sunflowers were the favoured subject matter of Dutch post-impressionist painter Vincent van Gogh. Having seen the vividly coloured works of the impressionists in Paris, he used still lifes of flowers to experiment with colour, often choosing to paint blooms that were already wilting.

In this period, Van Gogh went from a fairly traditional use of colour to painting dramatic combinations of striking yellows with intense blue backgrounds. Today, however, these famous canvases have faded to muted yellow-browns, likely due to the instability of the yellow paint he used: a mixture of yellow lead chromate and white lead sulphate. Though widely in use at the time, the colour degraded in sunlight, giving his canvases an aged quality much like his sunflowers.

**Now**

The nostalgic quality of this faded colour is key today. Worn, mustardy yellows speak of well-used colour, like finding a faded pressed flower from summers past inside the pages of a book. With fast fashion and fashion waste becoming more of a contemporary concern, a colour palette of well-worn and grounded hues serves a positive, conscious aesthetic.

**Use**

Tap into the popularity of baked, earthy tones and faded, muted sky blues – ideal for a fashion collection developing staple garments that transcend seasonal purchasing.

**Colour Values**

Hex code: #f8cd76
RGB: 248, 205, 118
CMYK: 3, 21, 62, 0
HSB: 40º, 52%, 97%

**Common Connotations**

- Warm
- Grounded
- Nostalgia

**Faded Sunflower in Art, Design & Culture**

- Tie-Dye Snack Shirt in Yellow by STORY mfg, *fashion*, 2020

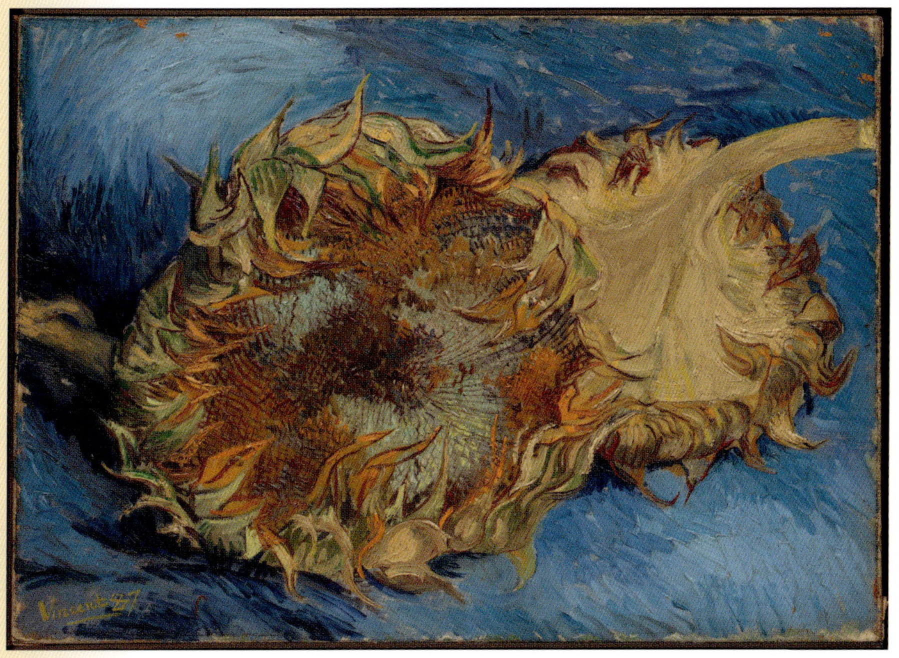

*Sunflowers* by Vincent van Gogh, 1887

# Wheat

**Then**

Humans have scavenged wild grains and grasses since the Stone Age, but the ability to domesticate and cultivate crops began only around 12,000 years ago in the Levant. One of the most important developments in our history, agriculture took our ancestors beyond a hunter-gatherer subsistence, but it also tied us to the land in a new way.

Ever since, until very recently, the harvest was a seasonal event that every member of society had a stake in. A good harvest meant there would be enough food for all, even surplus, while a bad one meant people would go hungry. Thus, the colour of golden ripe wheat fields has come to symbolize wealth and abundance across the Western world. While it's not a colourant in itself, the hue was important enough to be distinguished from other shades. In the late 17th century, 'wheat' began to be officially added to early colour naming systems.[*]

**Now**

An on-trend colour for interior design and fashion in the latter half of the 20th century and early 21st, wheat's soft yellow-brown shade has gained popularity as an inclusive neutral. In the 1980s, Max Mara's wheat-coloured trench coats provided a universally wearable statement piece, while Donna Karan brought a monotonal aesthetic to her Spring 2011 women's collection with silky wheat-colour gowns and down-to-earth jute details. More recently, French fashion designer Porte Jacquemus's Spring 2021 collection saw models treading a catwalk in a literal wheat field, dressed in a palette of hues inspired by the crop.

**Colour Values**

Hex code: #e6d29b
RGB: 230, 210, 155
CMYK: 12, 16, 46, 1
HSB: 44º, 30%, 90%

**Common Connotations**
- Authentic
- Idyllic
- Abundance

[*] Maerz, A. and Paul, M. Rea, *A Dictionary of Color*, New York: McGraw-Hill Publishing Co., 1930.

**Wheat in Art,
Design & Culture**
- *Garbes* by Josep Benseny Piñol, *painting*, 1951
- Womenswear collection by Donna Karan, *fashion*, S/S 2011
- Flourist bakery and flour mill, Vancouver, by Ste Marie, *interior design*, 2019

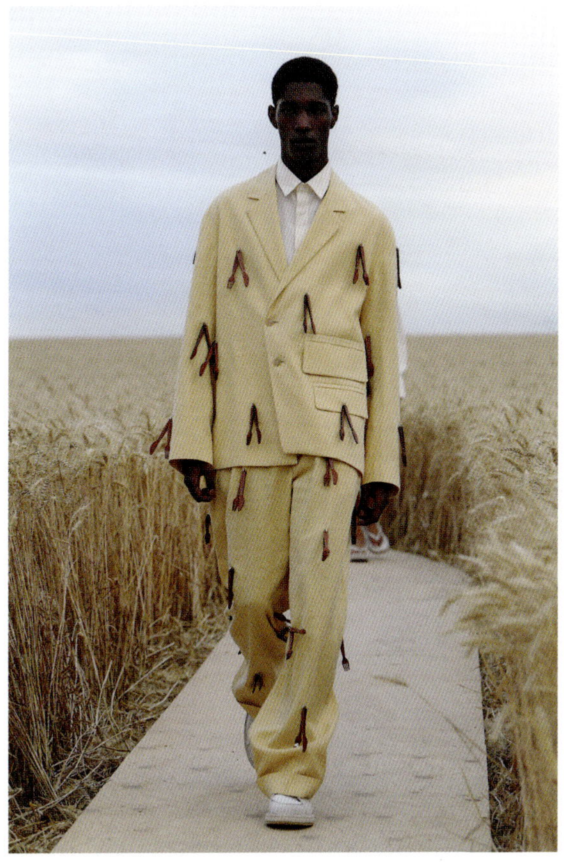

'L'Amour' collection by Jacquemus, Paris, Spring/ Summer 2021

## Use
Wheat is an optimistic modern neutral. A sunny combination with pale blue, sage, clay and soil brown creates a flattering palette suggestive of a more straightforward, authentic way of life.

 # Gold

**Then**

Gold fever goes back to ancient times and the brilliant yellow metal seems to have been almost universally treasured, with beautiful, sometimes holy objects crafted from it, civilizations destroyed for it, and thousands of myths attached to it. Gold has long been associated with divinity – Catholic churches and Hindu and Buddhist temples are known for liberal use of the material – and with royalty. In 18th-century France, Louis XIV, known as the Sun King, employed gilder Pierre Gouthière to apply a thin layer of gold leaf to every visible surface and object of his palace in Versailles, attesting to the wealth and power of his country.

In early religious painting of the Byzantine era, thin leaves of gold would be applied to the halos of saints and other details, and finely worked. In the Baroque period of the 17th century, however, it became a challenge for artists to prove their skill by capturing the effect of the metal by mixing other hues, as demonstrated by works such as Rembrandt's glowing *Belshazzar's Feast* (1636–8).

**Colour Values**

Hex code: #9b7a41
RGB: 155, 122, 65
CMYK: 32, 43, 77, 24
HSB: 38º, 58%, 61%

**Common Connotations**

- Perfection
- Excess
- Value

**Gold in Art, Design & Culture**

- Ladurée London, Burlington Arcade, decorated by Roxane Rodriguez, *interior design*, 2006
- iPhone 6S in Gold, *product design*, 2015
- *America* by Maurizio Cattelan, *sculpture*, 2016

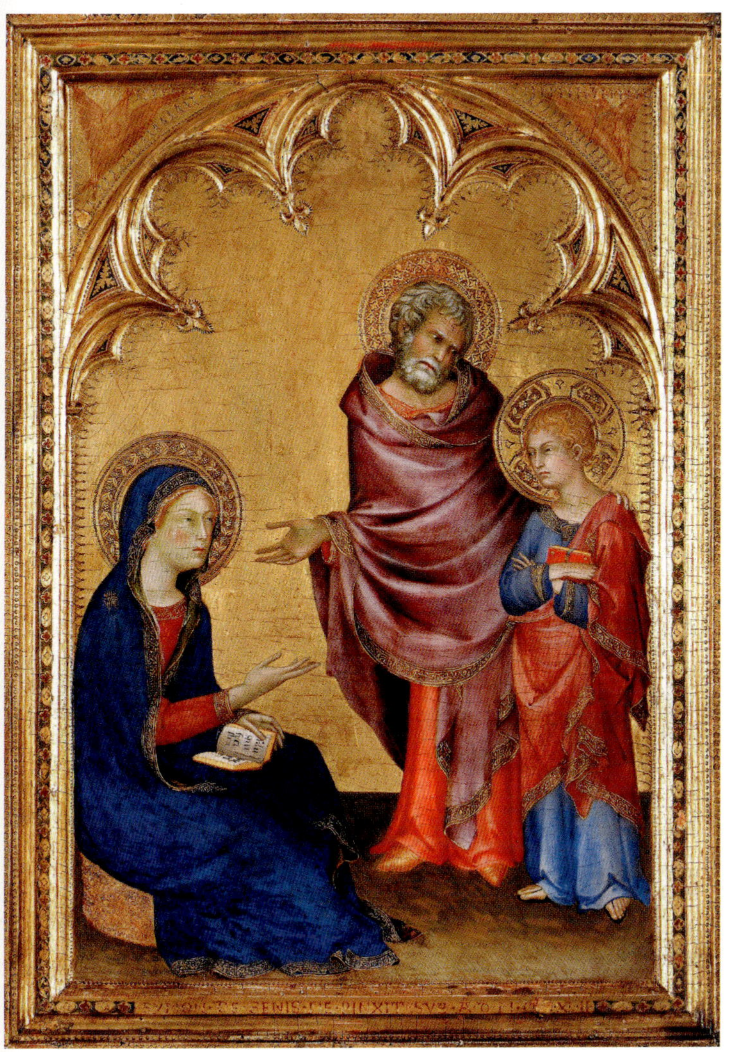

*Christ Discovered in the Temple* by Simone Martini, 1342

**Now**

Since ancient civilizations first connected the glowing metal with the sun, it has been hard to think of gold without drawing on its cultural and symbolic associations. But there is another side to gold, if we focus on its natural properties and practicality. For instance, architects and designers have found uses for its temperature-regulating properties, creating gold-coated glass windows to reflect sunlight during the summer and bounce internal heat back into rooms during winter.

The world has also taken notes from *kintsugi*, the Japanese art of repairing ceramics that uses gold to bind a broken vessel, wasting nothing and making the object more beautiful than before. The principles behind this practice have made gold an unlikely champion of restrained and appropriate application in a post-consumerist society.

**Use**

Gold's modern association with corrupt leaders and blinged-up celebrities has transformed it into a sign of excess, cultural domination and even tackiness. Small accents of the colour add a glint of rarity rather than excess to a palette.

'The principles behind *kintsugi* have made gold an unlikely champion of restrained and appropriate application in a post-consumerist society.'

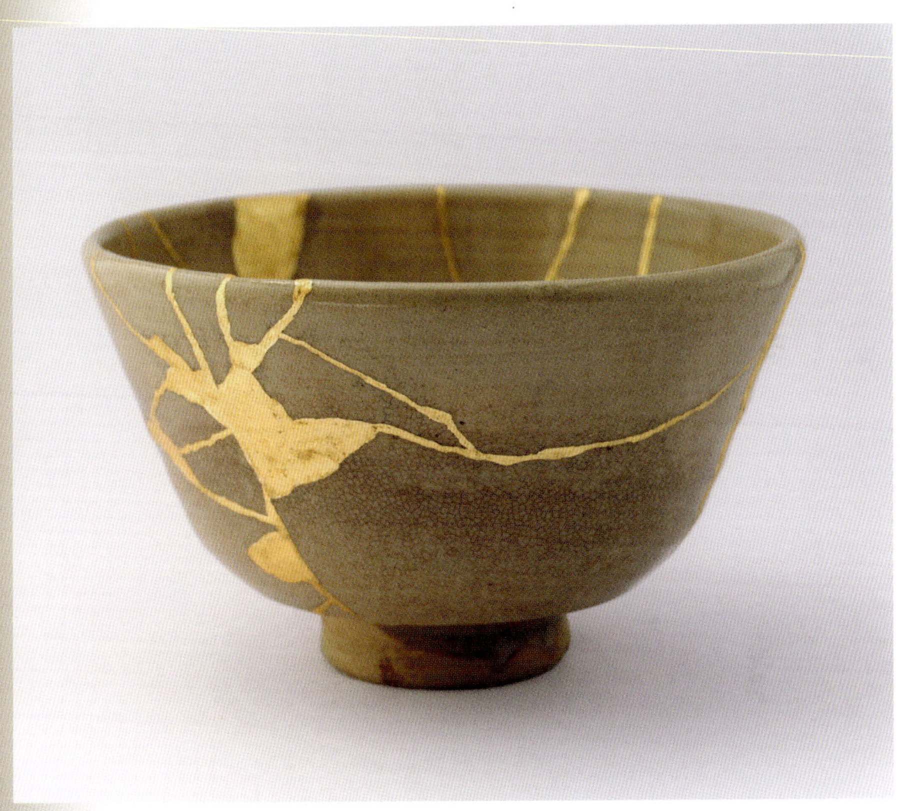

*Kintsugi* beige tea ceremony bowl, restored with gold (undated)

# Mindaro

**Then**

Thoroughly modern mindaro has its origins in chartreuse, which takes its name from the French liqueur that was in vogue in the mid-18th century. The original yellow-green colour was created using Scheele's green, a warm green pigment invented in 1775 by German-Swedish chemist Carl Wilhelm Scheele. Packed with arsenic, the pigment was highly toxic, yet commercial demand was high, with applications in paintings, wallpaper, fabric and even toys. By the late 1800s, silk and velvet fabrics were being produced in the distinctive shade, which became a quirky fashion choice among European society. Chartreuse-like shades, this time without the toxic tinge, had a resurgence in popularity in the late 1950s as an everyday colour choice for ceramics and furniture, and by the 2000s, it was firmly established on interior paint cards.

**Now**

The vibrant, tennis-ball-like yellow-green of chartreuse has been brought down a shade or two in common contemporary usage to a tempered and slightly off-kilter mellowed mindaro. In fashion, it is still a bold, slightly rebellious and eccentric colour; however, endorsement from former First Lady Michelle Obama, frequently seen wearing this shade, has ensured that mindaro carries a positive message. Packed with personality, in design, it can make an eye-catching statement or fade back to a forgiving neutral that can provide a break from homogeneous, unblended colours.

**Colour Values**
Hex code: #ddd582
RGB: 221, 213, 130
CMYK: 10, 4, 56, 10
HSB: 55°, 41%, 87%

**Also Known As**
- Chartreuse

**Common Connotations**
- Authentic
- Independent
- Eccentric

**Mindaro in Art,
Design & Culture**
- *Woman Combing Her
Hair* by Edgar Degas,
*pastel drawing*, c.1888–90
- Ready-to-Wear collection
by Jason Wu, *fashion*,
A/W 2009

## Use

Explore hand-applied colour to bring out mindaro's authentic nature. Try blending into rose pink to create sensitive colour gradients, highlighted with deep mustard or gold; ideal for distinctive one-off design and craft applications.

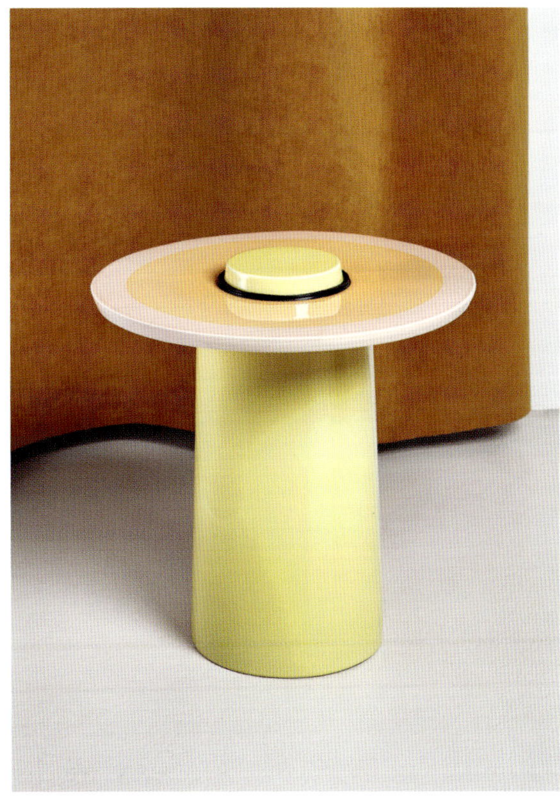

Table Top Yellow, Studio
RENS x Cor Unum
Ceramics, 2020

# Marigold

**Then**

In Mexican folklore, the souls of the dead follow the scent of marigolds. Deeply symbolic to the nation, the Aztec marigold has been used for medicinal purposes and as a bright offering on altars during Day of the Dead celebrations.

Bold and optimistic, marigold has long been used as a colour to make striking fashion statements. In the 1960s, Jackie Kennedy's marigold yellow ball skirt was an iconic part of her brightly coloured wardrobe, itself an era-defining symbol of aspiration and success. Since then, marigold has remained a faithful fashion companion, appearing in modern collections from Nina Ricci to Phillip Lim. Yellow naturally reflects lots of light, so adding a splash of marigold is effortlessly uplifting and catches attention.

**Now**

Leaning almost into orange, marigold's striking saturation cuts through the grey as a visceral reminder of the natural world around us. In 2016, artistic duo Christo and Jeanne-Claude employed the shade on colossal walkways they placed across the contrasting blue-green Lake Iseo, Italy, allowing 1.2 million visitors to walk on water.

**Use**

Harness the power of marigold for an uplifting effect. Use in bold proportions to raise energy levels and mood.

**Colour Values**

Hex code: #fb9614
RGB: 251, 150, 20
CMYK: 0, 49, 92, 0
HSB: 34°, 92%, 98%

**Common Connotations**

- Traditional
- Youthful
- Aspirational

**Marigold in Art, Design & Culture**

- Ready-to-Wear collection by Altazurra, *fashion*, S/S 2021
- *Yellow Roseline* from the series *Between These Folded Walls, Utopia* by Cooper & Gorfer, *photography*, 2020

Right: Altar in San Miguel de Allende with food, photographs and marigolds for Day of the Dead celebration, Mexico

Overleaf: Floating Piers by Christo and Jeanne-Claude, 2016

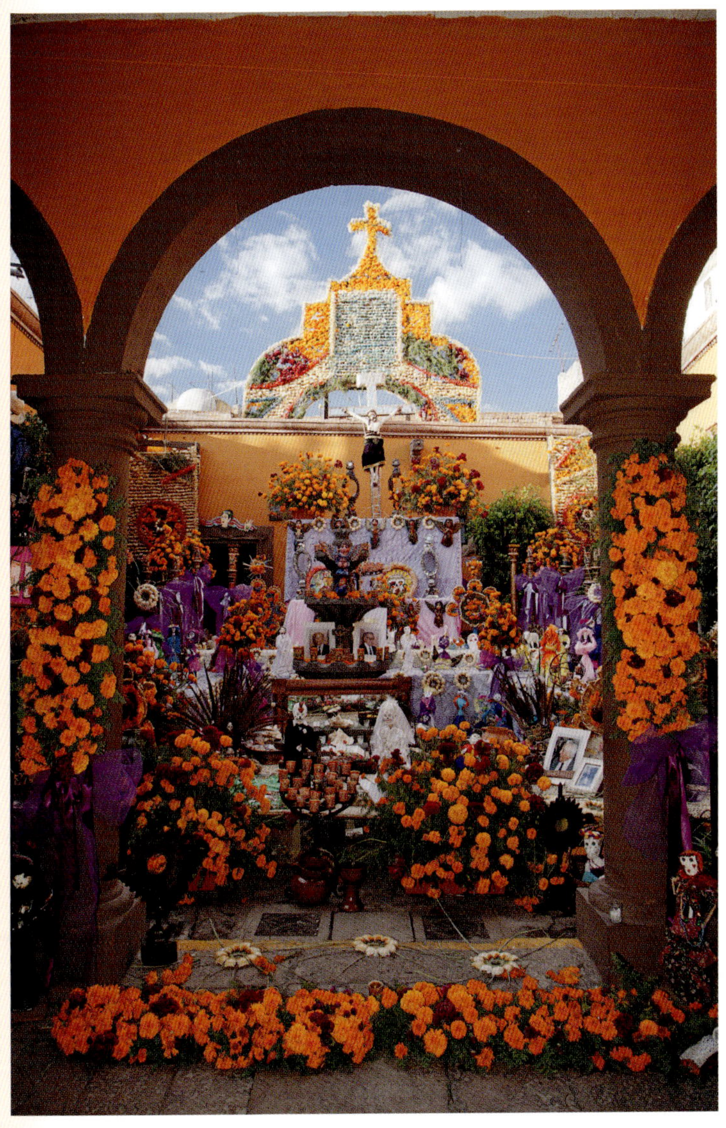

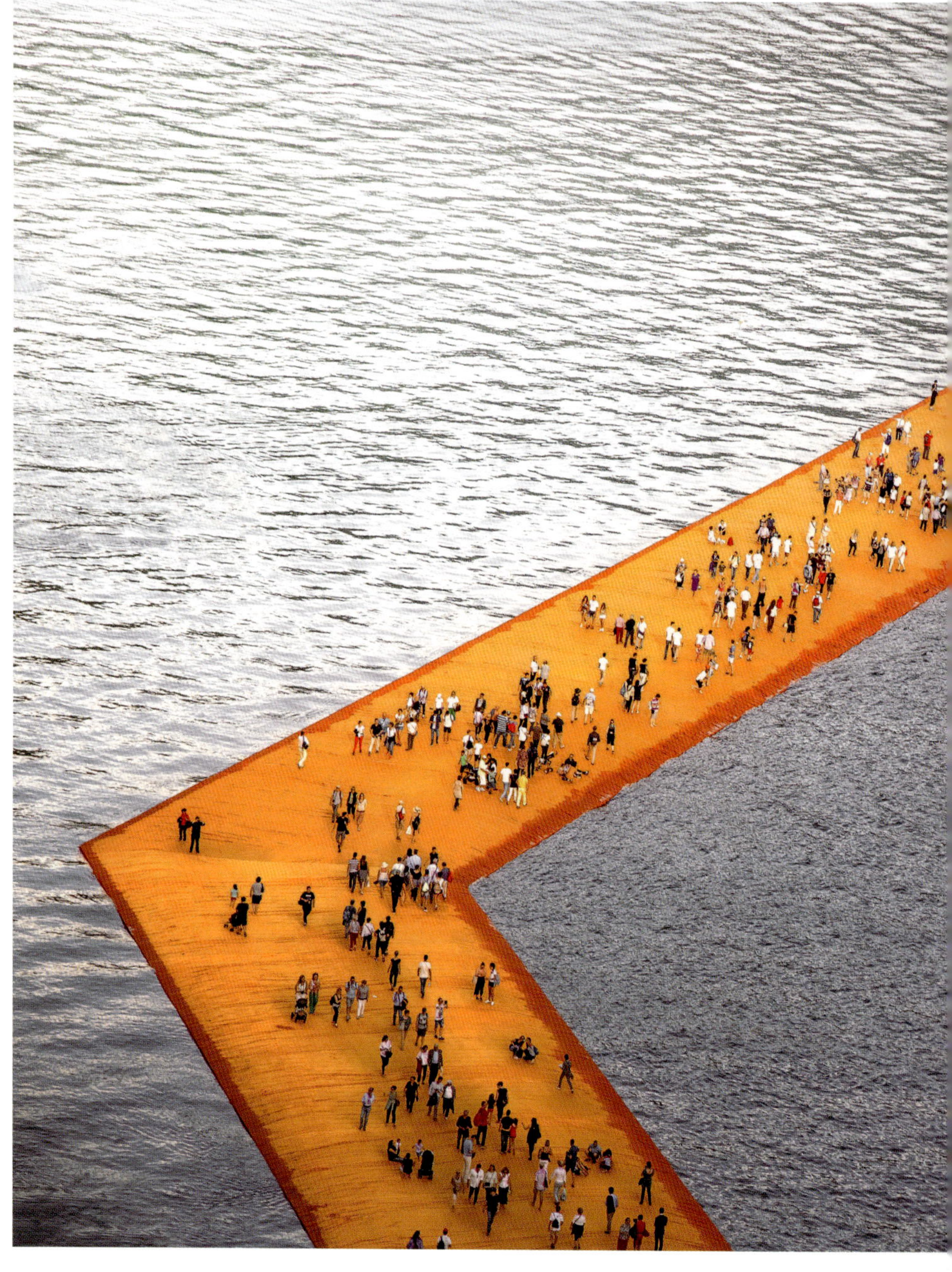

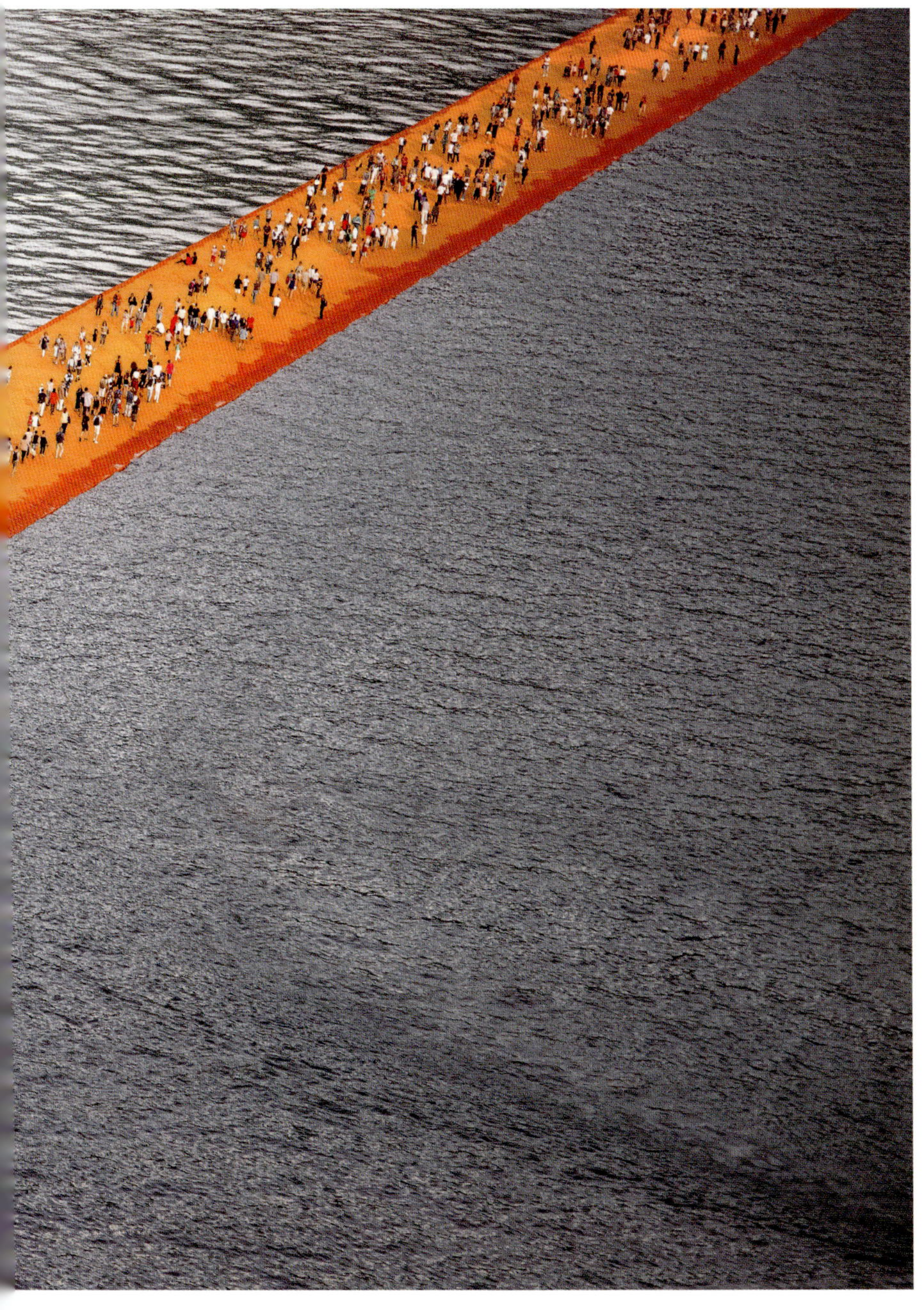

 # Green

There are not more greens in the world than any
other shade, as a common misconception has it;
however, our eyes have evolved to be especially good at
distinguishing the nuances of green light wavelengths.
We can see this for ourselves when observing foliage
in the natural world: what looks like one shade at first
glance offers almost infinite subtlety under further
inspection. Because our eyes are so adept at seeing
green, it is also a particularly comfortable shade for us
to look at. Today, the health benefits of being in nature
are well known, and we can bring some of this indoors
with us when we use green in our interior palettes.
T.S. Eliot once described his personal green space as
'my still point of the turning world'.[*]

From vivacious yellow- and leaf-greens to mysterious
and soothing dark greens; from murky olive-greens to
bright and jewel-like emerald and turquoise hues, the
green family contains a vast range of shades to choose
from, and it has been equally prolific in generating
associations. In Japan, green is traditionally highly
regarded as the giver of life. Strongly connected with
the prophet Muhammad and signifying paradise,
fertility, luck and wealth, it appears in the flags of many
predominantly Muslim countries. On the other hand,
green is the colour of decay as well as rebirth, and it
is commonly linked with putrefaction and disease. In
Thai, the word *kheīyw*, besides denoting 'green', also
means 'foul' and 'smelly' and holds other unpleasant
connotations. In Christian countries, green was also
associated with paganism – with the Celtic Green Man,
for example – and it has since often been used to signify
evil, in contrast with sacred and valorous reds.

Despite its frequency in nature, for a long time green
proved elusive as a pigment. Until the advent of synthetic
pigments, most greens were made by mixing blue and
yellow pigments due to the difficulty in extracting a

* Eliot, T.S, 'Burnt Norton',
*Poems*, London: The Hogarth
Press, 1919

stable and charismatic green, and even then greens proved hazardous. In 1775, chemist Carl Wilhelm Scheele concocted an artificial green that was quickly adopted into textiles and wallpapers. However, laced with arsenic, Scheele's green was toxic and caused an unknowable number of deaths throughout the 19th century.

Despite its chequered history, green is now making up for lost time. In the latter half of the 20th century, the colour gained popularity alongside the rise of the global environmental movement. Traditionally associated with ecological groups such as Greenpeace and the UK's Green Party, today it has also been adopted into the branding of any organization wishing to associate itself with environmentally sustainable practices. Most recently, advancements in science and biomaterials have unlocked new potentials in the natural pigments found in plant life, taking green's association with a sustainable future from the symbolic to the material.

**Colours in this chapter:**

# Green Earth

**Then**

This pallid, eponymously earthy green sits somewhere between a sea mist at first light and a dewy moss. It comes from naturally occurring minerals, including celadonite and glauconite, that are as abundant as they are inexpensive.

Green earth rose to fame in Europe in Renaissance times, when painters such as Giotto used it as a glaze under semi-transparent layers of crimson to create lifelike skin tones. Unfortunately, time reveals unstable pigments, and as the paintings have aged, so too have the flesh tones, often taking on a rather insipid, deathly green appearance.

In the 17th century, Japanese artisans exported stingray skins as decorative surfaces, which became known as 'shagreen'. They were often coloured with lucent *terre verte* so as not to distract from the scaly texture.

**Now**

More recently, the wash-like nature of green earth has allowed for the exploration of transparency as a form of materiality by minimalist painters such as Robert Mangold. Using a handmade tint in his painting series *Ring H*, the artist explores the soothing, subtle colour and curvilinear abstract forms.

**Use**

The non-opposing nature of this neutral green makes it a perfect grounding base tone. Layer to create peaceful, luminous washes, and balance with rosy hues and clean white for a calming, modern colour scheme.

**Colour Values**

Hex code: #8ba26c
RGB: 139, 162, 108
CMYK: 49, 23, 70, 2
HSB: 86º, 33%, 64%

**Also Known As**

- Terre Verte
- Verona Green

**Common Connotations**

- Vulnerable
- Supportive
- Soothing

**Green Earth in Art, Design & Culture**

- Japanese wood and shagreen spectacle case by Rinkomoru Yoshigawa, *accessory*, c.1890
- Clay Green by Studio RENS x Moooi Carpets, *carpet*, 2020

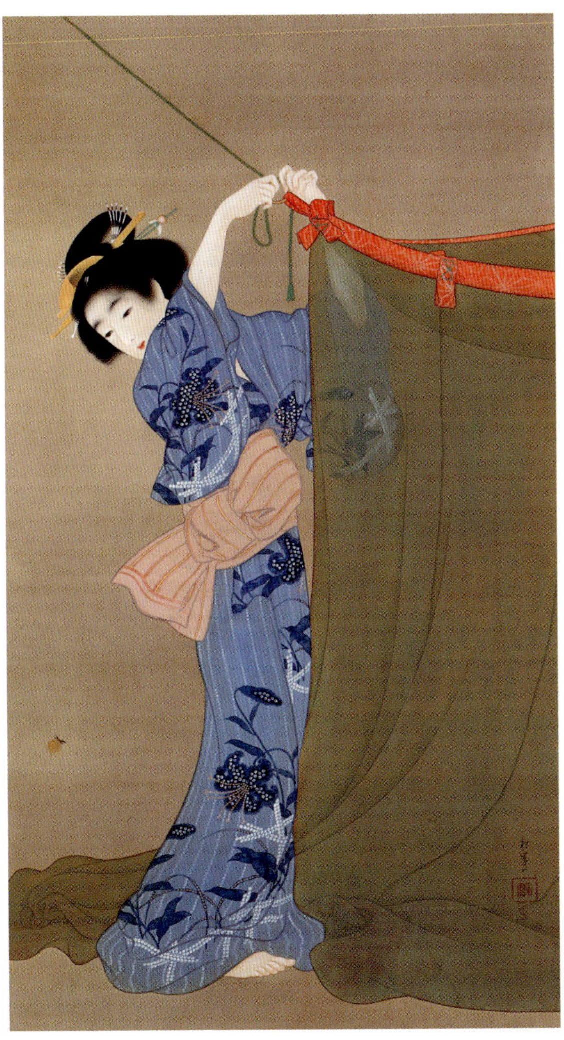

*Firefly* by Uemura Shōen, 1913

 # Verdigris

## Then

Unstable, reactive and even toxic, verdigris offers a perfect example of all the difficulties we have had in harnessing green. This amorphic green-blue colour is a byproduct of an ancient chemical reaction: the oxidization of copper and bronze. Described as the 'green of Greece' (the name comes from the French *vert de Grèce*), the scraped-off surface patina of this verdant 'rust' was ground down and made into a painter's medium, first appearing in Europe in medieval artworks.

Despite its poisonous nature and tendency to discolour, as the only truly vibrant green pigment available it remained in use until the 19th century. A common practice in Indian and Persian cultures to prevent the colour from turning brown or black was to introduce saffron. In the end, the fugitive colour was made obsolete once modern methods brought the creation of more stable, long-lasting tones.

## Now

Today, the naturally occurring verdigris can still be seen gracing elegant copper roofs and landmarks such as the Statue of Liberty. Unlike its corrosive red cousin, rust, which eats away at iron, verdigris provides a layer of protection to the copper that hosts it.

Meanwhile, as contemporary tastes have evolved – in particular with reference to Japanese principles of *wabi-sabi*, increased value placed on the natural world and the desire for uniqueness – the use of verdigris has become popular once more. London-based design studio Yenchen & Yawen's Landscape of Oxidation project features three homeware collections based on rust, Verdigris and *kintsugi* (the Japanese practice of filling cracks in pottery with gold, making the broken piece even more beautiful than the original). Pieces in the 'Blue Patina' collection are made by mixing jesmonite with glass, copper, brass and iron powders, and burying the vessels in wet dust for days to generate a unique verdigris patina that will alter over time.

**Colour Values**
Hex code: #27a1a4
RGB: 39, 161, 164
CMYK: 77, 16, 38, 0
HSB: 181°, 76%, 64%

**Common Connotations**
- Fickle
- Alluring
- Individual

## Use

Embrace verdigris' imperfect beauty by building translucent washes of this beautiful green-blue that interact with each other. Try pairing with minimal and modern proportions of other metallic shades such as copper and brass.

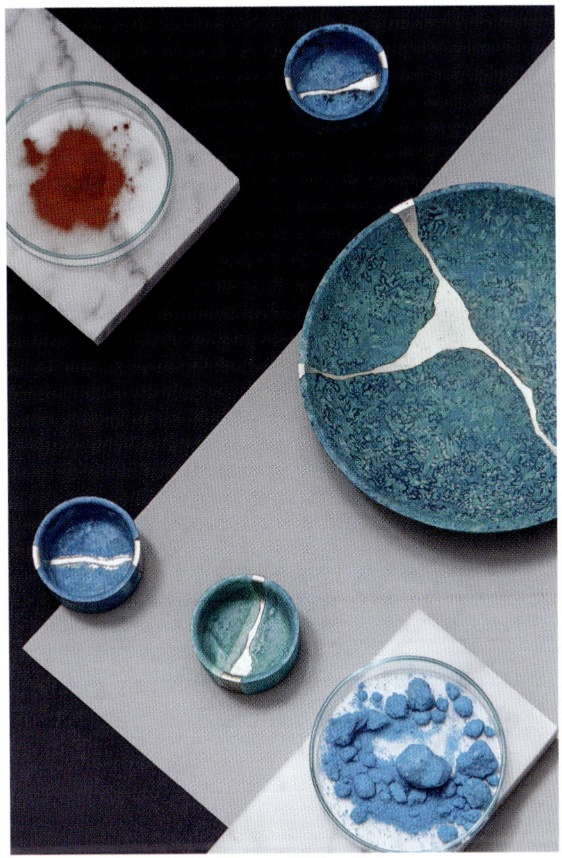

Landscape of Oxidation by
Yenchen and Yawen, 2018

# Malachite

### Then

The deep green, copper-based mineral malachite, ground down to form a pigment, is known to have been used as eyeshadow and decorative paint by ancient Egyptians, who gave the substance heavenly status, linking it to the goddess Hathor, 'the lady of malachite'. ancient Aztec civilizations mined malachite and created decorative accessories with slices of the green striated material, giving the deeply coloured substance talisman status. Japanese artist Watanabe Kazan's 1821 *Portrait of Sato Issai (Age 50)* shows malachite green at its finest, adding depth and shade to the subject.

It is one of the oldest green pigments known, readily available in its mineral form and giving a vibrant and lightfast (if toxic) green, but malachite did not find wide use in Europe. To retain its vibrancy, malachite does not want to be ground too fine, and while it would remain effective in paintings made with egg tempera or plaster, it becomes insipid in the fine consistencies required by oil paint, which supplanted the older tempera method during the Renaissance.

### Now

Now phased out as a pure pigment, the glamorous green of ancient cultures has made a comeback in the modern world thanks to an increased appreciation in art and design for material qualities. In 2020, Italian design company Fornasetti gave malachite a new outing by pairing patterns derived from the cut surface of the mineral with modernist shapes and forms, gelling the past and the present together in a new luxury aesthetic.

**Colour Values**
Hex code: #126d64
RGB: 18, 109, 100
CMYK: 87, 37, 61, 20
HSB: 174º, 84%, 43%

**Also Known As**
- Mountain Green
- Green Verditer
- Green Bice

**Common Connotations**
- Otherworldly
- Precious
- Luxury

Right: 'Malachite' living room, from the Unusual Living Rooms collection by Fornasetti, 2020

**Malachite Green in Art, Design & Culture**

- Headdress or helmet with mosaic of turquoise, malachite and thorny oyster shell, Aztec, Mexico, 1400–1521
- Chrysanthemums by Pierre-Auguste Renoir, *painting*, 1881–2
- Stelis Bag by Montunas, *accessories*, 2019

**Use**

Malachite's evocative association with ancient cultures, and the beautiful hue and delicate banded patterns of its gemstone, are what appeal today. Take a cue from Fornasetti's palette and pair deep malachite green with factory yellow and delicate oyster grey for luxury branding or packaging.

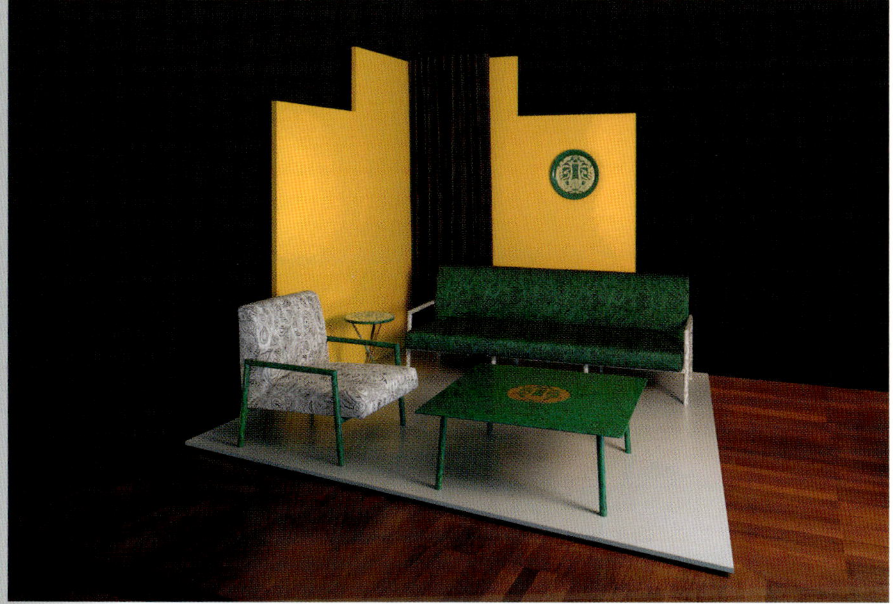

# Celadon

**Then**

In the 12th century, Chinese scholar Hsu Ching visited Korea to uncover the nature of Goryeo celadons. He was impressed with what he saw, remarking, 'With regard to ceramic wares, that which is of green colour is described by the natives as of *fei si* ('kingfisher colour')… their colour and glaze are particularly good.'* Made by applying a wash (or 'slip') of diluted clay containing a high proportion of iron, this green ceramic glaze was perfected in China around 25–220 CE.

As Hsu Ching's comment suggests, ceramics made from the celadon technique might vary from grey-green to greenish blue or a murky olive green, according to the region it was produced in and the techniques used to make it. Despite its material origin, the colour itself is insubstantial, as attested to by the seemingly arbitrary manner in which it came to be named: it is believed that 'celadon' was coined as a colour in the 17th century in reference to the hero of a French pastoral comedy, whose delicate green costume put viewers in mind of the distinctive green ceramics being imported from China.

**Now**

Still linked conceptually to the beautiful ceramics of China and South and East Asia, contemporary design often prefers a more delicate, glaze-like tone of celadon. Inspired by Chinese and Korean aesthetics and Bauhaus principles, British ceramicist Edmund De Waal uses the colour on porcelain vessels in atmospheric architectural spaces where its enigmatic and ephemeral nature sings.

* Gompertz, G. St. G. M., 'The "Kingfisher Celadon" of Koryo', Artibus Asiae, vol. 16, no. 1/2, 1953

**Colour Values**
Hex code: #90b7af
RGB: 144, 183, 175
CMYK: 45, 15, 32, 0
HSB: 168°, 21%, 72%

**Common Connotations**
- Enigmatic
- Graceful
- Peaceful

**Celadon in Art,
Design & Culture**
- Chinese funerary urns,
  stoneware with glaze,
  Yuan dynasty, *ceramics*
  1279–1368
- *Another Sky* by Edmund
  de Waal, *sculpture*, 2016
- Ready-to-Wear collection
  by Vince, *fashion*, S/S 2021

## Use

Pair celadon with other soft hues such as porcelain
whites and creams, duck-egg blues and butter yellows to
bring an airy and quietening mood to interior spaces.

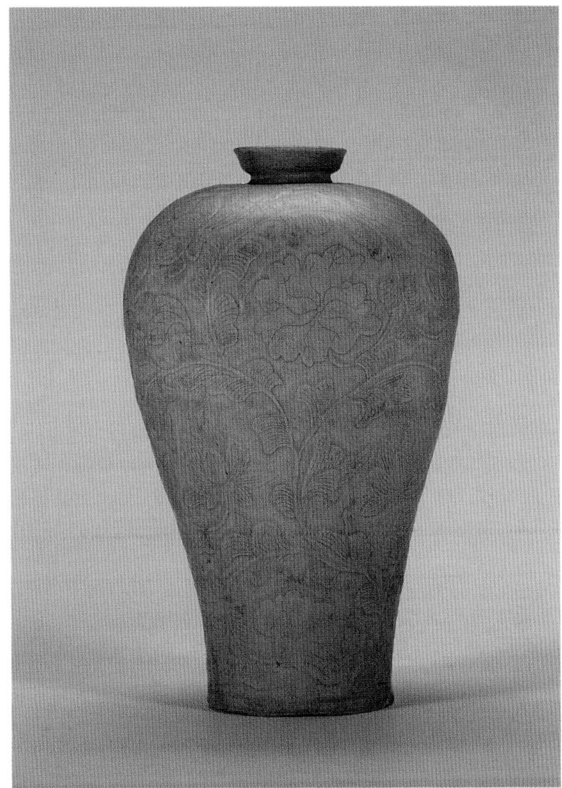

Celadon Maebyong from
the Goryeo Dynasty (glazed
ceramic). Korean School,
12th century.

# Hooker's Green

**Then**

A lush, saturated colour, this painterly green was created by William Hooker, who was employed by the Royal Horticultural Society (RHS) in 1815 as a botanical illustrator. In pursuit of a true leaf green, he mixed the recently invented Prussian blue (see page 178) with gamboge – a yellow pigment made from the sap of a deciduous tree found in Cambodia and the surrounding regions. The result was a complex green that altered according to its consistency, making it perfect for depicting a wide variety of natural foliage.

Over the hundreds of illustrations he made for the RHS, Hooker demonstrated his green's particular aptitude for depicting the myriad hues of fruit trees and became known as one of the 'greatest pomological artists of all time',* but his botanical green had, and indeed has, the potential for much wider application. Painters and colour-makers alike saw the value in Hooker's green and the colour was quickly adopted into palettes and commercialized to make a paint that is still in production today.

**Now**

A burgeoning interest in the natural world combined with a nostalgia for the authenticity of traditional design and production has ensured this green's continuing relevance. 'Greenery', a shade surely inspired by Hooker's green, was Pantone's 2017 colour of the year, dubbed 'nature's neutral'.

The traditional botanical illustrations of Hooker's era have recently experienced a resurgence in interior design, while in 2015 contemporary botanical artist Katie Scott worked with Nike on a campaign that imagined trainers sprouting stylized foliage.

**Colour Values**
Hex code: #00a63d
RGB: 0, 166, 61
CMYK: 82, 6, 100, 0
HSB: 142°, 100%, 32.5%

**Also Known As**
• Botanical Green

**Common Connotations**
• Nourishing
• Nurturing
• Natural

* Blunt, Wilfrid and Stearn, William T., *The Art of Botanical Illustration* (Revised 2nd edition), Suffolk: ACC Art Books, 1994

**Hooker's Green in Art, Design & Culture**

- *Jack-in-the-Pulpit No. 3* by Georgia O'Keeffe, *painting*, 1930
- *Tree of Plant Life* from *Botanicum* by Katie Scott, *print*, 2016
- Pantone 15-0343 'Greenery', Pantone Colour of the Year, *design*, 2017

## Use

Botanical greens are firmly part of a modern palette. The hue's connection with nature means it can feel deeply nourishing in environments and spaces. Pair with earthy pinks, raw sienna tones and perhaps charcoal for balance.

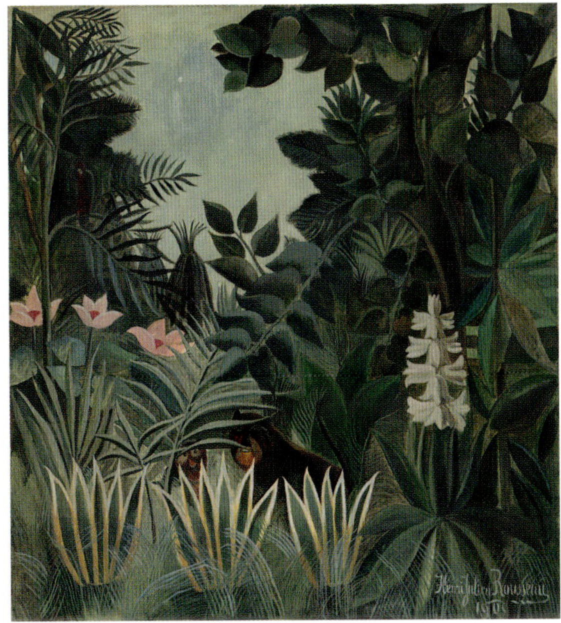

*The Equatorial Jungle* by Henri Rousseau, 1909

 # Emerald Green

**Then**

Vivid, rare and captivating, emeralds are evocative of envy as well as status, and in times past they were revered for their theoretical healing powers. In the 1st century CE, Roman historian Pliny the Elder wrote of them, 'nothing greens greener,' and noted the soothing effect of the stone's shade on the eyes. The emperor Nero supposedly liked to observe his gladiators' bloody combat through emerald sunglasses, perhaps for this reason.

The first 'emerald green' pigment was created in the 18th century, known as Paris green, a resplendent dye with a deadly edge. This coveted shade was one of the many similar greens, including one invented by Carl Wilhelm Scheele, the inventor of Prussian blue (see page 178), formed by mixing copper with arsenic. Brighter and longer-lasting than other greens on the market, impressionist painters' such as Paul Gauguin used these colours to depict stylized vegetation and fantastic verdant scenes. In Victorian England, emerald-hued clothes, patterned wallpaper, curtains, candles and even fake flowers and plastic toys, cut through the industrial grey. However, the pigments were often poorly applied and would easily flake off, producing toxic dust and leading to many deaths. Despite this, Scheele's green was used as an artist's paint until the 1960s.

**Now**

Today, arsenic-based greens are a thing of the past and emeralds come with much more positive connotations. Modern synthesized chromatic green-blue shades are hugely popular in art, interiors, and fashion for their jewel-like elegance and soothing effects. By splitting cooler and warmer combinations, tantalizing vistas of colour create dynamic interplay on modern artist Ptolemy Mann's paintings and woven landscapes.

**Colour Values**
Hex code: #439876
RGB: 67, 152, 118
CMYK: 89, 4, 63, 28
HSB: 156°, 56%, 60%

**Also Known As**
- Scheele's Green
- Paris Green

**Common Connotations**
- Opulence
- Jealousy
- Soothing

## Emerald Green in Art, Design & Culture
- *Te Fare* by Paul Gauguin, *painting*, 1892
- Celia's dress by Jacqueline Durran, worn by Keira Knightley in *Atonement, costume design*, 2007

## Use
Explore a split-complementary palette, with dark and chromatic green-blues meeting hot pinks and oranges. Experiment with a cool, pale lavender to temper and bring further balance to this striking combination.

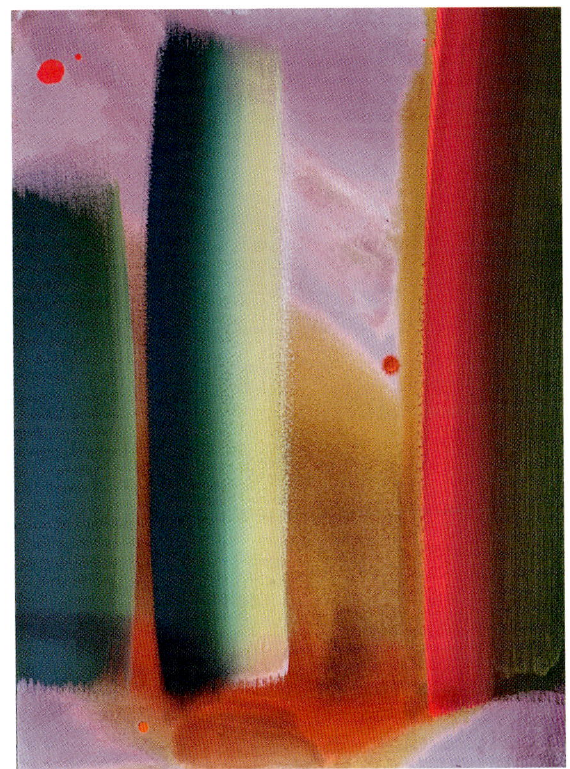

*Eclipse Painting (Ultraviolet Landscape)* by Ptolemy Mann, 2020

# Bottle Green

**Then**

From 'Ten green bottles sitting on a wall' to rows of green wine bottles sitting on supermarket shelves, the affiliation of bottles with greenery is so much part of our daily household palette that we likely don't think about it. But the history of this association goes back further than you might think. In ancient Indian and Hindu societies, the earliest *kumbha*, or 'water-pitcher', was also found decorated with deep green washes, while porcelain bottles of the Chinese Qing dynasty (1644–1912) were coated in green copper lead-based enamel, giving them a distinctive green colouring.

Ultimately, however, the hue's current association with the bottle form is down to pure function. Glass was not a common commodity until the Industrial Revolution, but wine had been bottled in glass as a luxury item for centuries before. In the 17th century, British adventurer and polymath Sir Kenelm Digby invented a new, stronger glass for wine bottles that was also darker. The darker glass protected the wine from UV rays and to this day many beverages are bottled in tinted glass to preserve them: traditionally brown for ales and green for wines.

**Now**

Still ubiquitous as the colour of wine and indeed many beer bottles, French designers Ronan and Erwan Bouroullec gave bottle green a fresh outing as one of the key colours in their Vases Découpage collection. Combining cylindrical vessels with abstract shapes in contrasting colours, the components are designed to be rearranged for different effects, each one creating its own 'fragile balance'.

**Colour Values**
Hex code: #1b5716
RGB: 27, 87, 22
CMYK: 84, 39, 100, 38
HSB: 115°, 75%, 34%

**Common Connotations**
- Quality
- Distinction
- Prosperity

**Bottle Green in Art, Design & Culture**
- Bottle, green glazed porcelain, Qing dynasty, *ceramics*,1736–1795
- *Green Coca-Cola Bottles* by Andy Warhol, *print*, 1962
- PET-art sculptures by Veronika Richteová, sculpture, 2004–ongoing

## Use
Use in branding as the primary hue to communicate quality and elegance. Try combining aqueous blue and yellowish sap green from either side of the colour wheel to create a lush harmony.

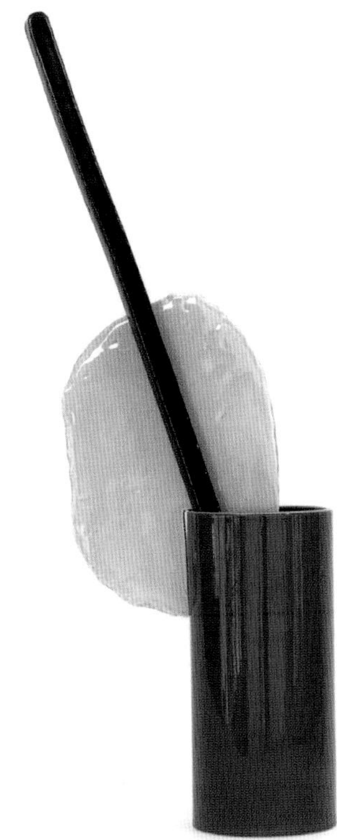

'Barre' from the Vases Découpages collection, by Ronan & Erwan Bouroullec for Vitra, 2020

 # Turquoise

**Then**

This family of brilliant blue-green colours derives originally from a stone that was used ornamentally as long as 6,000 years ago in ancient Egyptian and Persian societies, and from 200 BCE in Native American decoration. The name we know today comes from the French *pierre tourques*, or 'Turkish stone', as the stone was brought to Europe on the Silk Road around the 16th century.

A hydrous phosphate of copper and aluminium, turquoise is naturally occurring, wide-ranging in hue according to its mineral composition and soft enough to carve and work with easily, so it is no wonder it was appealing to ancient craftsmen. In Persia, where it was believed to have protective qualities, the stone was named *pirouzeh*, or 'victory'. Ancient Persians adorned daggers and bridles with it, as well as using it in amulets and, of course, religious architecture. An iconic vision of turquoise's most devout interpretations is the Sultan Ahmet Mosque in Istanbul, popularly known as the Blue Mosque for the traditional turquoise-coloured *İznik* tiles with which its interior is lined.

**Now**

As popular as ever, the 20th and 21st centuries have seen turquoise take on a multitude of new personalities and applications. The Palm Springs-fevered mid-century design scene of the 1950s and '60s saw the tone make a splash in interiors, with iconic designers such as Charles Eames and Verner Panton including the punchy bright tone in furniture and lighting collections. As modern consumerist culture broke out in the 1980s and '90s, bold style heroes such as the Memphis Group utilized the colour as a playful complementary tone to a brash, shiny retro-inspired palette.

**Colour Values**
Hex code: #40cecb
RGB: 64, 206, 203
CMYK: 62, 0, 27, 0
HSB: 179°, 69%, 81%

**Common Connotations**
- Wellness
- Escapism
- Optimism

**Turquoise in Art, Design & Culture**
- The Blue Mosque, Istanbul, *ceramics*, 1609–16
- *Silvered 2* by Bridget Riley, *silkscreen print*, 1981
- Dream Come True Building, Old Street, London, by Camille Walala, *mural*, 2015

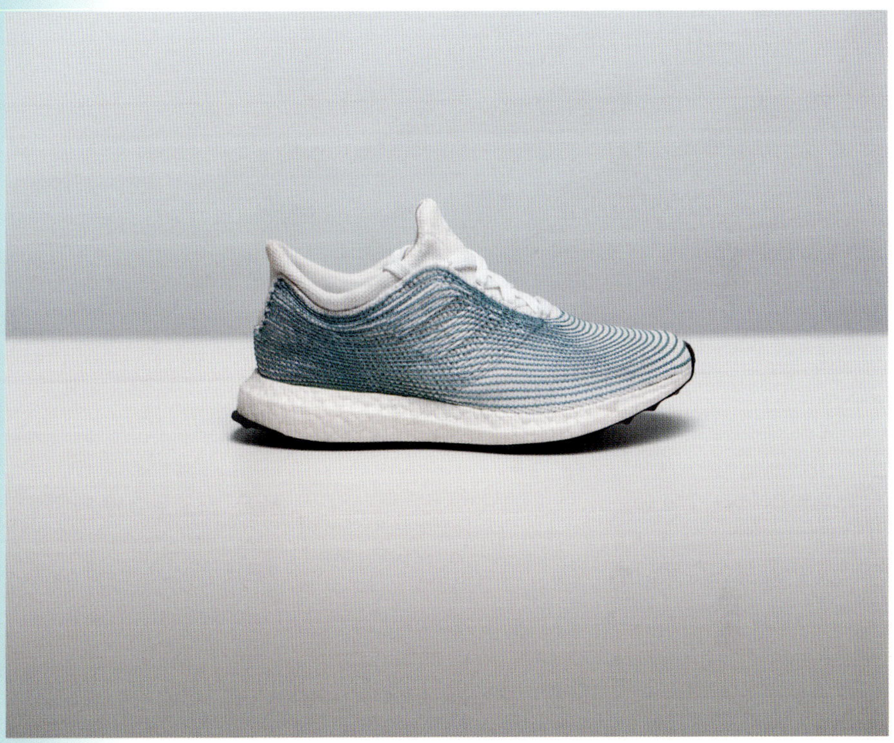



Ultra boost DNA Parley
shoe using Ocean Plastic
by Parley x Adidas, 2018

Turquoise now speaks of wellness and escapism, with the tranquil yet fresh aspects of the tone being applied to a range of lifestyle applications, bringing a sense of serenity. Adidas used turquoise to underscore its sensitive use of ocean plastic in its recent footwear launch, relying on the clean feel of the tone to convey environmental awareness.

**Use**
Unlock the shade's potential for composure and create a modern monochromatic palette that is as easy on the eye as it is mindful.

# Olive

**Then**

Named after the fruit of the tree whose branches have been extended in peace since the times of ancient Greece, olive is also the colour of modern warfare since armies ditched the bright costumes intended to differentiate them in favour of the subdued tones of olive as long-range warfare made camouflage more important (see also Khaki, page 302).

Aside from its associations with war and peace, this modest shade has also enjoyed an illustrious relationship with design. When the Art Nouveau movement of the turn of the 20th century brought its highly stylized vision of nature into design and architecture, olive green was a key member of the colour palette. Warm and unassuming, the shade continued to link interiors even in Bauhaus design, famed for its bold primaries: delicate muted shades like olive played a role on walls and ceiling to complement and accent the more strident tones. But it was with the explosion of mid-century modern design in post-war America that saw this colour in its most important interior role, with olive used alongside golds and corals to create a sense of grounding optimism for new open-plan interiors.

**Now**

Elegant, timeless and slightly quirky, olive green and the mid-century modern design aesthetic are still firmly in vogue in contemporary interiors. Today, olive green complements the 1950s-inspired furniture designs of Herman Miller and Eero Saarinen.

**Use**

Reboot the archive and employ olive as a warm neutral; try pairing with brass, and mustard yellow for a rich yet wholesome approach to an interior scheme.

**Colour Values**
Hex code: #868349
RGB: 134, 131, 73
CMYK: 47, 37, 83, 13
HSB: 57º, 46%, 53%

**Common Connotations**
- Growth
- Peace
- Strength

**Olive in Art, Design & Culture**
- *The Olive Trees* by Vincent van Gogh, *painting*, 1889
- *White and Textured Olive Green Tulip Side Chair* by Eero Saarinen, *furniture*, 1950s
- *Pasture* by Anni Albers, *textiles*, 1958

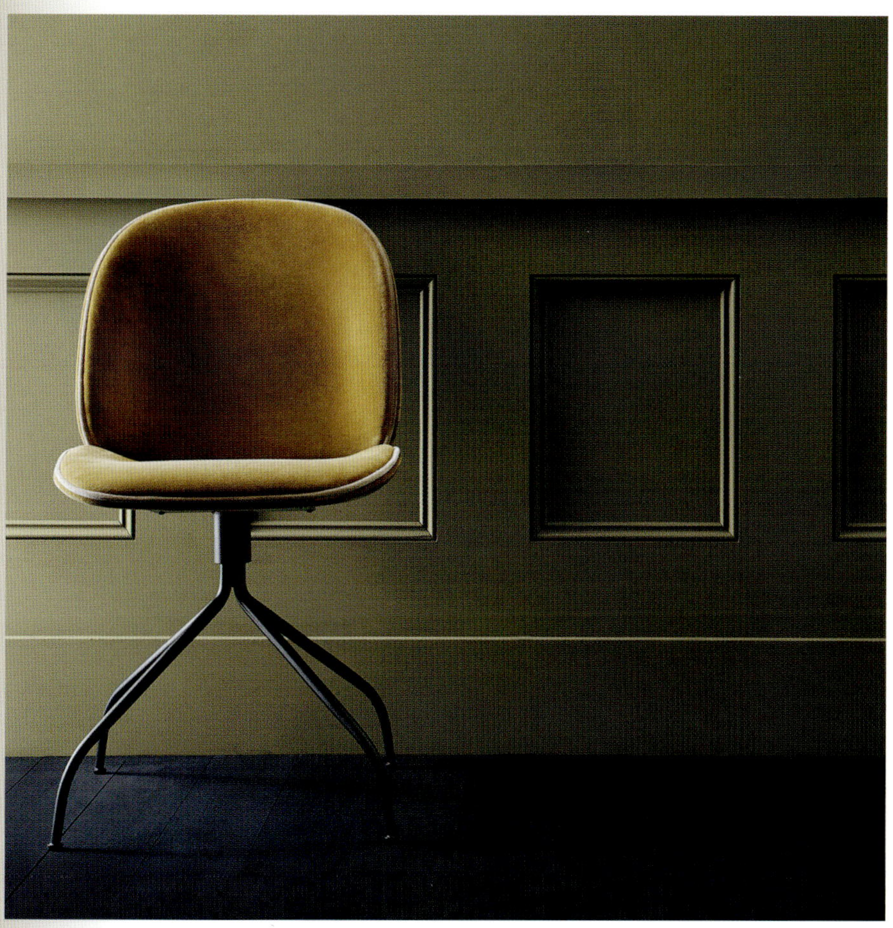

Olive Colour (72) by Little Greene

 # Vital Green

**Then**

A colour evolved for the modern world, vital green has its roots in the early days of personal computers when monitors produced pixels via cathode ray tubes shooting electron beams at phosphor dots behind the screen. Green was a cheap and long-lasting phosphor, better performing than red or yellow or white, which looked blurry on black. It was also easier on people's eyes than looking at white type on a black background – not only is green the most comfortable wavelength for our eyes but also, perhaps counter-intuitively, it has an eye-grabbing quality that can hold our attention.

Though screen technology advanced quickly, green on black became synonymous with all forms of digital life. In the 1980s and '90s, phosphorous green screamed from the inner labels of countless 12" singles as music embraced electronics in the age of synthesizers and autotune. Bright fonts greeted you from T-shirts, accompanied by smiley faces and alien heads.

But this shade is still ubiquitous in our contemporary world if we stop to consider it. It's the universal indicator for 'Go' in traffic lights, road signs and green switches, and points to first aid equipment, pharmacies and fire escapes. (See also Reactive Red, page 80.)

**Now**

Today, many designers are using vital green to communicate more than technological nostalgia. Since we live in a digital world where we generally see green on screen more times in a day than in nature, colour theory in this space has an ever-growing significance. A multitude of communication apps, including Snapchat, use this shade to indicate a message from

**Colour Values**
Hex code: #7cf135
RGB: 124, 241, 53
CMYK: 50, 0, 100, 0
HSB: 97°, 78%, 95%

**Common Connotations**
- Retro
- Digital
- Positive

**Vital Green in Art, Design & Culture**

- CRT screen by IBM, *computing*, 1972
- Fluorescent Green Medium Padded Nylon Clutch by Prada, *accessory*, A/W 2018
- Ready-to-Wear collection by Bottega Veneta, *fashion*, 2021

someone outside of the user's network; a calmer blue indicates a message from someone they know or have already accepted. In 2020, New York's High Line park introduced social distancing measures through the use of graphic, high-visibility vital green dots.

## Use

When creating websites or apps, bright greens can be particularly useful for making designs look compelling and clickable. Keep contrast in mind as interfaces with readable high contrast (black and green) make web content inclusive for a broader range of people.

Right: Pong video game by Atari, launched 1972

Overleaf: Social distancing graphics by Paula Scher, Pentagram, for Friends of the High Line, 2020

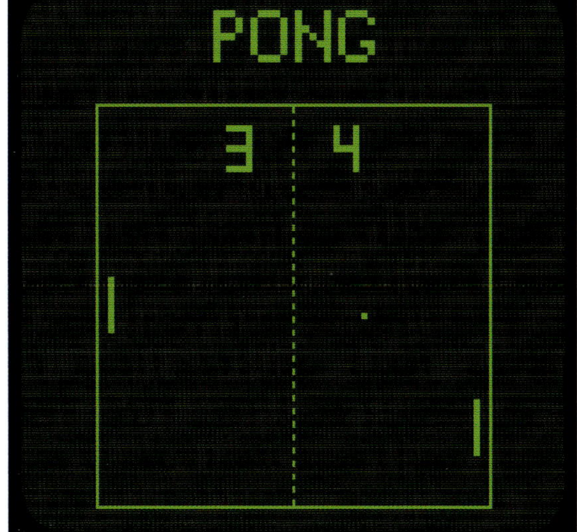

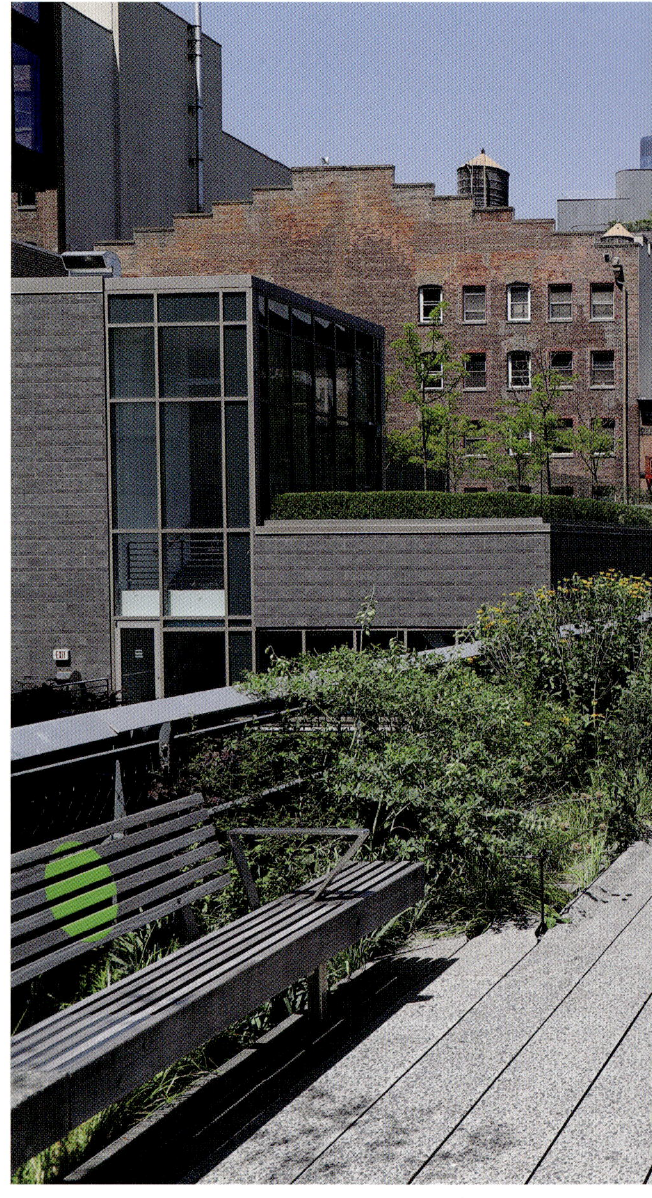

'This shade is still ubiquitous in our contemporary world if we stop to consider it. It's the universal indicator for "Go."'

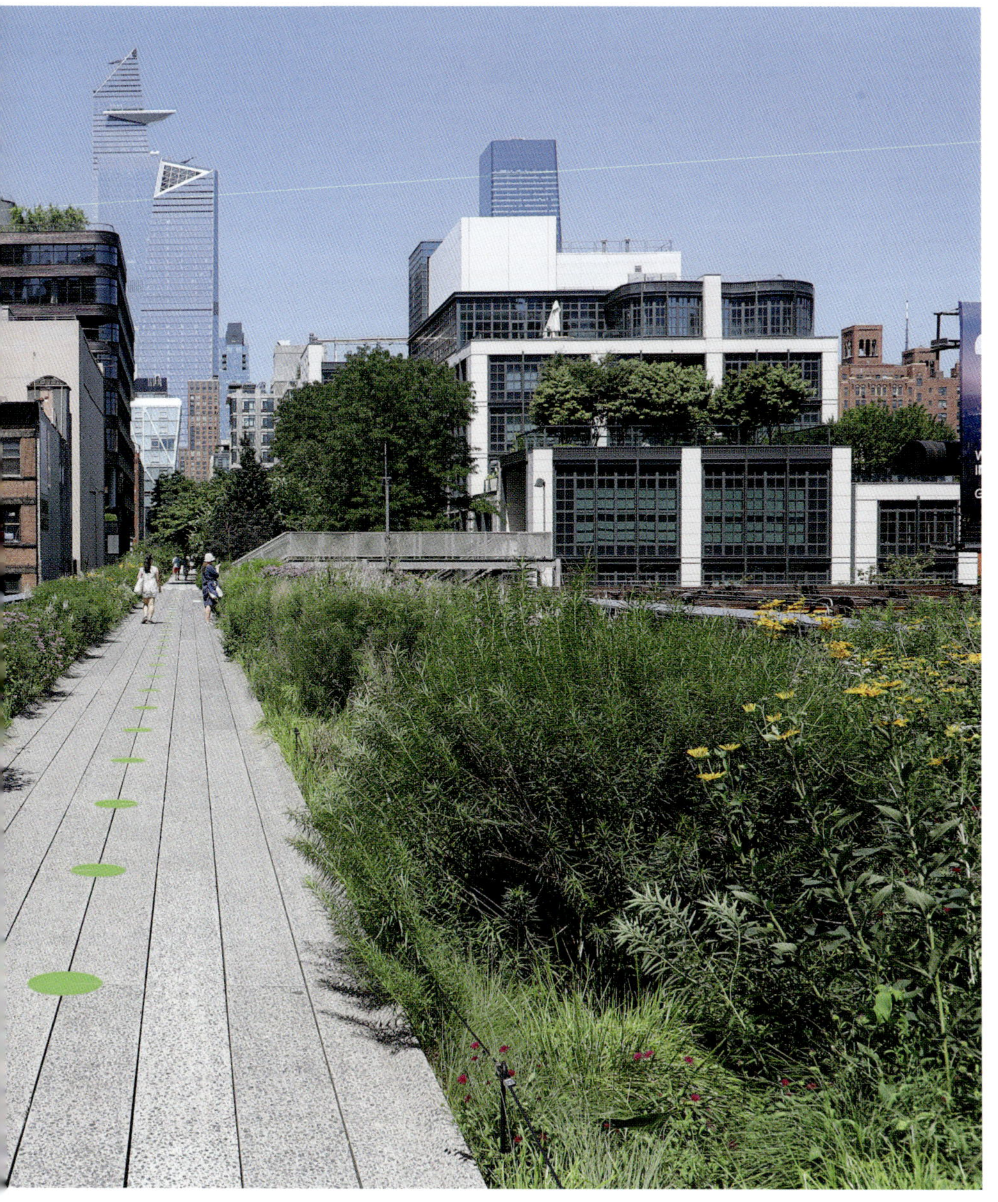

# Modern Mint

**Then**

Like many modern hues, mint was born out of technological evolution. Techniques such as powder coating, patented in the US in 1945 by Daniel Gustin, made solid-state colours like this bright pastel possible. With newly available plastics and the rise of the automotive industry, the middle of the 20th century was an era that grasped innovation with both hands and applied its principles to the products that defined the modern lifestyle.

In the 1950s, the use of gentle tertiary shades also helped encourage acceptance of startling designs by the likes of Jean Prouvé and Dieter Rams into home environments across the globe. Pastel pastiche continued to reign supreme into the 1990s, when mint lived in bathroom suites and Naf Naf streetwear, before taking a nosedive in popularity as the consumerist future envisioned in the '50s peaked around the turn of the millennium and a new generation began to define its own vision of modernity.

**Now**

Fresher, cleaner and futuristic, mint green has been synthesized far beyond its pastel heritage to become a thoroughly contemporary sensation. Capturing the zeitgeist of Instagrammable youth-driven colour trends and linking with plant life and nature in interiors, mint green has become a symbol of utopian optimism.

In fashion, the colour continues to align itself with the future, as Gucci sent male and female models down a mint-green travelator for Alessandro Michele's S/S 2020 show, while Irish designer Robyn Lynch chose the shade as the key note for her youth-inspired Fashion East collection.

**Colour Values**

Hex code: #9be9c2
RGB: 155, 233, 194
CMYK: 36, 0, 33, 0
HSB: 150°, 33%, 91%

**Common Connotations**

- Fresh
- Youthful
- Innovative

**Modern Mint in Art,
Design & Culture**
- Standard SP chair
  by Jean Prouve for Vitra,
  *furniture*, 1934/1950
- Cadillac Coupé deVille
  in 'Princess Green',
  *automotive*, 1956
- Primary school,
  Boom, Belgium,
  by Areal Architecten,
  *architecture*, 2016

## Use

Fresh greens are visually calming on the mind and
are often a good choice for welcoming people into
public spaces. Take a monochromatic direction with
mint green as the leading player on walls, floors and
surfaces. Pair with its opposite soft rose-pink to tempt
further interaction.

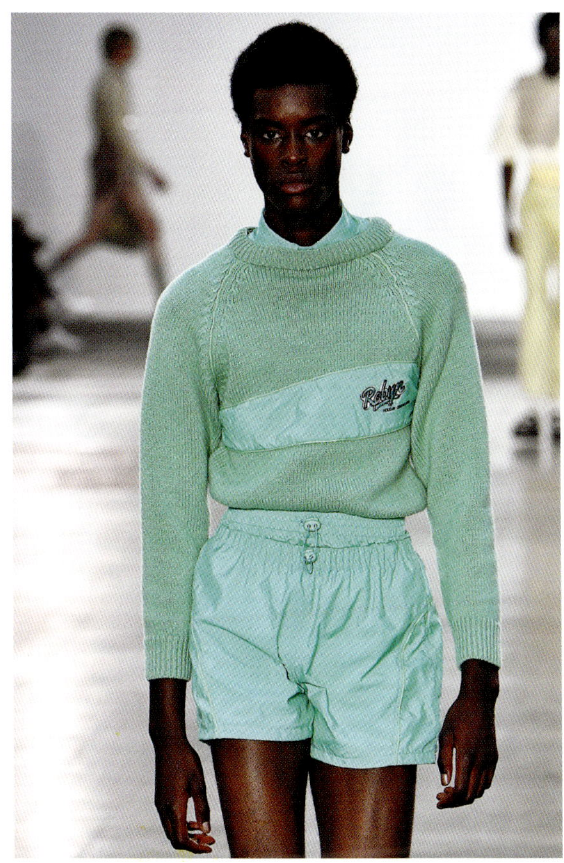

Menswear collection by
Robyn Lynch, Spring/
Summer 2020

# Electric Lime

**Then**

It was a workplace accident and the pursuit of stage magic that inspired two American teenagers to create the first fluorescent pigments in 1933. After hitting his head at the factory he worked at, 19-year-old Robert Switzer was forced to spend months in a dark basement; meanwhile, his younger brother Joseph was experimenting with fluorescent light for a glow-in-the-dark element to his magic show. The two mixed a concoction of luminous minerals with a gooey lacquer and created a series of new Day-Glo colours.

Lime green, named after the fruit of the same yellow-green hue, has an older and more dignified history, first coined as a colour in 1890 when it became popular in Victorian design. However, after its Day-Glo reinvention, the colour really came into its own in the futuristic 1960s and was seen in homewear and interiors, clothing and, perhaps most lastingly, the high-octane muscle car. Chrysler launched its optional high-impact paint colours in '69 in conjunction with PPG. What followed was a series of loud hues that stood out from the crowd, not least with its popular lime green 'Sublime'.

**Now**

The colour's link with performance cars continues; now with a sustainable ethos driving it. In 2016, Toyota launched 'Thermo-Tect Lime Green' for its Prius range; in this new paint, the black carbon particles have been removed, meaning the car heats up less, reducing the need for air conditioning and improving fuel economy. Nike has also gravitated to the shade for decades; in 2015, it paired the luminous shade with motion and movement, mixing performance with a burst of feminine pleats.

**Colour Values**

Hex code: #00bb74
RGB: 0, 187, 116
CMYK: 76, 0, 75, 0
HSB: 157°, 100%, 73%

**Also Known As**

- Neon Green
- Lime Green

**Common Connotations**

- Garish
- Exciting
- Inventive

**Electric Lime in Art, Design & Culture**

- Dodge in 'Sublime', *automotive*, 1970/2019
- NikeLab x Sacai, *fashion*, S/S 2015
- Thermo-Tect Lime Green by Toyota, *automotive*, 2016
- Menswear collection by Homme Plissé Issey Miyake, *fashion*, S/S 2021

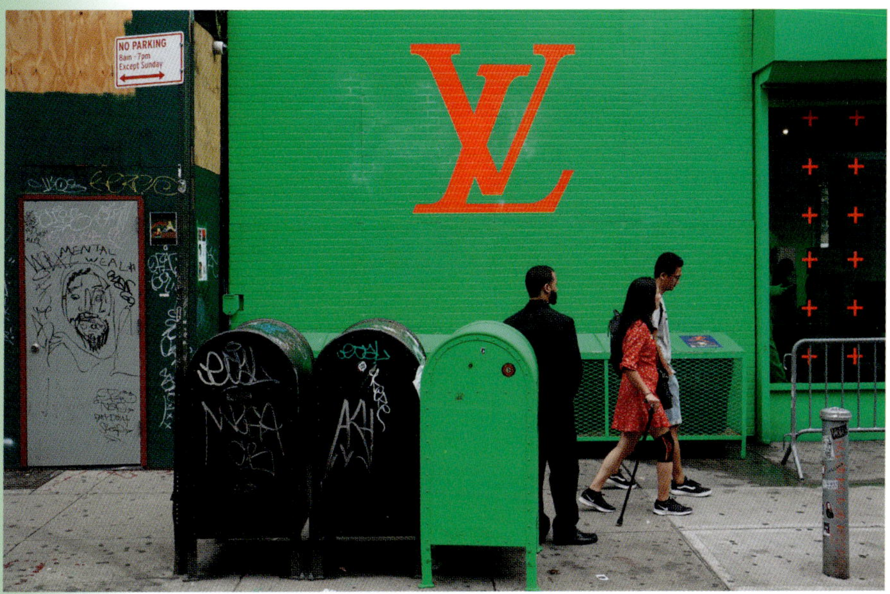

Louis Vuitton's neon green pop-up store, New York, with Virgil Abloh's menswear collection, Fall/Winter 2019

**Use**
Give electric lime a chic makeover by combining it's cool green tone with contrasting fiery orange for a classic contrast of temperature.

# Chlorophyll

**Then**

A transparent, clean green, chlorophyll is the photosynthetic pigment found in plants that absorbs blue and red lightwaves, reflecting green to give leaves their distinctive colouring. It is also this process that gives plants their energy to grow and respirate, meaning that leaf green will always summon associations with new life, health and verdant spring foliage.

First isolated in 1817 by French chemists Joseph Bienaimé Caventou and Pierre-Joseph Pelletier, the light-sensitive properties of the pigment played a role in the advancement of photography. In the 1940s, Sir John Herschel invented the 'anthotype' print, using flower petals, leaves and vegetable juices to produce light-sensitive emulsions that could be waxed onto paper to form a negative – '*anthos*' deriving from the Greek word for flower.

Today, chlorophyll is often used in food colouring, but one of the pigment's most infamous outings as a colourant dates to long before its discovery. Originating in late-18th-century Switzerland, absinthe, otherwise known as 'the green fairy', gets its natural colour from the chlorophyll in the botanicals it is made with.

**Colour Values**
Hex code: #96d69c
RGB: 150, 214, 156
CMYK: 42, 0, 51, 0
HSB: 126°, 30%, 84%

**Common Connotations**
- Growth
- Cleansing
- Vitality

**Chlorophyll in Art,
Design & Culture**
- *Holding #2* from the
*Immortality: The
Remnants of the Vietnam
and American War* series
by Binh Danh, *chlorophyll
print*, 2009
- Bamboo silk scarves
dyed with chlorophyllin
by Emily Mae Martin,
*textiles*, 2019

## Now

Often used as a colourant, chlorophyll is also popular
as a health supplement, with a host of potential benefits
including as an anti-ageing agent, a deodorant and in
some cancer treatments. Meanwhile, its photosynthetic
properties continue to drive technological innovation.
Inspired by photosynthesis, designer Marjan van Aubel
has created coloured glass panels made from dye-
sensitized solar cells that generate an electrical current
to charge household devices from USB ports integrated
into window ledges.

## Use

Chlorophyll's pure green evokes the calming and
health-boosting influence of being in the natural
world. It will always send a positive message in
wellness contexts, and its easy association with
plant life establishes its environmental credentials,
particularly in the growing realm of plant-based food.

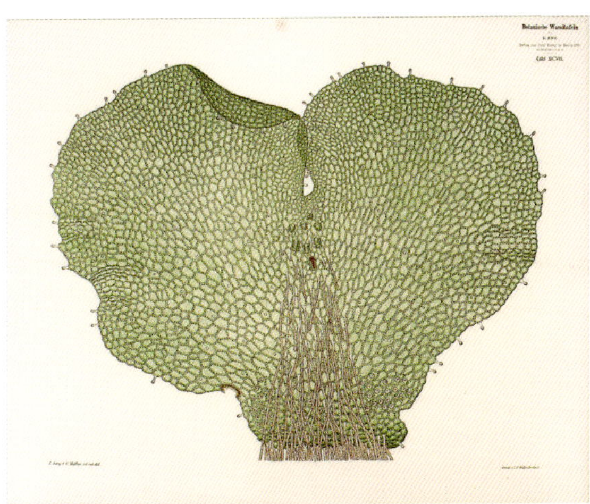

*Apidium Filix* from
*Botanische Wandtafeln*
by L. Kny, 1874

 # Algae

### Then

Historically, humanity has drawn on earth pigments from minerals, plant and animal matter and mud to create colours for dyeing and decoration, but the future of colour may lie in the sea. This is not an entirely new concept: the coastal lichen orchil was used by ancient Phoenicians to make a purple dye – a cheap alternative to Tyrian purple (see page 202) – while dulse, a red seaweed, and crotal, a rock-growing lichen, have been used for dyeing Scottish tartans for centuries; the latter also having an olfactory role, as it is said to be what gives Harris tweed its distinctive smell. However, it was not until the mid-20th century that scientists began to understand the pigment makeup and function of different algae, and only in recent years have we begun to understand their full potential. Of the microalgae making waves today, it is spirulina, a blue-green saltwater cyanobacterium, that has caused the biggest splash.

### Now

Packed with antioxidants, this humble alga has been used as a health supplement for years, but it is the drive for sustainable energy solutions that really kicked off the spirulina revolution. Bio-architect firm ecoLogicStudio has been looking at ways to harness spirulina's potential in built environments. Not only could it provide a food source with high nutritional content, but its photosynthetic processes mean it could be used to generate energy while at the same time breaking down environmental pollutants, consuming carbon dioxide and generating oxygen – a totally sustainable and symbiotic approach.

Back into the world of colour, algae are seeing increasing use as sustainable dyes, both as food colourants and textile dyes, to replace the less eco-friendly synthetic dyes that rose to prominence in the Industrial Revolution.

**Colour Values**
Hex code: #61c69b
RGB: 97, 198, 155
CMYK: 60, 0, 52, 0
HSB: 154°, 51%, 78%

**Also Known As**
- Phycocyanin
- Seaweed

**Common Connotations**
- Humble
- Organic
- Ecological

Right: Dyed yarn on a traditional loom ready for weaving Harris Tweed, Scotland

**Algae in Art,
Design & Culture**

- BIQ building with
  bio-adaptive façade
  by Arup, Hamburg,
  *architecture*, 2013
- Ooho edible water bottle
  by Skipping Rocks Lab,
  *product design*, 2013
- Vivobarefoot Ultra III by
  BLOOM, *footwear*, 2016
- Indus by Bio-Integrated
  Design Lab, *algae
  hydrogel tiles*, 2019

## Use

Synthetic dyes replaced earth-based pigments because they were cheaper to produce and less susceptible to fading. Tastes have changed, however, and the unique patterns and qualities resulting from exposure to light have come to be valued as an aspect of an organic beauty that is not harmful to the planet. Spirulina and other natural pigments favour use in similarly natural environments: avoid engineered precision and emulate nature's rough perfection.

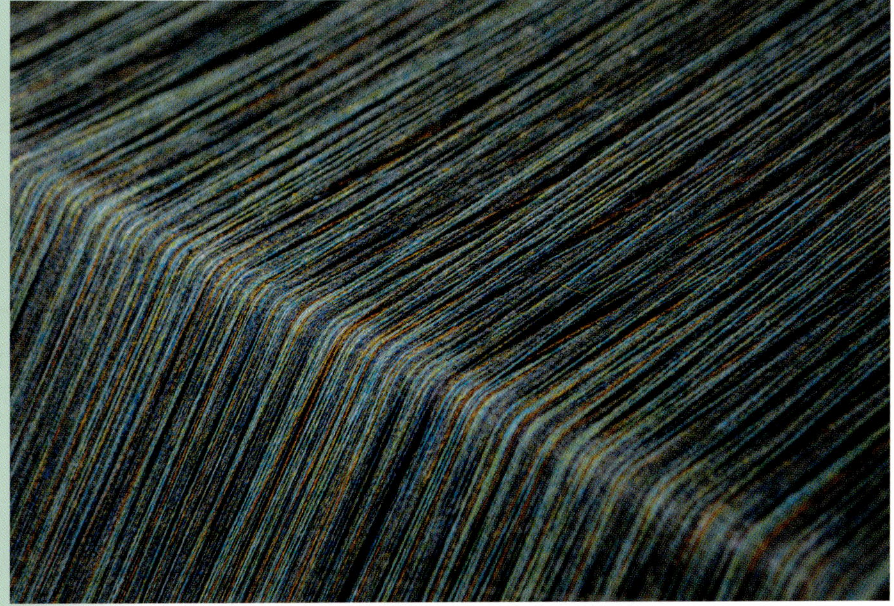

 # Blue

Blue is the colour that features most prominently in the natural world, and yet for much of history people have had difficulty extracting a blue pigment for use in art and design. In ancient times, the semi-precious stone lapis lazuli was mined in the mountains of Afghanistan and the resulting pigment was highly prized in Mesopotamia and Egypt; across the Middle East today the colour is associated with spirituality and immortality and it appears in sacred places such as mosques, where blue vaulted ceilings emulate the sky. Later, lapis lazuli was also coveted by European painters, for whom the ground-up stone yielded the best blue pigment; its name, ultramarine, suggesting its rarity and exotic, almost mythical provenance.

Over the course of history, artists in all media have sought perfection in blue. In the mid-20th century, in pursuit of the colour of the sky, the French artist Yves Klein famously developed a version of ultramarine that retained the pigment's pure intensity that traditional binding agents had diminished. Like many other artists, Klein believed that the colour blue could have a transformative effect on the mind. Studies have since shown that blue is indeed calming and improves mental wellbeing, which is why it is often used in interior design.

For many years, however, attractive blue pigments remained rare and so the colour was reserved for the rich and powerful, and set aside for artists' most worthy subjects and illustrious commissions. It was not until the 18th century, when a new pigment, Prussian blue, was discovered by accident and became the first synthetically produced pigment, that it became commonly available. In 2009, a new inorganic pigment, YInMn blue, was discovered – also by chance. The purest form of blue we are likely to be able to see, it also has unique cooling properties. Perhaps it is the connection with scientific innovation that has made the colour a popular choice in the logos of new media and tech companies.

Associated with both the rich elite and the working class of society – the blue-blooded or blue-collared – and with both spirituality and the world of science, the meanings attached to the colour blue are as endless as the sea and sky, but the popularity of the colour remains unwavering. Among hunter-gatherers, those drawn to clear skies and clean water were more likely to survive, so over time this preference may, in fact, have become hardwired.

## Colours in this chapter:

# Indigo

## Then

Indigo, a beautiful inky blue with a tinge of green and/or violet, depending on the light, has been coaxed from the seeds of the Indigofera plant for thousands of years. Its value as a dye made it an important commodity around the globe and led to some of the first trade routes being forged across Asia and Europe. In recent years, archaeologists unearthed a patterned indigo-dyed cloth sandwiched in between the wooden beams of an ancient Peruvian burial site, dated at nearly 6,200 years old.

Like ultramarine (see page 174), indigo was associated with wealth and luxury in many cultures, who developed distinct ways of using it to embellish clothing, costumes, domestic textiles and ritual objects. We can see its use from the ancient Kofar Mata dye pits of West Africa to the Indian indigo farms and Japanese block printers. In the 17th century, Isaac Newton named indigo the seventh colour of the spectrum.

## Now

Although it is rarely now given a place in the rainbow, indigo remains as iconic as the blue jeans it is used to dye. And while today it may be best associated with workers' clothing, its deep hue still brings luxury to contemporary interior design. In 2019, Japanese indigo pioneer Buaisou made a series of indigo-dipped wooden stools for Finnish furniture manufacturer Artek, employing techniques that have been used for thousands of years.

## Use

Ancient indigo is still beautifully relevant, particularly when used in monochromatic treatments – don't be afraid to use it in bold proportions. Deeper tones of indigo can help to focus your thoughts, while lighter tones calm the mind, making this an ideal addition to the palette for restful interiors and lifestyle settings.

**Colour Values**
Hex code: #0c426a
RGB: 12, 66, 106
CMYK: 100, 77, 34, 21
HSB: 206°, 89%, 42%

**Common Connotations**
- Calming
- Honesty
- Wisdom

**Indigo in Art, Design & Culture**
- Basinjom mask and gown, Banyang of Nigeria and Cameroon, *costume*, 1973
- 'State of Indigo', presented by the India Pavilion at London Design Biennale, *installation*, 2018
- *Symphony for Untold History* by Aboubakar Fofana, *textiles*, 2018

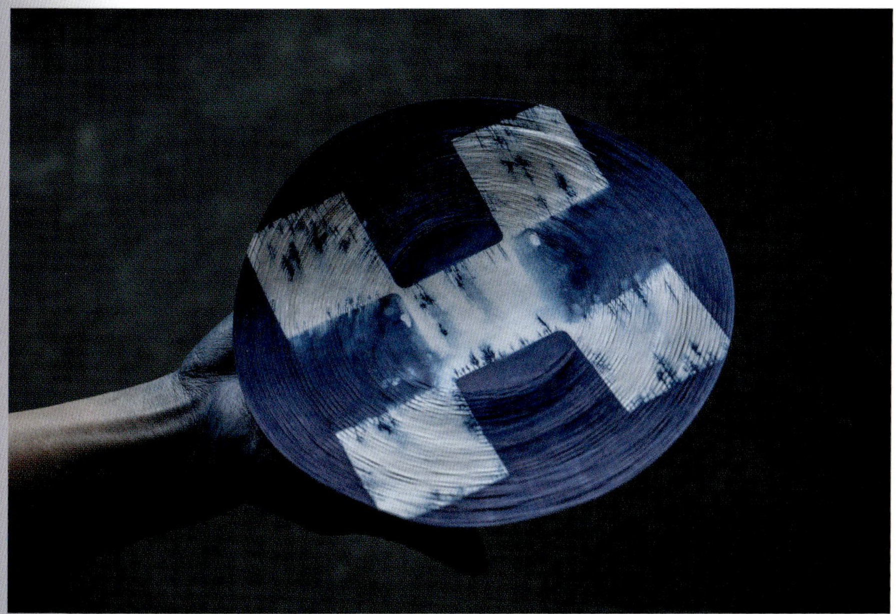

*Airvase* by Torafu Architects from the artist series. Dyed by Buaisou, Japan

# Woad

**Then**

Woad is a deep blue that is derived from the leaves of *Isatis tinctoria* using heat, oxygen and water in a slow process that creates a plethora of shades. Despite the rather pungent and dirty manufacturing process, woad was an important commodity in ancient Mediterranean and Middle Eastern civilizations. It became particularly significant in Europe because of the plant's ability to grow in the wild on the banks of hills and to survive in temperate climates, making it a cheaper and more readily available alternative to indigo (see page 168). The colour still conjures up images of ancient Celtic tribes terrorizing Roman invaders, their faces and bodies painted with fierce woad tattoos.

However, great quantities of *Isatis tinctoria* are required to produce woad, and a dye-fast version, in particular, could only be afforded by the wealthy, which later led to it being associated with nobility. Medieval tapestries depict French kings Charlemagne and Louis XI wearing rich robes of ermine fur, blue textiles and gold embroidery. In the 17th century, Frederick William, Elector of Brandenburg, was one of the first rulers to give an army a blue uniform. The reasons were economic: the German states were trying to protect their dye industry against imported competition.

Woad was eventually superseded when, in the European colonization of North America, a new indigo crop was developed and exported in great quantities from the 18th century onwards. However, wool continued to be dyed with natural woad up until the 1930s in the UK at least – in part due to the use of the colour in police uniforms.

**Colour Values**
Hex code: #20355c
RGB: 32, 53, 92
CMYK: 97, 84, 37, 29
HSB: 219°, 65%, 36%

**Common Connotations**
- Trustworthiness
- Strength
- Mystical

**Woad in Art, Design & Culture**
- 'The Unicorn Tapestries', France/The Netherlands, *tapestries*, 1495–1505
- Woad/Guado collection by Nudie Jeans, *fashion*, 2012
- Spiritual Glamour collection by Viktor & Rolf with Claudy Jongstra, *fashion*, A/W 2019/2020

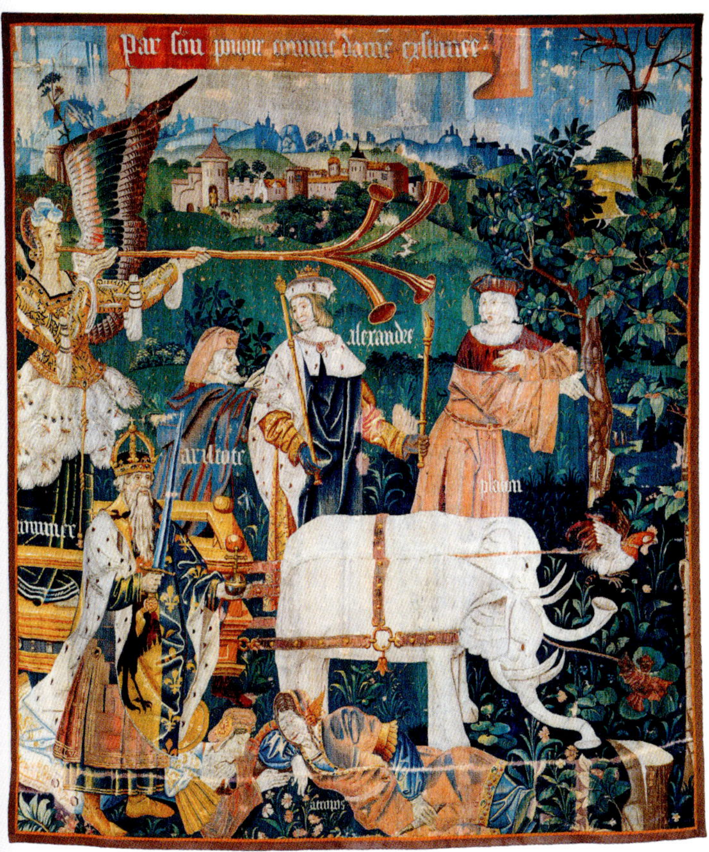

*The Triumph of Fame over Death*, South Netherlandish, 1500–1530

**Now**
Woad and other organic dyes have had a resurgence
in recent years. The rise of the 'slow movement' in
modern design and the ethics of sustainability have
brought attention to this natural, deep blue shade.
Fashion label Viktor & Rolf commissioned textile artist
and natural dye specialist Claudy Jongstra to create
several fashion pieces using the colour in uneven
quantities to great success for their Autumn/Winter
2019–20 collection.

**Use**
Take woad into the modern era by using a triadic
approach with shades of gold and bright red. What is
key here is the proportion of shades, with small accents
supporting this historical tone. This could be a good fit
for brands wishing to present a luxurious message that's
mindful of environmental impact.

# 'The rise of the "slow movement" in modern design and the ethics of sustainability have brought attention to this natural, deep blue shade.'

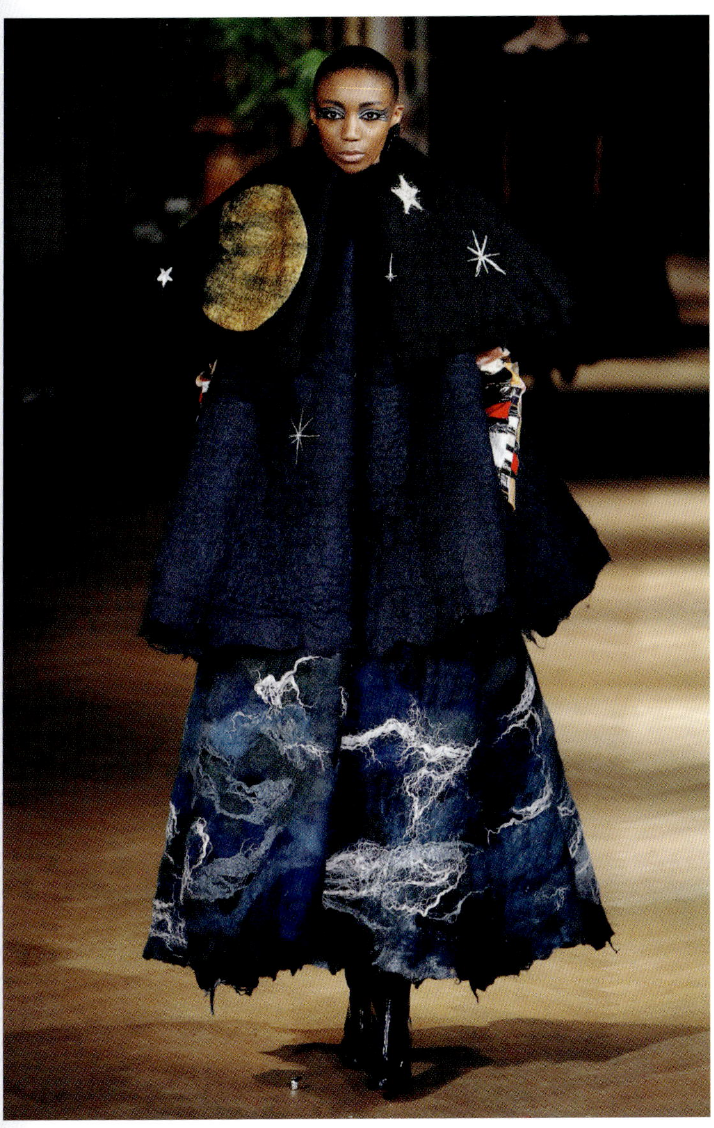

Viktor & Rolf, Paris, Autumn/Winter 2019–20

 # Ultramarine

**Then**

Once worth more than gold, ultramarine is derived from lapis lazuli, a semi-precious stone mined in the mountains of Afghanistan and ground into a powder. The method for obtaining lapis lazuli's intense colour – through purifying and kneading a combination of wax, resin and oil with the stone's naturally occurring mica and metallic amalgams – contributed to the pigment's price and its rarefied status.

Lapis lazuli first appeared as a pigment in the 6th century, used in Buddhist paintings in Bamiyan, Afghanistan. The Egyptian Book of the Dead recognizes lapis lazuli, carved in the shape of an eye and set in gold, as an amulet of inestimable power. It's no wonder that the colour was used to decorate the elite of ancient Egyptian society: Tutankhamun's sarcophagus was ornamented with the stones; later, Cleopatra wore powdered lapis lazuli as eye shadow.

Ultramarine was also used in 13th- and 14th-century Anglo-Saxon illuminated manuscripts, where the key elements of the universe were pictorially illustrated with the pigment. These works showcase some early examples of colour association, with the brilliant ultramarine used to depict God the Creator; vermillion red (see page 66) standing for the earth or nature; and lead white (see page 246) representing the flesh.

Because of its prohibitive cost, Italian artists of the same period, such as Cimabue, Duccio and Giotto, preserved their stocks of ultramarine for important religious subjects, notably depictions of the Virgin Mary. A particular shade was even named after her: Marian blue. The colour's alluring depth, radiant qualities and price led Baroque master Johannes Vermeer into monetary ruin. It remained expensive until a synthetic ultramarine was invented in 1826 by French chemist Jean-Baptiste Guimet, which was then aptly named 'French ultramarine'.

**Colour Values**

Hex code: #4166f5
RGB: 65, 102, 245
CMYK: 77, 63, 0, 0
HSB: 228°, 73%, 96%

**Common Connotations**

- Divinity
- Distinction
- Perfection

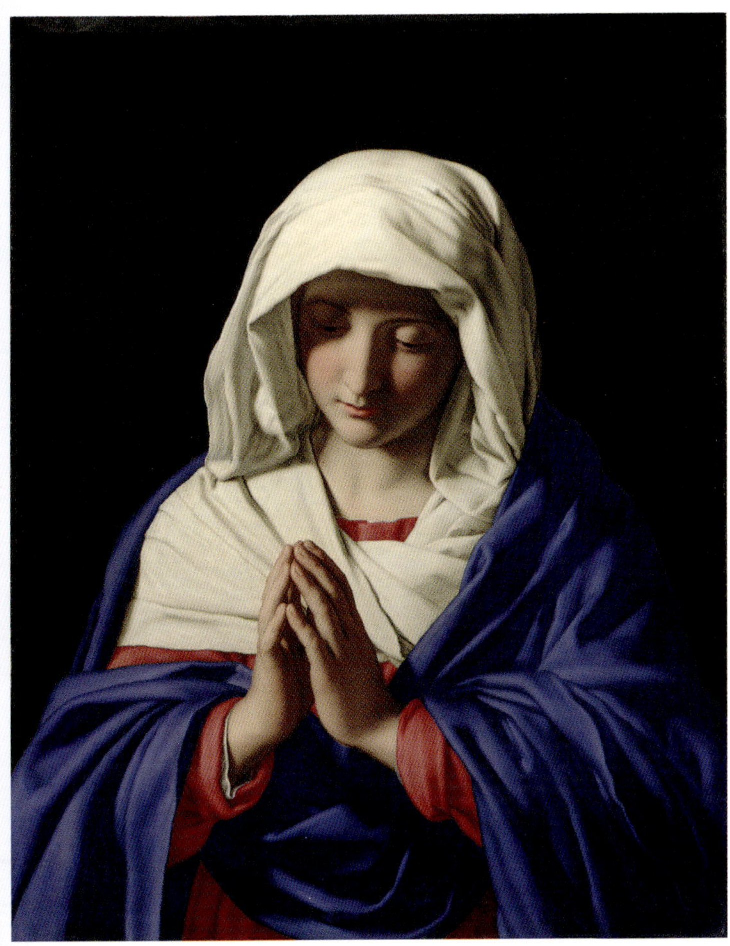



*The Virgin in Prayer* by Giovanni Battista Salvi da Sassoferrato, 1640–50

## Now

Although the development of synthetic dyes and
pigments have made a plethora of rich blues possible,
ultramarine has retained much of its power. Twentieth-
century artists Wassily Kandinsky and Yves Klein
both saw perfection and divinity in the rich colour,
the latter using it as the base for his superlative IKB
(International Klein Blue; see page 190). It remains
a potent symbol of power as well: the Queen of the
United Kingdom and the Chancellor of Germany often
wear a royal blue sash at formal occasions.

## Use

Play to the colour's richness by combining it with sun-
kissed yellows and accents of violet-pink in a powerful
triadic colour scheme.

**Ultramarine in Art,
Design & Culture**
- *The Dead Christ and the
  Virgin* by Neapolitan
  follower of Giotto,
  *painting*, c.1330–40
- *Hahn/Cock* by Katharina
  Fritsch, *sculpture*, 2013
- *Bluets* by Maggie Nelson;
  cover design by Suzanne
  Dean, *book*, 2017

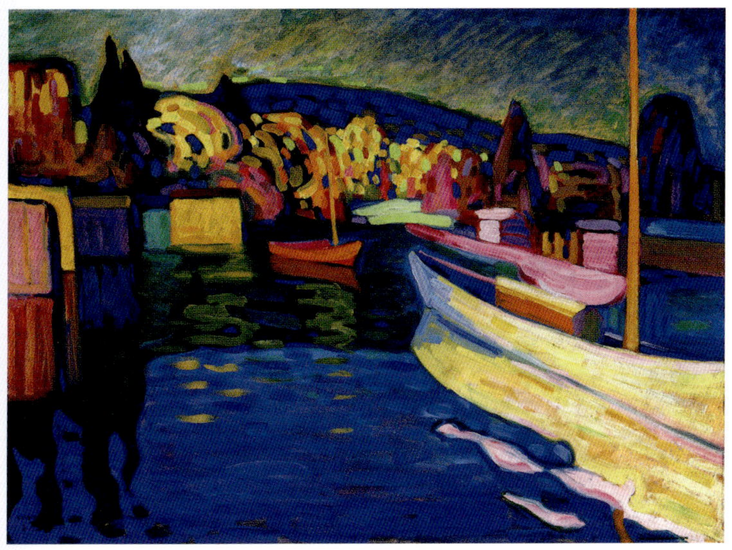

*Autumn Landscape with Boats* by Wassily Kandinsky, 1908

# Prussian Blue

**Then**

A deep, dark hue, Prussian blue is chemically created using prussic acid (hydrogen cyanide). The pigment version was synthesized by German-Swedish chemist Carl Wilhelm Scheele in 1782 and the result has an alluring, colour-shifting nature. In sunlight, this midnight hue is identifiably blue to the eye, but it can easily appear black, particularly under the limited gamut sometimes found in artificial lighting, due to its chemical composition and its ability to absorb specific wavelengths of visible light. As a result, the pigment colour cannot be accurately seen on a digital display.

One of the first modern synthetic pigments, Prussian blue was also possibly the world's first 'on-brand' colour, when it became the predominant colour worn by the infantry regiments of the Prussian Army in the 18th century. It was also quickly adapted for use in dyes, inks and oil paints, supplanting ultramarine and Egyptian blue thanks to its lightfast nature.

This new, intense hue was exported around the world and was quickly adopted by Japanese painters such as Hokusai, replacing native indigo in woodblock printing.

**Now**

At the turn of the 20th century, Pablo Picasso, while in his 'blue period', painted obsessively with this colour, finding in its dark and shifting nature a form of sincere emotional expression to describe his state of mind. This is perhaps its most compelling association today, as a thoughtful and intelligent colour.

**Colour Values**
Hex code: #010042
RGB: 1, 0, 66
CMYK: 100, 95, 31, 56
HSB: 241°, 100%, 26%

**Also Known As**
- Midnight Blue

**Common Connotations**
- Melancholy
- Introspective
- Trustworthy

**Prussian Blue in Art, Design & Culture**

- *The Great Wave off Kanagawa* by Katsushika Hokusai, *woodblock print, c.1830–2*
- *Photographs of British Algae: Cyanotype Impressions* by Anna Atkins, *photo book, 1843–53*
- *Slice Painting in Prussian Blue* by Cian Donnelly, *painting, 2004*

*Mère et enfant (Mother and Child)* by Pablo Picasso, 1902

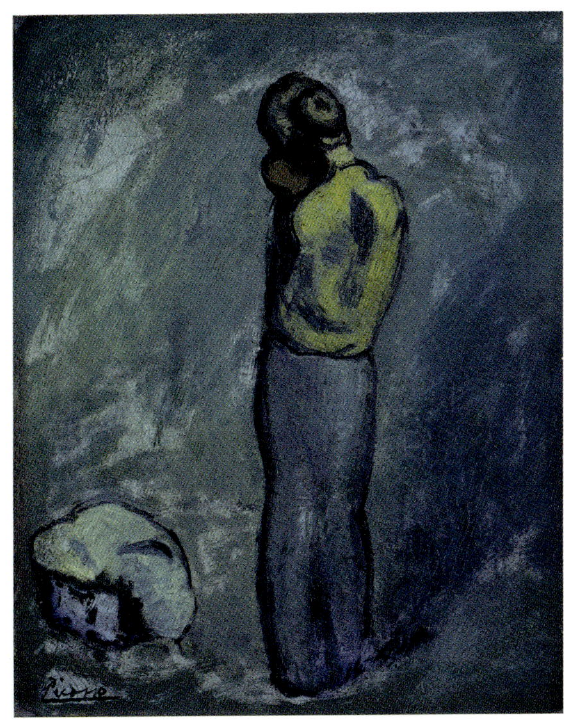

## Use

Prussian blue's tendency to reflect back very little light naturally draws us in to inspect further, giving the colour an intensity and almost melancholic nature. This serious colour is ideal for uses connected with mental wellbeing, working well in combination with soothing greens.

 # Smalt

**Then**

Smalt is a semi-transparent, earthy, mineral blue with a rich history. Ancient Egyptians drew smaltite ore out of the earth and first made a colourant by a process of experimentation, melting the ore together with quartz and potash, in much the same way as they made Egyptian blue (see Cerulean, page 184). The result was an intensely blue, glass-like substance that was cooled, splintered, ground up and sold to producers of glassware and porcelain.

In the 8th and 9th centuries, smalt gave Chinese pottery painters a colour with which to illustrate life, nature and day-to-day tales and scenes, giving us the classic blue-and-white chinaware that is ubiquitous today. When the blue-glazed porcelain was shipped back to Europe by Dutch traders in the 17th century, it inspired the famous blue-and-white Delftware. The centuries that followed saw smalt take on a range of shades, from light mineral blue to deeply intense cobalt, depending on the preferences of the ceramicware master artisans and the upper-class fashion trends of the time.

**Now**

Smalt faded, literally, and was shunted aside by the chemically stable and multifaceted synthetic cobalt in the 19th century (see page 182). However, smalt still has a place in art and design, if only in respect of its valued history. In 2016, Dutch designer Olivier van Herpt, working for the Kunstmuseum Den Haag, 3D-printed porcelain and smalt-cobalt pigments together for the first time, playfully absorbing the blue back into the material once again.

**Colour Values**

Hex code: #295ea0
RGB: 41, 94, 160
CMYK: 90, 67, 8, 1
HSB: 213º, 74%, 63%

**Common Connotations**

- Timeless
- Confident
- Elegant

**Smalt in Art,
Design & Culture**
- A Dutch Delft Dish
  from Het Moriaanshooft
  Factory, *ceramics*, 1679–86
- Arcanum by Olivier Van
  Herpt, *ceramics*, 2017
- *A Pair of Memory Vessels
  LXIV* by Bouke de Vries,
  *sculpture*, 2020

**Use**
Reference the liquid quality of glazed smalt by using it in transparent layers, softening with bone white and an accent of deep midnight blue to capture the elegance of the hue.

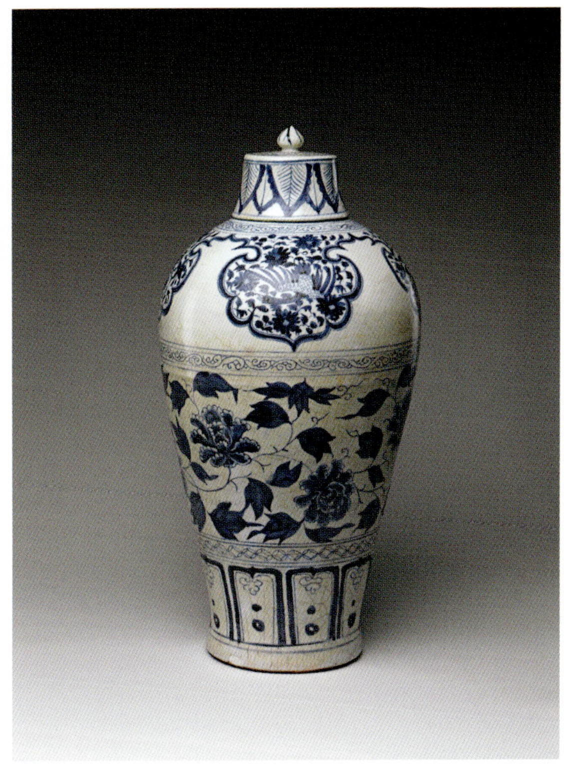

Bottle with peony scroll,
Jingdezhen ware, Yuan
Dynasty (1271–1368)

## Cobalt



**Then**

Cobalt is a bright and decorative hue associated with porcelain and impressionist paintings, but it has a dark past. An element, cobalt was historically extracted from mineral ores and was often found in combination with arsenic. Extracting it was so dangerous, causing strange, unexplained deaths, that in the 17th century, German miners named it 'kobold' after the evil mountain-dwelling spirits of Germanic folklore. It wasn't until the 18th century when Swedish chemist and smelting-plant owner Georg Brandt discovered its elemental nature and renamed it cobalt, to rid it of its devilish associations.

In 1802, French chemist Louis Jacques Thénard boiled the ore with alumina to create a stable pigment, and impressionist painters such as J.M.W. Turner, Pierre-Auguste Renoir and Vincent van Gogh took heed. Thénard's cobalt quickly replaced organic smalt (see page 180) and, alongside synthetic ultramarine (see page 174) and Prussian blue (see page 178), ushered in a new blue age, providing a nuanced vocabulary to describe deep waters and the purest skies. Van Gogh, who used all three new pigments in his masterpiece *The Starry Night* (1889), described cobalt as 'a divine colour and there is nothing so beautiful for putting atmosphere around things.'[*]

**Now**

Since its early beginnings, this luminous blue has continued to inspire artists. Cobalt literally predominates in William Scott's 1972 series of paintings *A Poem for Alexander*, alongside a limited palette of brown, black, white, yellow and green.

[*] Roskill, Mark (ed.), *The Letters of Vincent Van Gogh*, New York: Simon & Schuster, 1997

**Colour Values**

Hex code: #536fb0
RGB: 83, 111, 176
CMYK: 74, 57, 3, 0
HSB: 222°, 53%, 69%

**Common Connotations**

- Otherworldly
- Joyful
- Profound

**Cobalt in Art,
Design & Culture**
- Chefchaouen, Morocco, *architecture*, from 1492
- Limnos Wines: Krama Limnio Merlot, packaging by Luminous Design Group, *graphic design* 2019
- *Darkening* series by Lorna Simpson, *paintings*, 2019

## Use

Long since having thrown off its historical association with dark and deadly mines, cobalt is an established colour of bright, outdoor, summertime scenes. Combine with bright but natural impressionist colours – carmine, vermillion, pale yellow and leaf greens – to capture this atmosphere.

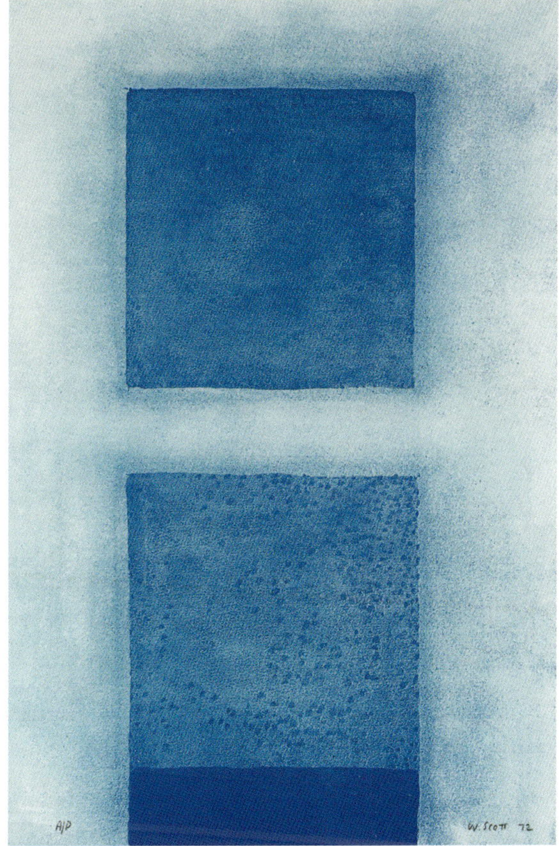


*Cobalt Predominates* from the series *A Poem for Alexander* by William Scott, 1972

 # Cerulean

## Then

The name 'cerulean' derives from a Latin word referring to the sky or heavens above, aptly describing this rich hue. It was the name the Romans gave to Egyptian blue. Historically important as possibly the first synthetic pigment, this blue was made by the ancient Egyptians from copper, which gave it its hue, combined with a mixture of silica, lime and an alkali. It remained in use until the means of making it were forgotten with end of the Roman Empire.

In 1805, a new synthetic cerulean was created by the Swiss chemist Albrecht Höpfner. The shade was popular with artists, especially with the rise of the impressionist movement in the middle of the century. Obsessed with capturing the quality of light, many impressionist artists followed developments in colour theory, notably the work of French chemist Michel Eugène Chevreul. Chevreul's theory of 'simultaneous contrast' suggested that a colour's visual appearance can be affected by neighbouring hues regardless of their material consistency. Instead of mixing colours on the palette, the impressionists painted dabs of pure colours on the canvas, placing analogous or complementary shades side by side. This technique relies on the optical effects of the colours to do the work of mixing, as demonstrated so effectively in Claude Monet's *Water Lilies* paintings.

## Now

When you look closely at Monet's works, you will often find a garish spectrum of colours dabbed over the canvas – but it appears natural enough when you stand back. The colour combinations blend in the eye, drawing out each other's subtle nuances, mimicking the effects of light and shadow. More recently, 'colour field' painters such as Mark Rothko and Willem De Kooning have explored a similar approach to create balanced sonatas of colour.

**Colour Values**
Hex code: #6aa9de
RGB: 109, 169, 222
CMYK: 55, 22, 0, 0
HSB: 208°, 51%, 87%

**Also Known As**
- Egyptian Blue
- Sky Blue

**Common Connotations**
- Sanctuary
- Tranquillity
- Creativity

Right: *Water lilies, water study, morning* (detail) by Claude Monet, from a series of eight large canvases painted at Giverny, c.1914–18

**Cerulean in Art, Design & Culture**

- *Girl on a Divan* by Berthe Morisot, *painting*, c.1885
- Cinderella's ballgown by Jane Law, worn by Lily James in *Cinderella, costume design*, 2015
- Couture collection by Elie Saab, *fashion*, S/S 2016

**Use**

In Monet's skyscapes and lily ponds, you will often find colours and tints of violet beside blue, analogous on the colour wheel, offset with a tiny dab of complementary yellow to enliven the whole palette. His example inspires us to understand the way colours interact, to consider the effects of our palettes and proportions holistically.

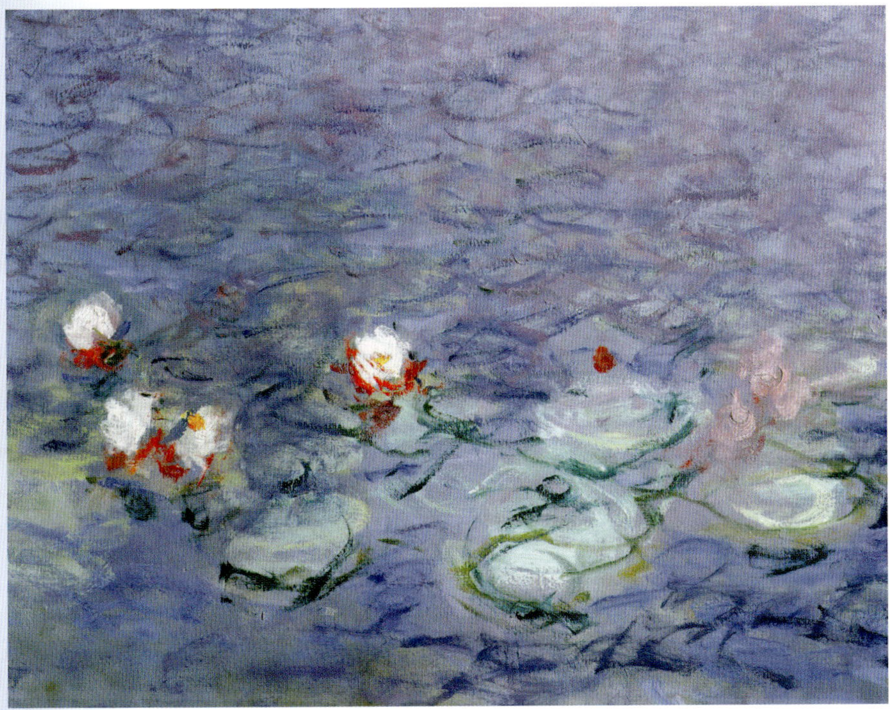

 # Glaucous

**Then**

Sometimes green and sometimes blue, the ancient
Greeks – who famously did not distinguish between
the two hues – used the word *γλαυκός*, or *glaukós*, to
describe the pale grey or blue-green appearance of
aloe leaves. Later, the colour would be identified in
the fleeting storm-grey feathers of the glaucous gull,
as well as the grey-green haze of glaucoma. Poets of
the ancient world loved this colour for its mutability,
sometimes applying the name to browns and yellows,
as well as the more common greys, greens and blues.

Over the centuries, the ephemeral colour
persisted: in Latin, it took the spelling we use today,
becoming 'glauk' in Middle English, and it enjoyed
a revival among Romantic artists and poets who
revered both the ancient Greeks and the natural
world that glaucous blue evokes.

**Now**

Both its restless changeability and its eye-pleasing
harmony have kept this shade relevant and useful. In
the 1950s the shade found a renaissance when Italian
typewriter manufacturer Olivetti and Danish architect
Arne Jacobsen both used the shade to soften the forms
and encourage acceptance of their progressive designs.

Readily found in nature but difficult to pin down,
this colour remains important, if obscure, for artists
of all fields. In a 2018 multimedia performance
commissioned by Tate St Ives, Cornish artist Nina Royle
explored the contradictions and unclassifiable nature of
the colour blue through her work entitled *Glaucous*.

**Colour Values**

Hex code: #849bab
RGB: 132, 155, 171
CMYK: 51, 31, 25, 0
HSB: 205º, 23%, 67%

**Common Connotations**

- Natural
- Ambiguous
- Meditative

**Glaucous in Art, Design & Culture**

- Room 606, SAS Radisson Hotel (formerly Royal SAS), Copenhagen, by Arne Jacobsen, *interior design*, 1950
- Eventbrite offices, San Francisco, by Rapt Studio, *interior design*, 2014
- Cosm Chair by Studio 7.5 for Herman Miller, *furniture*, 2020

Room painted in Coastal Grey from the Dulux Colour Futures palette, 2021

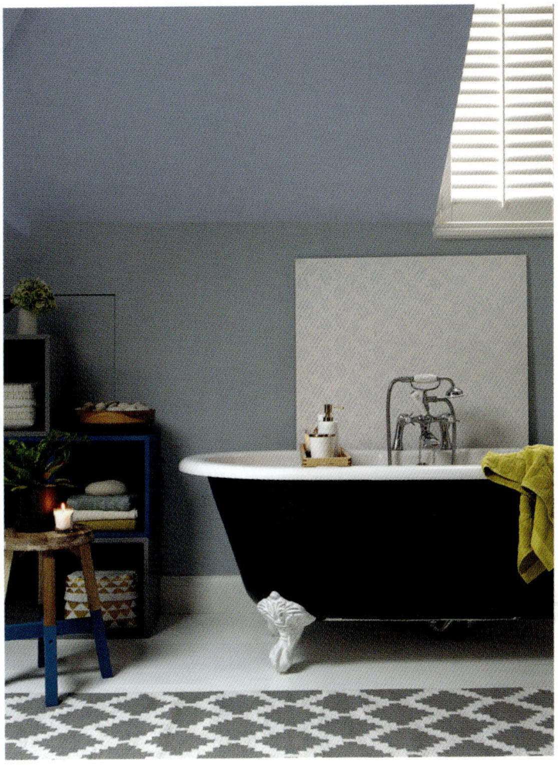

## Use

Born out of the observation of the natural world, this shade is uniquely suited to instilling the meditative quality of the blue-green sea wherever it is found. A calming and understated shade, it can be given prominence without overpowering or offending the eye. Try balancing the cool sea-blue of glaucous with its warm, complementary terracotta to create a balanced and restorative atmosphere.

 # Teal

**Then**

A modern-day hero, teal got its first outing as a colour
in 1917, the name deriving from the Eurasian teal – a
freshwater duck with a distinctive blue-green marking.
Mexican artist Leonora Carrington, born the same year
as the colour, made great use of this opulent shade in
her surrealist landscapes, often pairing it with golds,
blues and reds in jewel-like combinations. The colour
also found rich expression in the works of master
colourist Henri Matisse, who often paired it with
orange to sensationally bold and playful effect.

However, it was post-war Europe that really
embraced the colour: hungry for the new, Vespa
launched its first scooter in teal in 1946 and generated
a media frenzy around its fresh use of the shade.
Two years later, in 1948, the *Plochere Color System*, a
publication for interior designers, added 'Teal Blue'
to its repertoire, thrusting the colour into the interior
design scene of the 1950s and '60s. Italian designer Gio
Ponti made glamorous use of the colour for interiors
by pairing it with modernist architecture, chic vintage
pinks, wingback chairs and sleek teak accents, turning
teal into a modern yet approachable design statement.

**Now**

The popularity of this modern colour has been building
steam for decades. Thought to promote and support
our ability to concentrate and think clearly because of
its calming effects on the nervous system, the hue was
one of the first 16 colours in HTML/CSS web coding
and the background screen colour of Windows 95. It's
no surprise that when Apple launched its iconic iMacs
in 1998, teal was one of the chosen shades.

**Colour Values**
Hex code: #367589
RGB: 54, 118, 137
CMYK: 81, 43, 36, 8
HSB: 194°, 61%, 54%

**Common Connotations**
- Clarity
- Creativity
- Luxury

**Teal in Art,
Design & Culture**
- *Virginia Woolf* by Vanessa
  Bell, *painting*, 1912
- Vespa 98 by Enrico
  Piaggio, *automotive*, 1946
- iMac G3 by Apple in
  Bondi Blue, *product
  design*, 1998

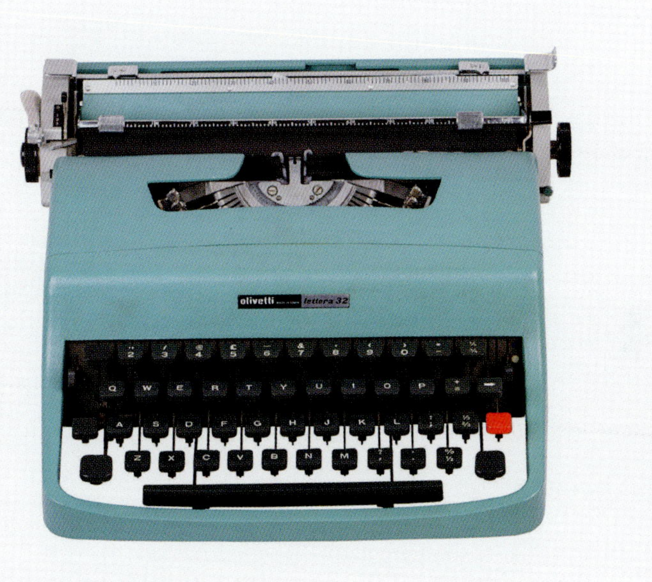

Lettera 32 typewriter, designed by Marcello Nizzoli for Olivetti in 1963

Not only has teal found favour in the innovative field of information technology, it has also been a darling of the fashion industry for years. Perhaps due to its association with the charismatic eras of the '20s, '50s and '60s, or perhaps because it pairs well with gold and elegant rose hues, teal seems a natural fit for the red carpet.

## Use
Modern and versatile, teal can both blend in as a neutral to soothe and bring tranquillity to interior and product design, or work its chic magic in bolder outings. Hark back to Gio Ponti's retro sophistication by pairing teal with a complementary mid-tone pink, and ground it with darker and lighter neutrals.

# Process Cyan

## Then

Along with yellow, magenta and black, cyan is one of the four inky pillars of the CMYK colour model that is used in most modern printing. As such, cyan really came into its own with the development of modern printing techniques in the early 1900s that allowed colour illustrations to be printed cheaply and accurately, in particular with the rise of mass-market comic books from the 1930s onwards.

By the 1970s, the garish colours that characterized most comics were beginning to show more nuance and restraint as a result of improved printing techniques; it was in this decade also that Italian-born graphic designer Massimo Vignelli redesigned New York's subway map. His map married modern typography with a rainbow of primary and secondary colours, including cyan, and used a healthy pinch of graphic license to create a system that was clear and easy to use. Although Vignelli's map was not immediately loved – the abstraction from reality he employed being too much for many at the time, who could not recognize the physical city in the diagram – it has since become a classic example of the use of simplified colour and design to transform the user experience.

## Now

As one of the CMYK's four fundamental pigments, cyan will always have a place in design. The halftone technique that underpins the CMYK printing process involves printing tiny dots that vary in size, space and colour – either cyan, magenta, yellow or black – and combine to create a virtually infinite number of colours. As a subtractive colour model (see page 10), the more colours that are combined, the darker the result – just as when children (or adults) mix all the colours on a paint palette and inevitably end up with a disappointing muddy brown. Therefore, the simplest combinations will always be the brightest, and you will often find pure cyans, magentas and yellows wherever designers want to showcase clean colour or reference the printing process.

**Colour Values**
Hex code: #00aeef
RGB: 0, 174, 239
CMYK: 100, 0, 0, 0
HSB: 196°, 100%, 94%

**Also Known As**
- Printer's Cyan
- Process Blue

**Common Connotations**
- Optimism
- Simplicity
- Inspiration

**Process Cyan in Art,
Design & Culture**

- *Colour Sound* by Karl
  Gerstner, *silkscreen print*,
  1973
- 'Winston Churchill:
  The Wilderness Years'
  poster design by Ivan
  Chermayeff, *lithograph*,
  1983
- *Amsterdam Urban Nature
  Map* by Urban Good/
  Nature Desks, *map*, 2019

## Use

Colour can help users follow what would typically be a
complicated sets of instructions. Use distinct primaries
such as cyan to help guide the eye and promote
confidence in navigating physical locations, printed
plans or instruction manuals.

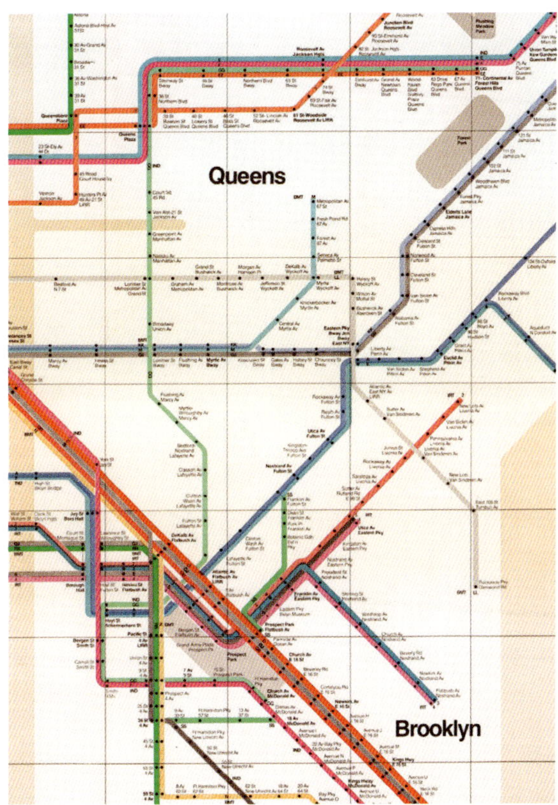


New York Subway Map by
Massimo Vignelli, 1972

 # International Klein Blue

**Then**

'Blue is the invisible becoming visible,' French artist Yves Klein once said.* It was, for him, not just a colour, but a pure expression of the infinite, and his obsession with it led him to invent a new blue pigment.

In order to achieve his perfect blue, he worked with paint specialist Edouard Adam to create a new binder for ultramarine that preserved the intensity of the pigment in its pure, powdered form. The result was a luminous, matt blue paint, which Klein patented under the name International Klein Blue (IKB) in 1960. Klein went on to make a series of rich and radiant artworks with the colour, not only nearly 200 IKB monochrome paintings, but also his *Anthropometries*, a performative series that involved painting a naked woman (or women) with IKB, who would then lie upon the canvas as a 'human paintbrush'.

**Now**

Klein was following in a long tradition of artists who had, since the Renaissance, and even earlier in the Middle East and Africa, reserved the colour for their most holy and illustrious subjects. But in making the colour the subject – rather than the means of representation – he inspired a new way of looking that continues to reverberate in the art world. IKB has been adopted by artists, creatives and fashion houses right up to the present day: for Spring 2017, fashion giant Céline launched a collection of *Anthropometries*-inspired prints with IKB, while John Galliano's Spring 2019 collection for Maison Margiela was linked by the motif of a distinctly IKB poodle.

**Colour Values**

Hex code: #3b3ff6
RGB: 59, 63, 246
CMYK: 81, 73, 0, 0
HSB: 239°, 76%, 96%

**Common Connotations**

- Infinite
- Playful
- Mesmerizing

* Weitemeier, Hannah, *Yves Klein*, Cologne: Taschen, 2016

**International Klein Blue
in Art, Design & Culture**
- *Blue* by Derek Jarman,
  *film*, 1993
- Ready-to-Wear collection
  by Céline, *fashion*, S/S 2017
- Couture collection by
  Maison Margiela, *fashion*,
  S/S 2019

**Use**
For the 90th anniversary of Klein's birth, the Yves Klein Archives partnered with paint manufacturer Ressource to create an official IKB paint. A transformative shade that commands attention, IKB is also ideal for product design, and graphic, typeface and user interface design. To realize its full impact, IKB wants to be used alone or on white.

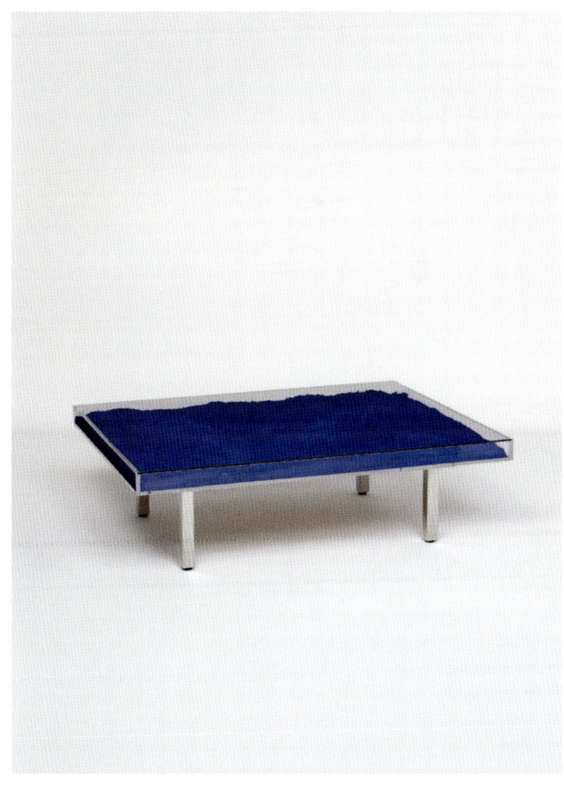

Table IKB® by
Yves Klein, 1961

'Blue has no dimensions, it is beyond dimensions ... blue suggests at most the sea and sky,

and they,
after all, are
in actual,
visible
nature what
is most
abstract.'
– Yves Klein

# Electric Blue

**Then**

People have been describing shades of blue as 'electric' since the late 19th century, inspired by Thomas Edison using electricity to produce light. A shade often connected to technology and advancement, David Bowie's 1977 song 'Sound and Vision' spells out what the interior design of the future might look like: 'Blue, blue, electric blue / That's the colour of my room / Where I will live.'

**Now**

Electric blue remains the go-to colour for representing the future. Science fiction films such as *Minority Report* (2002), *Tron* (1982) and *Wall-E* (2008) have all utilized the colour when depicting futuristic technology, while energetic and pulsating shades have been used to represent the promise of innovation across a range of industries. It has been used in advertising campaigns for 5G connectivity, and Ford's 2020 'Go Electric' campaign features electric blue vehicles and visuals. Other brands including Volkswagen, Mercedes-Benz and Virgin have also embedded this luminous colour in various advertising campaigns.

If electric blue is the colour of the future, however, it also comes with a warning. A study by Harvard Medical School has recently shown how blue light wavelengths produced by electronics, such as smartphones, suppress melatonin levels, making it hard to fall asleep and potentially causing other health issues.

**Use**

Use electric blue sparingly to call attention to key features. Ideal for branding and UI/UX applications, balance this vivacious colour with a grounding navy background. Use accents around interaction points and buttons for easy usability, while fonts and graphics could be offset with a complementary hot violet.

**Colour Values**
Hex code: #0091ff
RGB: 0, 145, 255
CMYK: 73, 40, 0, 0
HSB: 206°, 100%, 100%

**Common Connotations**
- Connectivity
- Technology
- Speed

**Electric Blue in Art, Design & Culture**
- *276. (On Colour Blue)* by Joseph Kosuth, *light installation*, 1990
- ID.R electric racing car by Volkswagen, *automotive*, 2018

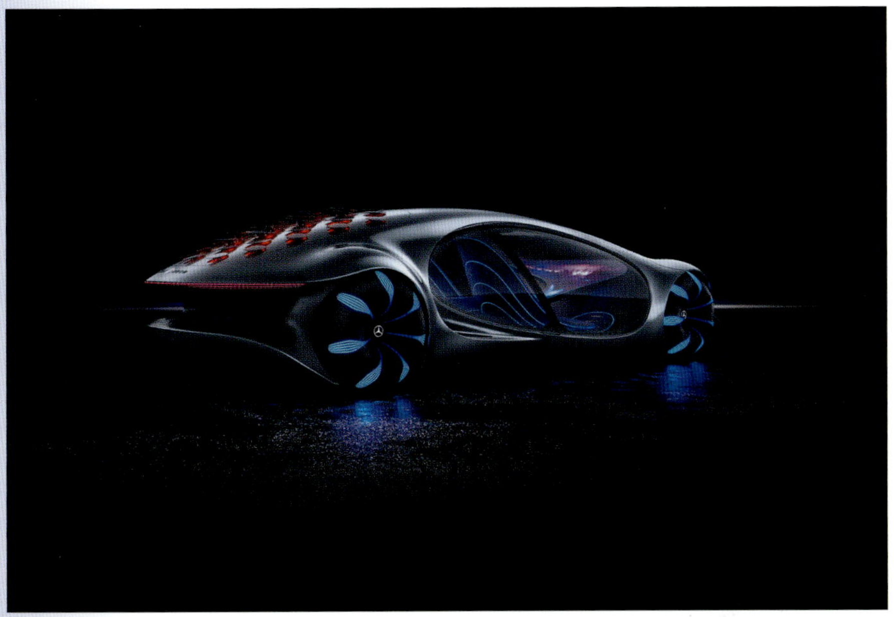

Vision AVTR concept car by Mercedes-Benz, 2020

# YInMn Blue

## Then

In 2009, chemist Mas Subramanian of Oregon State University made a real-life, out-of-the-blue discovery, of which we are only now just beginning to see the fantastic potential. This was all thanks to a lab accident in which a super-heated mixture of the elements yttrium, indium and manganese fused in an evaporation dish within moments to reveal a tantalizing new shade of blue. Even more remarkable, it is the first truly new blue to surface since cobalt in 1802, over 200 years ago.

## Now

What's key about this new artificial pigment is that it is almost completely unmuddied by other colours. It doesn't fade over time, is stable when mixed with oil or water and it reflects a high proportion of infrared light. The colour is one of the purest forms of blue we are likely to be able to see, as its crystalline structure absorbs red and green light wavelengths while reflecting blue wavelengths almost exclusively. In 2015, a licensing agreement was reached for commercial production. The shade is already yielding a high-performance value and a proven ability to keep temperatures down when used with tech devices, cars and aircraft.

## Use

This vibrant shade can be paired with greens and violet pastels to provide a cooling environment. A bright red could juxtapose the blue in a high-contrast scheme, ideal for wayfinding or controls.

**Colour Values**
Hex code: #00289b
RGB: 0, 40, 155
CMYK: 100, 94, 4, 2
HSB: 225°, 100%, 61%

**Common Connotations:**
- Cooling
- Futuristic
- Balanced

YInMn Blue by Kremer Pigmente

 # Pink & Purple

A little bit redder, a tiny bit bluer, very few truly spectral violets appear in the natural world, and violet is also the colour wavelength that is hardest for our eyes to detect, making it a deeply mysterious and elusive hue. Pinks, meanwhile, make up a fluid, shapeshifting family adopting many faces: pinks can be gentle and soothing, but they can also be shocking, rebellious and powerful. Both pinks and purples are mixes of key primary colours; as a result, these hues run the gamut of personalities, associations and moods.

Throughout history, pink has assumed a range of guises, at various times being considered masculine, feminine, sensual, tasteless, chic and opulent. In 17th-century China, it was not recognized as a colour at all, the word for pink meaning 'foreign colour'; it was eventually brought into the culture under increasing Western influence. However, we know that ancient Egyptians were making natural rose-tinted dyes for cloth, probably from limestone, long before today's shades and associations came along.

In the West today, pinks are typically entrenched with ideas of femininity, but this association did not come about until the early-to-mid 20th century. When pink and blue pastel hues were created in the 19th century, pink was seen as a boyish version of masculine red; a stronger colour than the dainty blue that at the time was thought to be more appropriate for girls. By the 1950s, this had changed thanks to the rise of consumerism in post-war America and branding that used pink as a symbol of hyper-femininity. However, its countercultural leanings in the 1970s and '80s and the emergence of millennial pink make it a case study in how perceptions of colour are entangled with the concerns and contexts of each generation.

Exploring the purple family reveals a similar story of evolution. Purple gained fame with Julius Caesar who, influenced by Cleopatra's use of the colour, adopted it as the colour of emperors. Subsequently, it became a royal colour, with a strict monopoly around who was allowed to wear it. This can't have been hard to enforce, as scientists have estimated that it would have taken around 12,000 harvested Murex snails to create just 1.4 grams of Tyrian purple, barely enough to cover a small swatch of fabric, and so the pigment was extravagantly expensive.

Purple is still associated with royalty, status and luxury across much of the world, but it is also commonly linked with mysticism and divinity. As the colour most commonly used to represent the crown or Sahasrara chakra in Ayurvedic and Tantric Buddhist meditation, it is also linked to pure consciousness and the highest spiritual states. In the West, it has long been connected with the supernatural. Today, we are seeing the magic of purple pigments in action, with violet-tinged bacterial dyes presenting extraordinary new opportunities for sustainable textile production.

## Colours in this chapter:

# Tyrian Purple

**Then**

This rich purple dye comes from predatory Murex snails, specifically the odorous secretions of a mucous gland located near the anus, dried and boiled. Legend has it that it was first discovered when the Greek hero Hercules' dog chewed on a Murex shell on the shores of Tyre. When his mouth turned purple and the dye was revealed, Hercules' amorous nymph 'companion' demanded a garment of the same colour. When Hercules told King Phoenix of his encounter, the monarch decided that the rulers of Phoenicia would wear purple as a symbol of royal status.

The Romans named the shade *sacer murex* ('sacred purple'), and it was heavily priced and restricted, with severe penalties for those who wore it without imperial permission. The Vestal Virgins, chaste priestesses responsible for the wellbeing of Rome, wore headdresses with purple stripes signalling that their person was sacrosanct, and any transgression considered a crime. In fact, the Romans were so obsessed with the purity and status of the colour that *adoratio purpurae* ('the kissing of the purple') was an act of kissing purple cloth at the feet of the emperor to honour its value and worth.

**Colour Values**

Hex code: #472a4c
RGB: 71, 42, 76
CMYK: 72, 87, 42, 39
HSB: 291°, 45%, 30%

**Common Connotations**

- Royalty
- Exclusivity
- Power

**Tyrian Purple in Art, Design & Culture**

- New Balance x Concepts 990v2 'Tyrian', *footwear,* 2016
- 'The Soft Enfilade' show space by AMO for Miu Miu, *set design,* 2017
- *Purple Poem for Miami* by Judy Chicago, *performance art,* 2019

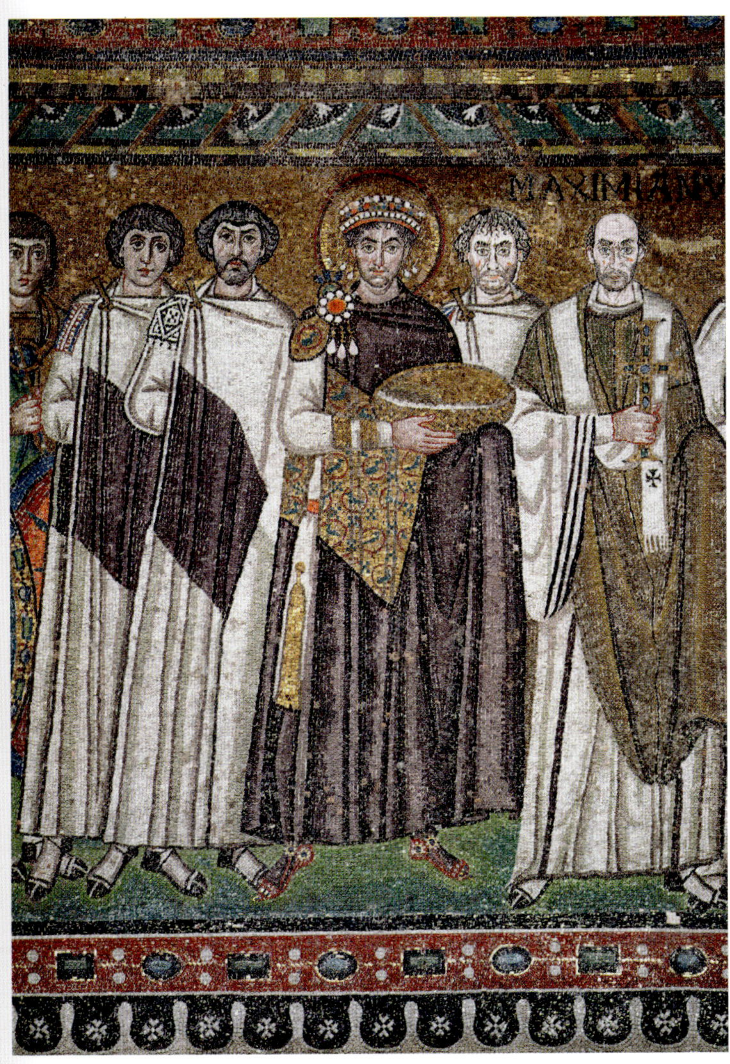

Justinian I and his retinue, from a mosaic in the Basilica of San Vitale,
Ravenna, Italy, c.547 CE

**Now**

In the late 1850s, British chemist William Perkin accidentally derived the pigment mauve out of coal tar, a readily available substance during the Industrial Revolution. When Queen Victoria and Empress Eugénie were seen wearing elaborate mauve dresses, 'mauve mania' saw the shade enjoy a new, widespread popularity.

While purple may have become common with Perkin's discovery, the hue has lost none of its cachet. Worn by ordinary people, the colour has supported radical ideas including feminism: it was used alongside green and white to mark the Suffragettes' 'Votes for Women' campaign at the turn of the 20th century. In more recent times, it has regained a sensual mystique in the hands of luxury brands such as Dior and Yves Saint Laurent, who used it in the branding of their dangerous-sounding perfumes Poison and Opium.

**Use**

Create a powerful, modern combination using this exclusive tone matched with vibrant emerald green for trustworthy statements and attention-grabbing messaging.

'While purple may have become common, the hue has lost none of its cachet. Worn by ordinary people, the colour has supported radical ideas.'

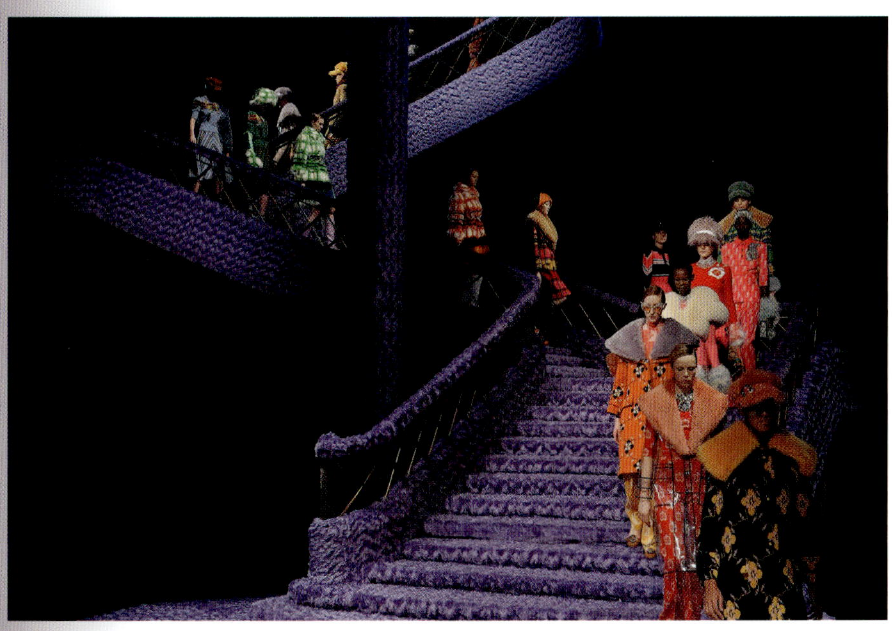

Interior design by AMO for Miu Miu Womenswear Fall/Winter 2017/2018 at Paris Fashion Week

# Magenta

**Then**

The success of William Perkin's mauve prompted the European scientific community to embark on a race that would result in the discovery of over 50 further distinct colour dyes. French chemist François-Emmanuel Verguin was the first to infuse aniline and tin chloride, a process that in 1858–9 resulted in a reddish purple dye that Verguin called fuchsine (or fuchsia), after the flower.

At the same time, two British chemists, George Maule and Chambers Nicolson, discovered a virtually identical dye that they named roseine. Fuchsine and roseine were later renamed magenta by dye manufacturers to commemorate France and Sardinia's recent victory at the Battle of Magenta, one of the bloodiest and most important skirmishes of the Second Italian War of Independence.

This weird and wonderful shade was embraced by Victorian fashionistas, who splashed it onto dresses, petticoats, bonnets, stockings, shoes, gloves, parasols, fans and jewellery. Like many early dyes, however, magenta's allure concealed a deadly secret: traces of arsenic were discovered in textiles dyed with the original magenta synthesis. After a less poisonous process was adopted, magenta dye found itself used in numerous consumer products, from wines and syrups to pharmaceutical drugs and wallpaper.

**Colour Values**

Hex code: #ec008c
RGB: 236, 0, 140
CMYK: 0, 100, 0, 0
HSB: 324°, 100%, 93%

**Also Known As**

- Fuchsine
- Fuchsia

**Common Connotations**

- Revolutionary
- Assertive
- Flamboyant

**Magenta in Art, Design & Culture**

- *Les Toits de Collioure* by Henri Matisse, *painting*, 1905
- Foyer of Teatro Regio Torino Theater, Turin, by Carlo Mollino *interior design*, 1965–73
- The American Restaurant by Warren Platner, Kansas City, *interior design*, 1974

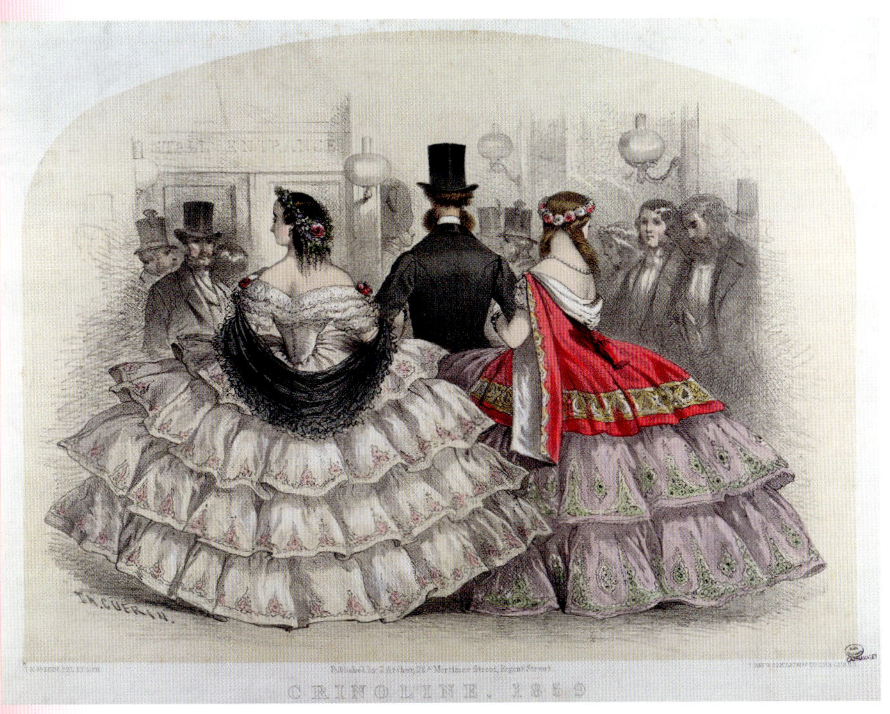

Ladies Wearing Crinolines at the Royal Opera House,
Covent Garden, London, by T.H. Guerin, 1859

**Now**

Increased production of cheap dyes resulted in a market flooded with bright, garish magentas. American artist Jeff Koons' use of the colour in his *Sacred Heart* (1994–2007), *Balloon Dog* (1994–2000) and *Balloon Rabbit* (2005–10) sculptures highlights its association with warmth and romance, riffing on the tokens we give each other in celebration.

Today, magenta plays a key role in the CMYK printing process, sitting snugly between red and blue and directly opposite green on the colour wheel, making it a versatile colour with sass and style to spare.

**Use**

Pair with deeper, grounding shades of berry, gold and oatmeal. This luxurious combination foregrounds the approachability of magenta when used in a balanced way, making it ideal for packaging and branding.

'This weird and wonderful shade was embraced by Victorian fashionistas, who splashed it onto dresses, petticoats, bonnets, stockings, shoes, gloves, parasols, fans and jewellery.'

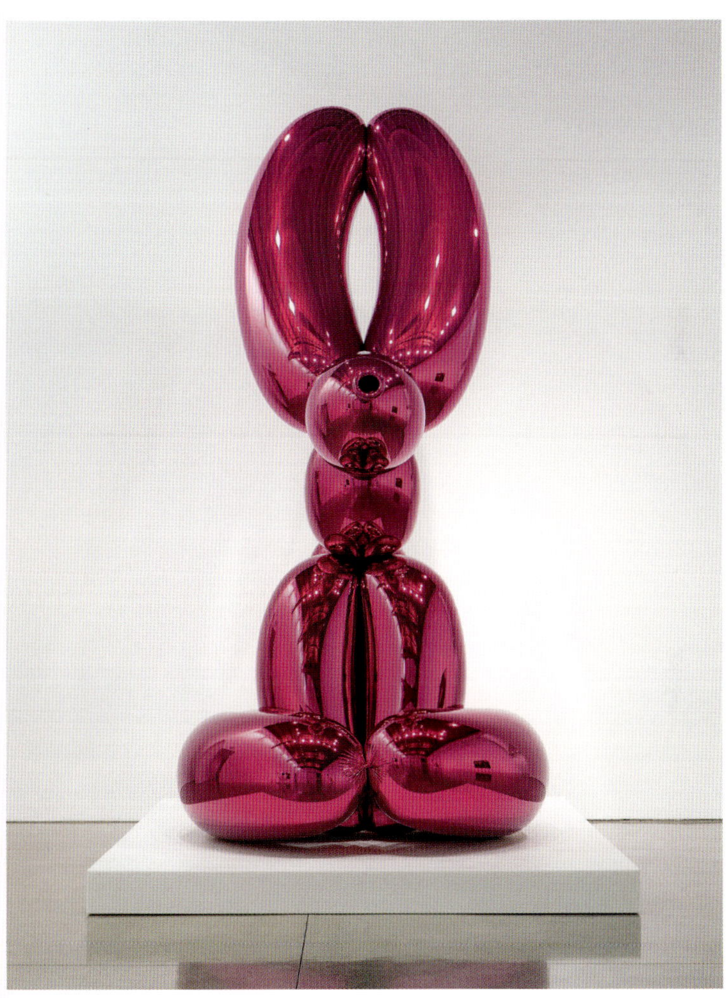

*Balloon Rabbit (Magenta)* by Jeff Koons, 2005–10

 # Violet

## Then

What differentiates violet from other purples is its purity: violet is a spectral colour, not a red-blue mixture, and as such it is rarely seen in nature. Nevertheless, the earliest evidence of the colour dates to 25,000 years ago when Neanderthals discovered a deep, dark violet shade by grinding the mineral manganese – a substance and process still used by the Hopi Native Americans of Arizona to colour ritual objects.

After the invention of mauve in 1856 and the subsequent popularity of purple hues, it was not long before new violets followed. These included the highly saturated but toxic cobalt violet in 1859 and a synthetic manganese violet in 1968. The new colours ignited the imagination of artists and specifically the impressionists, whose uninhibited use of them led to the term 'violettomania' being coined. Working outdoors, or *en plein air*, impressionists strived to capture the effects of light and shadow using complementary colour pairings, which  made violet vital: if the sunlight was yellow, then its direct opposite shadow was not black but violet.

## Now

Violet has the shortest wavelength and our vision is relatively insensitive to its colour, often just seeing black even though violet is present. Perhaps it is this elusive quality that connects the hue to mystery and spirituality: in Ayurvedic tradition, the Sahasrara chakra, indicating our highest spiritual centre, is represented with violet. The musician Prince branded his music and unique style with the mystical force of deep violet which he dubbed 'purple rain'. In 2018, 'Ultra Violet' 18-3838 was Pantone's Colour of the Year, referencing the need for mystery and meditative connection in a world oversaturated with information and immediacy.

**Colour Values**
Hex code: #6f6cb7
RGB: 111, 108, 183
CMYK: 63, 62, 0, 0
HSB: 242°, 41%, 72%

**Common Connotations**
- Spirituality
- Intuition
- Eccentricity

**Violet in Art,
Design & Culture**
- Pantone 18-3838 'Ultra Violet', Pantone Colour of the Year, *design*, 2018
- Le Creuset 'Ultra Violet' collection, *homeware*, 2019
- Pegasus XP-2 by Virgin Hyperloop with BIG and Kilo, 2020

**Use**

'Rare' can be translated as 'unusual', and violet is often seen as an eccentric shade. Use in confident, monochromatic schemes to win the trust of the viewer or user.

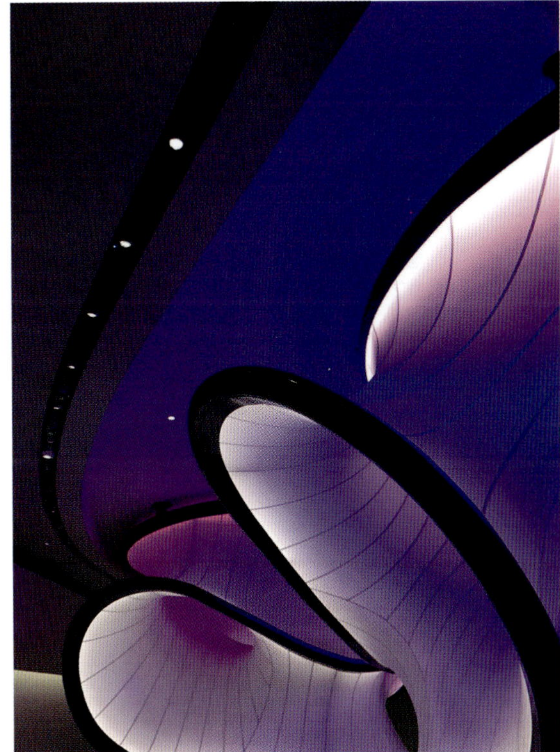

Mathematics: The Winton Gallery, Science Museum, London by Zaha Hadid Architects, 2016

'I have finally discovered the true colour of the atmosphere.

It's violet. Fresh air
is violet.'
– Monet

# Heliotrope

**Then**

A head-turning shade of pure wonder, heliotrope was coined as a colour in 1882. The petals of the flower for which the shade is named gain their radiant appearance from the presence of anthocyanins, natural pigments that are found in the leaves, roots, stems and flowers of certain plants. Today, we know that fruits and vegetables with the distinctive red, purple and blue colourings, such as blueberries, that indicate anthocyanins are rich in antioxidants, but people have used such plants for medicine long before we understood this. Traditional Indian healers in the Kancheepuram district of Tamil Nadu, for example, have used the root and leaves to cure skin diseases and poison bites for centuries.

**Now**

Material forms of this colour in dyes and pigments are rare, and humans have sought to reproduce it over the years. Finally, in the 2000s, thanks to the discovery of YInMn blue (see page 198), a new form of the inorganic purple dye has entered our palette.

Today, the interior design scene's adoption of the shade's playful, spirited nature can be seen in the work of Adam Nathaniel Furman, while in fashion, Nina Ricci utilized it as a stimulator in a modern, bold and eclectic palette in its 2020/21 collection.

**Use**

Pair heliotrope with its opposite, a sunny marigold, for a bold bouquet that expresses individuality and fun.

**Colour Values**

Hex code: #9a7ccf
RGB: 154, 124, 207
CMYK: 43, 55, 0, 0
HSB: 262°, 40%, 81%

**Common Connotations**

- Ethereality
- Healing
- Individualism

**Heliotrope in Art, Design & Culture**

- *Ziff* by Frank Bowling, *painting*, 1974
- *The Colour Purple* by Alice Walker, *book*, 1982
- 'Piggy Ring Box' by Wang & Söderström, *sculpture*, 2018

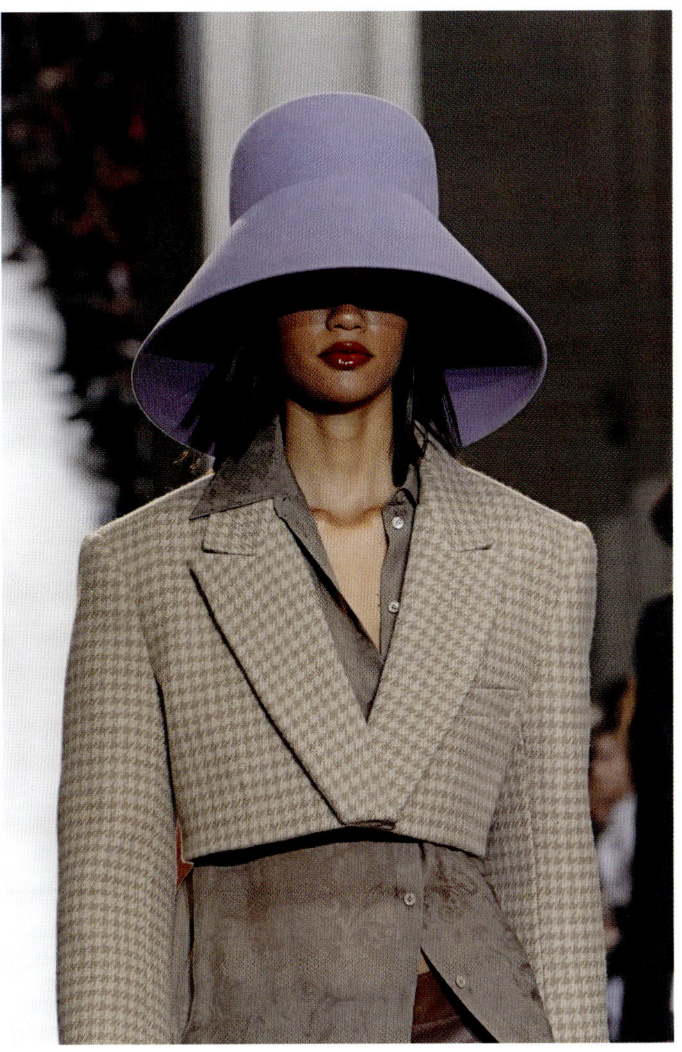

Nina Ricci, Paris Fashion Week, Womenswear Fall/Winter 2020/21

# Rose

**Then**

The consummate pink since ancient times, Homer defined this hue as the colour of morning light in *The Odyssey*, which includes no fewer than 20 mentions of the 'rosy-fingered dawn'. A moment of wonder and awe, that gentle first light gives us a sense of optimism towards the day ahead – and perhaps a rose-tinted viewpoint on the past.

In its history since, this blush shade has pinballed between associations with masculinity and femininity, extravagance and innocence. Raphael used the sweeter side of the colour to depict tender, almost spiritual moments between mother and child, but rose was also used to represent staunch masculinity, as can be seen in the illuminated manuscript *Nova Statuta*, c.1400, which shows King Henry V posing in a rosy pink tunic. The colour gained a more feminine status among 18th-century European nobility when Madame de Pompadour, the chief mistress of Louis XV, loved the colour so much that, in 1757, French porcelain manufacturer Sèvres named its exquisite new shade of pink Rose Pompadour in her honour.

In early-20th-century America, rose pink was again associated with masculinity (this time with male sports) and extravagant wealth. The 2013 film interpretation of F. Scott Fitzgerald's 1925 novel *The Great Gatsby* picks up on this in the three-piece suit worn by Leonardo DiCaprio, playing the sanguine Jay Gatsby. The rose hue of this costume emphasizes Gatsby's status while also softening the impact of his outrageous behaviour.

**Colour Values**
Hex code: #d0747c
RGB: 208, 116, 124
CMYK: 16, 66, 40, 0
HSB: 355°, 44%, 82%

**Also Known As**
- Rosa Pink
- Rococo Rose

**Common Connotations**
- Tenderness
- Sweetness
- Privilege

Right: Elephant Candelabrum Vase (*Vase à Tête d'Eléphant*), Sèvres, 1757–8

Overleaf: 'Community is Kindness' billboard campaign by the BUILDHOLLYWOOD family of JACK, JACK ARTS and DIABOLICAL, London, 2020

**Rose in Art,
Design & Culture**
- *Nova Statuta*, UK, *manuscript*, c.1400
- *The Swing* by Jean-Honoré Fragonard, *painting*, 1767
- Nous restaurant and florist, Dongguan, China by Studio 0321, *interior design*, 2018

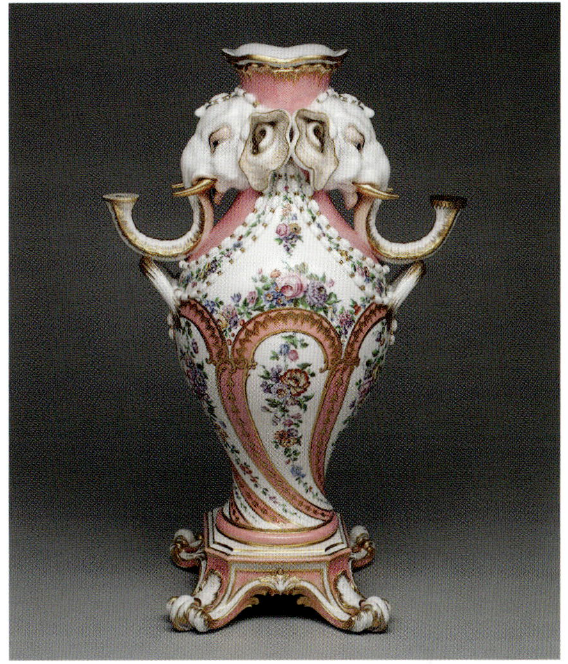

## Now

In our modern world, rose is used to soften a moment or message and to stand for optimism in times of need. This worked to great success in the 2020 'Community is Kindness' billboard campaign in London by the BUILDHOLLYWOOD family of JACK, JACK ARTS and DIABOLICAL, which called for empathy in the community in the face of the Covid-19 pandemic.

## Use

For a contemporary twist, pair naturalistic petal hues with a more daring, darker purple to hint at deeper networks, particularly for digital communication channels.

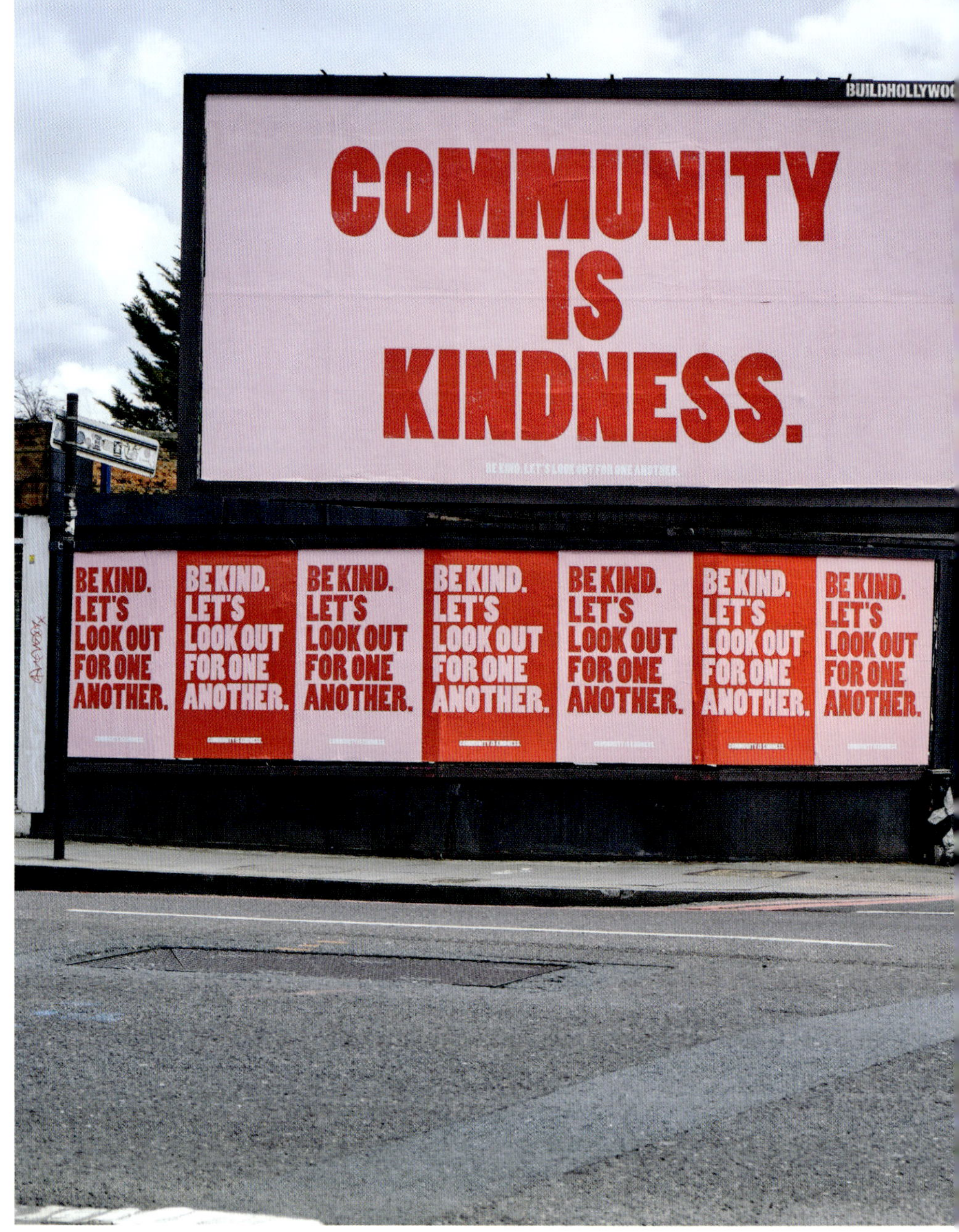
BUILDHOLLYWOO
COMMUNITY
IS
KINDNESS.
BE KIND. LET'S LOOK OUT FOR ONE ANOTHER.
BE KIND. LET'S LOOK OUT FOR ONE ANOTHER.
BE KIND. LET'S LOOK OUT FOR ONE ANOTHER.
BE KIND. LET'S LOOK OUT FOR ONE ANOTHER.
BE KIND. LET'S LOOK OUT FOR ONE ANOTHER.
BE KIND. LET'S LOOK OUT FOR ONE ANOTHER.
BE KIND. LET'S LOOK OUT FOR ONE ANOTHER.
BE KIND. LET'S LOOK OUT FOR ONE ANOTHER.

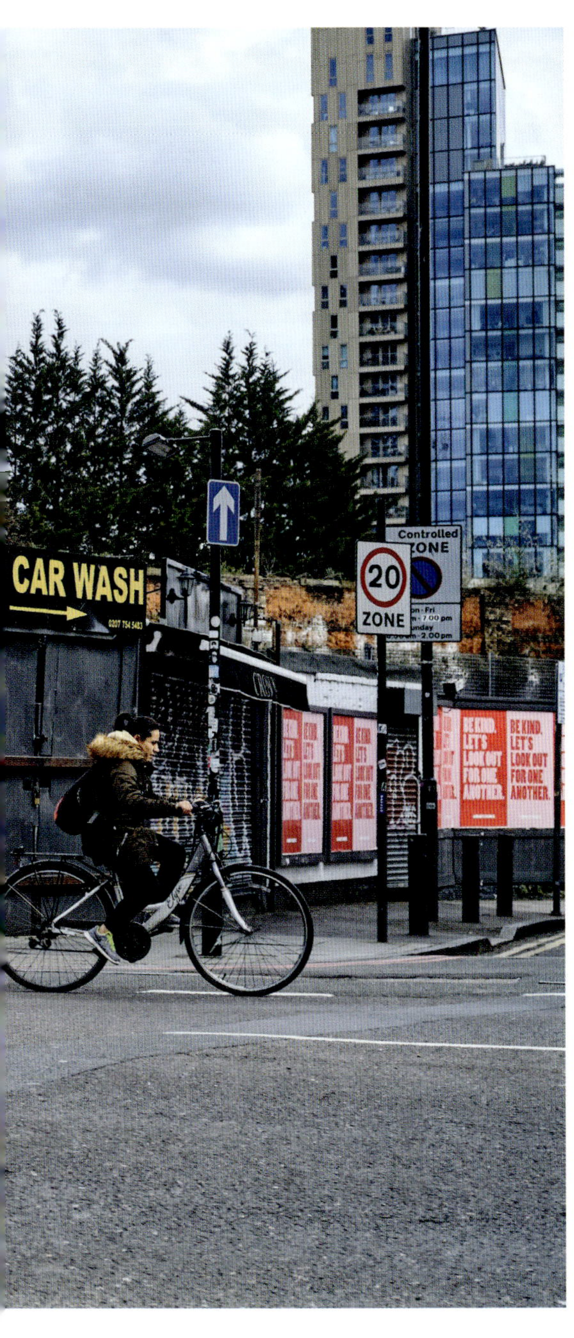


'In our modern
world, rose is used
to soften a moment
or message and to
stand for optimism
in times of need.'

# Shocking Pink

**Then**

It was in 1937 that fashion designer Elsa Schiaparelli coined this determinedly outrageous colour. With this bold shade, her designs stood out against the restrained palettes that defined fashion during Second World War. Bright colours, especially pink, were a means to both distract from and take a sartorial stance against the fear, loss and deprivation that accompanied the global conflict.

In the decades that followed, shocking pink fell out of favour. The post-war '50s idealized pastel shades, while '60s America rejected the colour, which was linked to anti-establishment feminist movements. But in the '70s, the colour regained relevance in punk-era London when Vivienne Westwood and Malcolm McLaren branded their famous King's Road clothing boutique with a four-foot-high pink rubber sign announcing the name of the shop: SEX.

From this moment, the colour was established as the shade of counterculture and political action. Its use by punk bands including the Ramones and The Clash established its edginess, and fashion designer Zandra Rhodes dyed her hair hot pink. Meanwhile, the pink triangle became a symbol of solidarity in the face of the AIDS crisis, after the important, awareness-raising 'Silence = Death' poster campaign in 1987.

**Colour Values**

Hex code: #b51366
RGB: 181, 19, 102
CMYK: 25, 100, 36, 3
HSB: 329°, 90%, 71%

**Common Connotations**

- Empowerment
- Passion
- Energy

**Shocking Pink in Art, Design & Culture**

- 'Silence = Death' project by Avram Finkelstein, Brian Howard, Oliver Johnston, Charles Kreloff, Chris Lione, and Jorge Socarrás, *lithograph print*, 1987
- Do Women Have To Be Naked To Get Into the Met. Museum by Guerilla Girls, *screenprint*, 1989
- Lady Gaga in Brandon Maxwell at the Met Gala, *fashion*, 2019

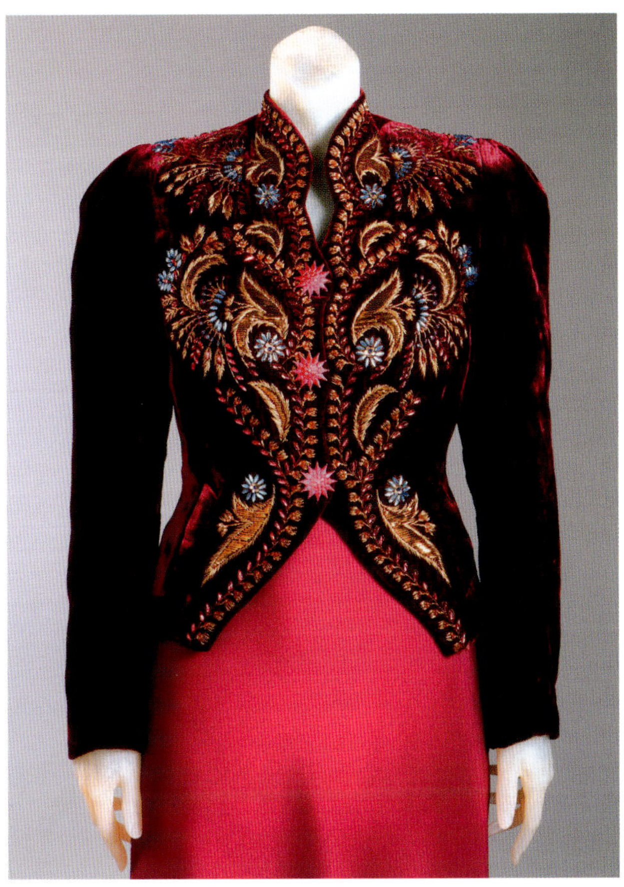



Evening Jacket, Winter (silk velvet, silk & metallic thread embroidery
with sequins) by Elsa Schiaparelli, 1937–8

**Now**

In modern times, activism and shocking pink remain entwined, from the Pussyhat Project that turned women's marches against Donald Trump's presidential inauguration into a 'sea of pink' to the signature colour of the feminist vigilante Gulabi Gang in India, as well as the current Extinction Rebellion campaign.

**Use**

Use the power of shocking pink with a series of equally contrasting off-beat allies to create powerful branding or messaging to emphasize online and offline campaigns.

'I gave to pink, the nerve of the red, a neon pink, an unreal pink.'
– Elsa Schiaparelli

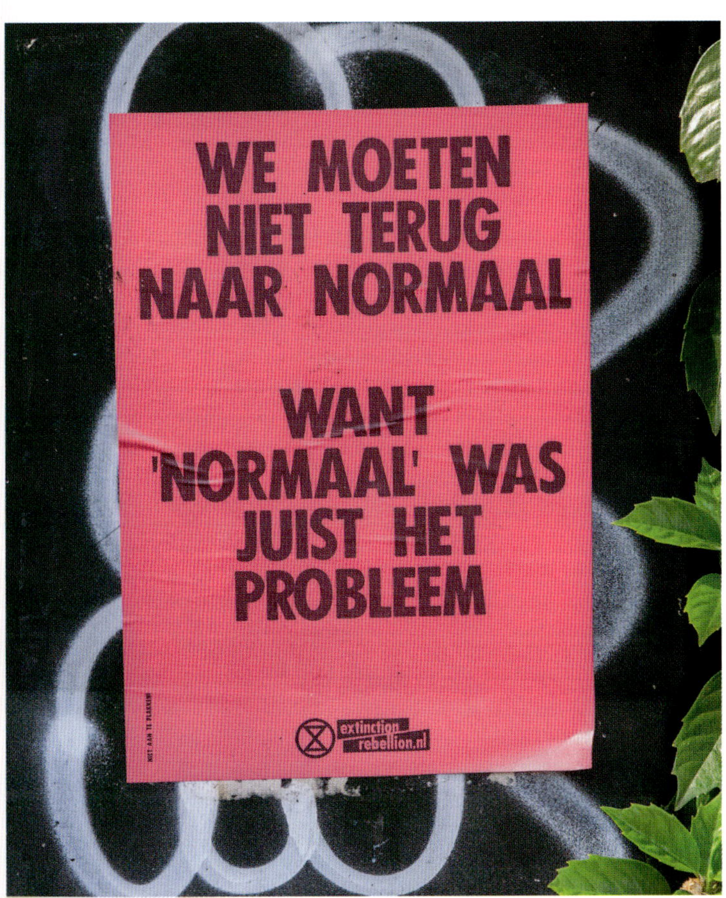


Poster from the Rebellion Extinction group in Amsterdam,
the Netherlands, 2020

# Baker-Miller Pink

224

**Then**

Even fleeting moments with colour can be all that is needed to transform mood and improve user experience. In the late 1970s, Alexander Schauss, director of life sciences at the American Institute for Biosocial Research in Tacoma, studied psychological and physiological responses to colour. His research on inmates at the Naval Correctional Facility in Seattle led to findings that appeared to show that a particular shade of pink – which he created himself by mixing pure white paint with red semi-gloss paint – had a calming effect on those exposed to it. He named the shade after the institute directors, Gene Baker and Ron Miller, who allowed the walls and railings of the prison cells to be painted to create an immersive environment. According to the study, over 156 days, no violent incidents took place, where previously the prison had been rife with fights and violent attacks.

**Now**

The validity of the original Baker-Miller experiments has been challenged in the decades since they first took place, but the story has continued to inspire designers. Interior brand Normann Copenhagen used the shade to entice users into its stores, where it found that people relaxed and considered what they would purchase for much longer. The Vollebak Baker-Miller pink hoodie was designed specifically to help athletes prepare for endurance events. When zipped up and enveloped in the colour, the wearer's heart rate lowers, suggesting the colour's effect helps the heart work more efficiently.

**Use**

Create a calming equilibrium using lightly tinted neutrals and Baker-Miller pink. You could also experiment with other colours known to have a calming effect, such as turquoise.

**Colour Values**

Hex code: #e68d8d
RGB: 230, 141, 141
CMYK: 7, 54, 34, 0
HSB: 0°, 39%, 90%

**Common Connotations**

- Relaxing
- Calming
- Reassuring

**Baker-Miller Pink in Art, Design & Culture**

- Normann Copenhagen flagship store, Copenhagen, Denmark, by Hans Hornemann and Britt Bonnesen, *interior design*, 2016
- Museum of Ice Cream, New York, USA, by Maryellis Bunn and Manish Vora, *interior design*, 2016

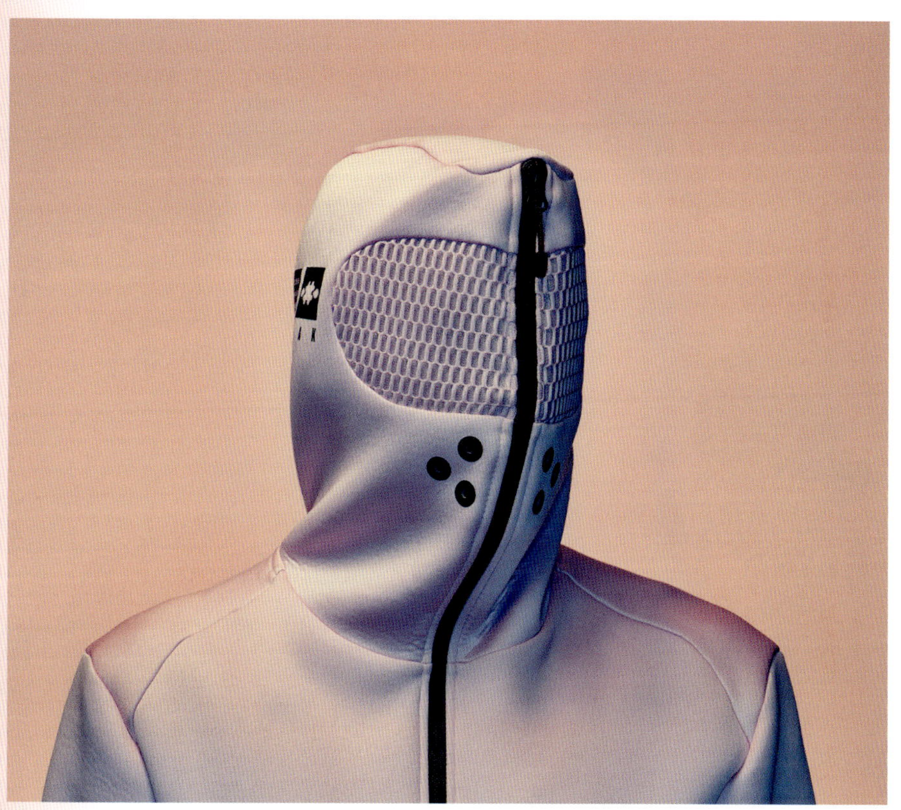

Relaxation Hoodie in Baker-Miller Pink, by Vollebak, 2016

# Neon Pink

## Then

The word neon can broadly apply to a wide range of ultra-bright, fluorescent colours that have come to symbolize modernity, innovation and sometimes even spirituality. In the 1960s and '70s, American minimalist Dan Flavin used fluorescent-light tubing and coloured gels to create simple geometric installations that mixed light and colour like never before. In the same era, another American artist, James Turrell, began experimenting with immersive light-and-space environments. Some were lit with deep, diffused but intense monochrome pink. Audiences reported the experience of entering these spaces to be profoundly moving.

From the psychedelic pink-and-orange swirls of the '60s to the acid house music movement of the '90s, neons have had a place in many counter-culture movements of the last 50 years. The first issue of *i-D* magazine, released in 1980, was a hot pink spot-printed paper zine stapled together by founders Terry and Tricia Jones.

## Now

The turn of the new millennium saw a nostalgic throwback to the music, movies and video games of the previous decades. Flashes of neon pink are associated with synthwave electro sounds and glitching screens in this resurgence in fluoro-inspired graphic design, clothing and branding.

## Use

Be wary of neon saturation: a pure black or white base and/or typography will help to temper a hot pink for a contemporary, graphic look.

**Colour Values**
Hex code: #f600ca
RGB: 246, 0, 202
CMYK: 17, 87, 0, 0
HSB: 311°, 100%, 96%

**Common Connotations**
- Psychedelic
- Playful
- Innovative

**Neon Pink in Art, Design & Culture**
- *Untitled/Night-Time Traffic (Pink and Red Traffic Stream with White Sparks)* by László Moholy-Nagy, *photography*, c.1937–46
- *End Around: Ganzfeld* by James Turrell, *light installation*, 2006
- Ready-to-Wear collection by House of Holland, *fashion*, S/S 2019

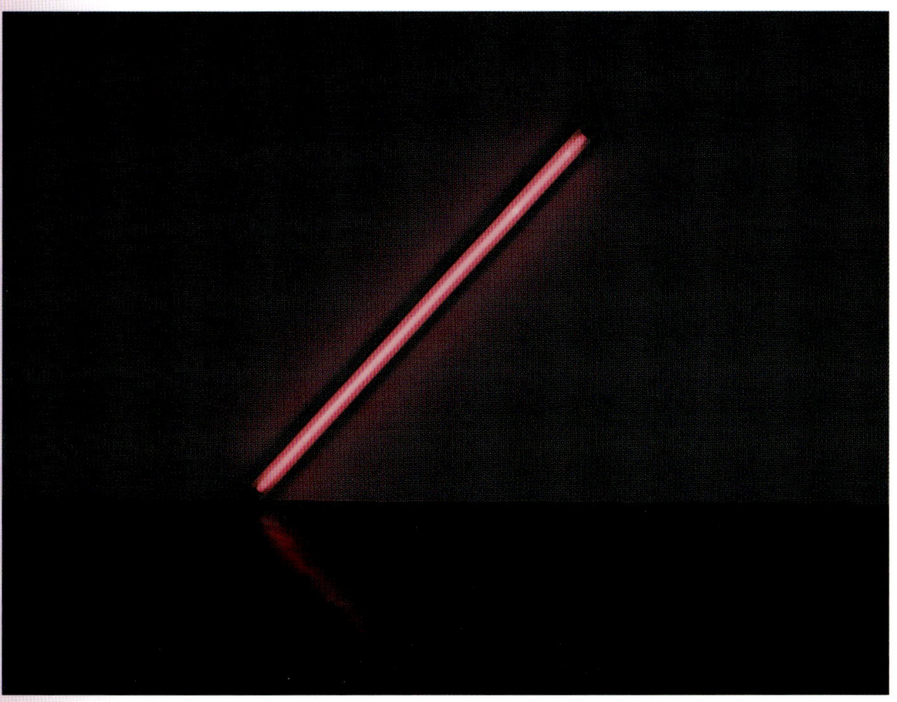

*The Diagonal of May 25th* by Dan Flavin, 1963

# Pinkish

**Then**

When we think of Bauhaus, it is usually primary-coloured palettes and imposing concrete buildings that come to mind. Yet a warmer, earthier rose shade can be found at the base of many a Bauhaus palette, as well as in photography, wallpaper designs and printed posters.

This modern pink can be seen as a neutral underscore to support domestic life, following the example set by Bauhaus artists and designers. A recent restoration of Wassily Kandinsky's house revealed that the living room was once coloured in mustard-toned yellow and pinkish rose, and adorned with gold leaf details, with great thought and consideration given to texture and placement. In the internal hallways and entrances of Walter Gropius's Dessau-Törten Housing Estate, the ephemeral pinkish tone was used to provide a warm and welcoming atmosphere to the social housing project. Paul Klee used pinkish to explore space and dimension in *Three Houses* (1922), and Anni and Josef Albers carried the hue's friendly connotations over into domestic wallpapers and textiles.

**Now**

Perhaps the reason this colour passed relatively unnoticed in the Bauhaus canon could be its resistance to classification – it is hard to pinpoint the exact pinkish shade, as it was probably mostly mixed by hand. Nevertheless, this colour, or range of colours, is inextricably linked with modernity and style, and we can still see the ripple effects today, with designers and architects picking up a pink-led neo-neutralism in architectural elements and retail interiors.

**Use**

Use pinkish as a neutral, warming base for any interior scheme. Block with complementary botanical greens and saturated accents of deep red or orange for a modernist nod.

**Colour Values**

Hex code: #ceafb2
RGB: 206, 175, 178
CMYK: 19, 31, 21, 0
HSB: 354º, 15%, 81%

**Common Connotations**

- Intelligent
- Soothing
- Friendly

**Pinkish in Art, Design & Culture**

- *Three Houses* by Paul Klee, *painting*, 1922
- 'A Tribute to Bauhaus' collection by Sarit Shani Hay, *furniture/textiles*, 2019
- The Webster flagship store, LA, USA, by Adjaye Associates, *architecture*, 2020

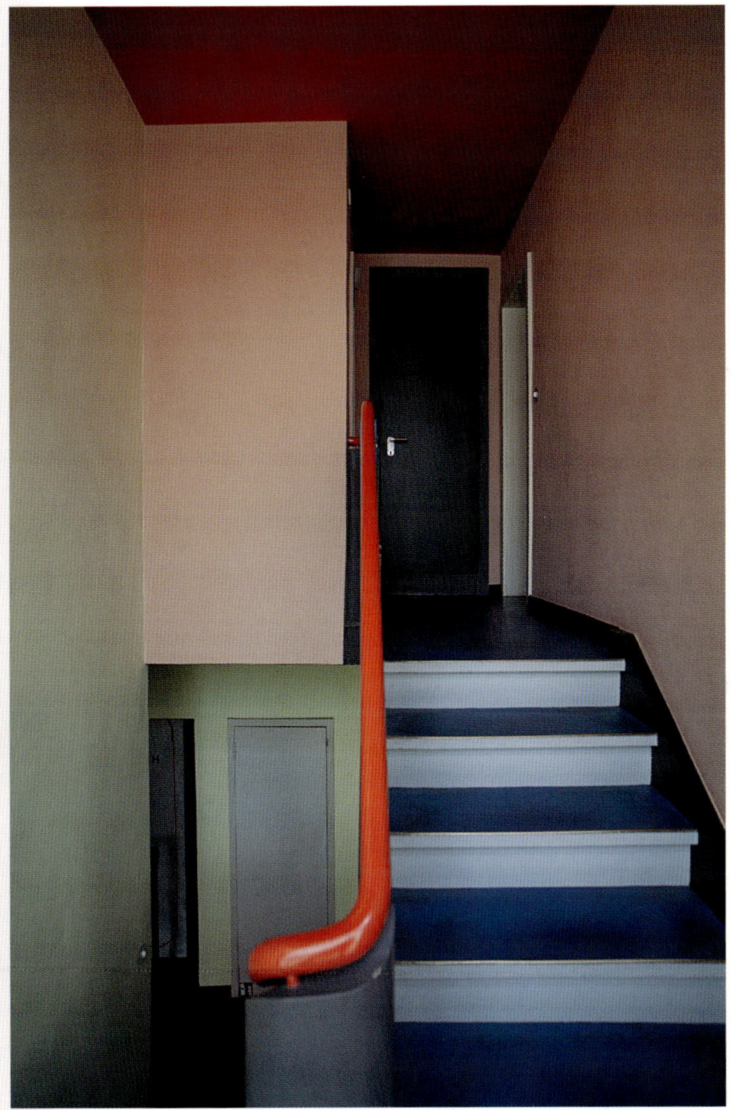

Master House No. 3, Bauhaus Dessau, interior

# Millennial Pink

## Then

Millennial pink, an amorphous hue, was mentioned over 32,000 times online in 2017. With incredible media presence, the colour soared to popularity as savvy lifestyle brands, social media and Generation-Y consumers propelled this indistinct shade into the limelight. Hovering somewhere between rose gold and dusty pink, even its name was contested, with Tumblr pink and Scandinavian pink as hashtag challengers.

Perhaps the first glimpse of the shade's coming importance was in Juergen Teller's 1998 shot of Kate Moss with once-bright-pink hair, washed out to salmon at the roots, spilling over a pillow. When British fashion designer Paul Smith opened his LA store in 2005, the entire exterior, painted in a punchy pastel pink, was a strong style statement. But it was in the 2010s, with the rise of the Instagram aesthetic, that this pink wall became a landmark for a generation. In 2014, Paul Smith's spring menswear collection was replete with pinks. That same year, interior designer India Mahdavi curated the restyling of London restaurant Gallery at Sketch with a show-stopping display of delectable rose quartz pink, helping it to become the most Instagrammed restaurant in the world.

What happened after that was design history, and a conglomerate of brands including Nike, Acne, Celine and Jonathan Saunders shared in the commercial, if short-lived, success.

## Now

The rise of millennial pink was a watershed moment, as with it, the pink family took a new stand against conventional ideas around gender while at the same time gaining mass commercial adoption.

**Colour Values**
Hex code: #efc7c5
RGB: 239, 199, 197
CMYK: 4, 29, 19, 0
HSB: 3°, 18%, 94%

**Also Known As**
- Tumblr Pink
- Scandinavian Pink
- Rose Quartz

**Common Connotations**
- Youthful
- Challenging
- Aspirational

Right: Fenty x Puma by Rihanna, Spring/ Summer 2017

**Millennial Pink in Art, Design & Culture**
- iPhone 6S in Rose Quartz by Apple, *product design*, 2015
- Pantone 13-1520 'Rose Quartz', Pantone Colour of Year, *design*, 2016
- Peggy Porschen flagship, London, UK by Kinnersley Kent Design, *interior design*, 2019

**Use**
Play with monochromatic tonal schemes to create a more sophisticated and contemporary millennial pink palette. This modern colour invites us to consider its use in many applications, challenging conventional ideas of how and where we use pink.

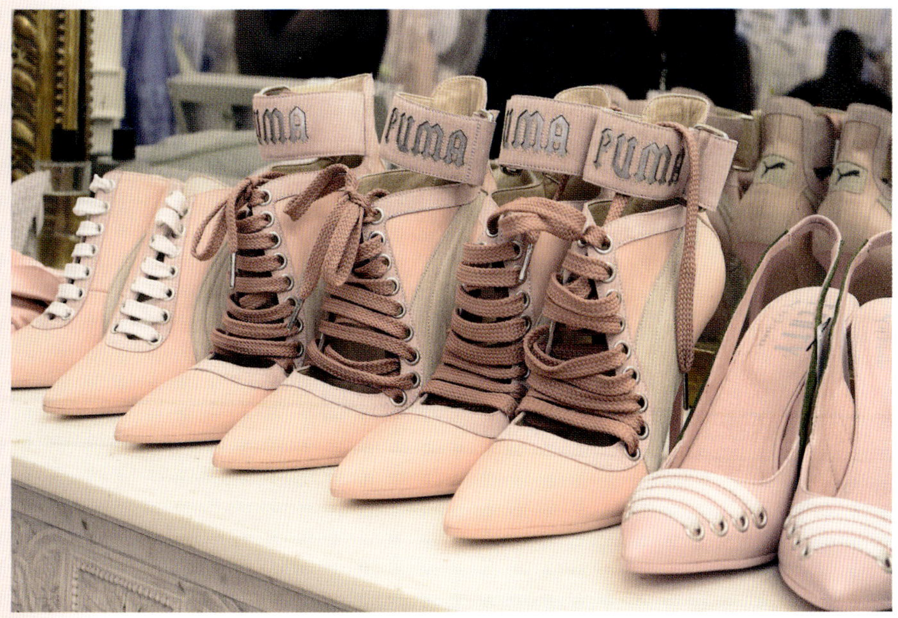

 # Pale Pink

**Then**

Once the glow of millennial pink had faded, what remained was a less ostentatious, more considered shade. As we turn our back on the excess of the previous decades' hyper-consumerism, we seek more meaningful, inclusive products – and that includes our colour choices.

In the summer of 2017, two grid-like buildings sprung up in King's Cross, London. The new office buildings were part of a massive construction scheme to regenerate the area, but what made them stand out from other prestigious architectural projects being developed at the time were their rose pink and pale pink exteriors. The pinks, emulating the bricks of the nearby St. Pancras Renaissance Hotel, talked to each other; they were connected but distinct and created an enhanced sense of place.

**Now**

The use of pale pink is as intuitive as it is useful for architecture and urban planning, as demonstrated by the Secondary School Romanshorn in Switzerland, completed in 2019. Designed by Bak Gordon Arquitectos and Architekturbüro Bernhard Maurer GmbH, its pink concrete exterior with deeper pink window shutters combines with beige tiles to soften the otherwise austere exterior while reflecting light, creating a cool and bright environment for learning.

Colour in architecture can be smarter and more sustainable when used intelligently. By selecting lighter colours in crucial areas of the buildings we occupy, we can harness natural light to create visually open and welcoming spaces – even in dense urban environments.

**Use**

Use inviting pale pink with contrasting supportive tones of green and sky blue to promote a gentle but dynamic dialogue.

**Colour Values**

Hex code: #efded4
RGB: 239, 222, 203
CMYK: 5, 12, 13, 0
HSB: 22°, 11%, 94%

**Also Known As**
- Modern Pink
- Neo-Pastel Pink

**Common Connotations**
- Calming
- Inviting
- Connecting

**Pale Pink in Art, Design & Culture**
- *Untitled* by Agnes Martin, *painting*, 1963
- COS + Snarkitecture pop-up store, LA, *interior design*, 2015

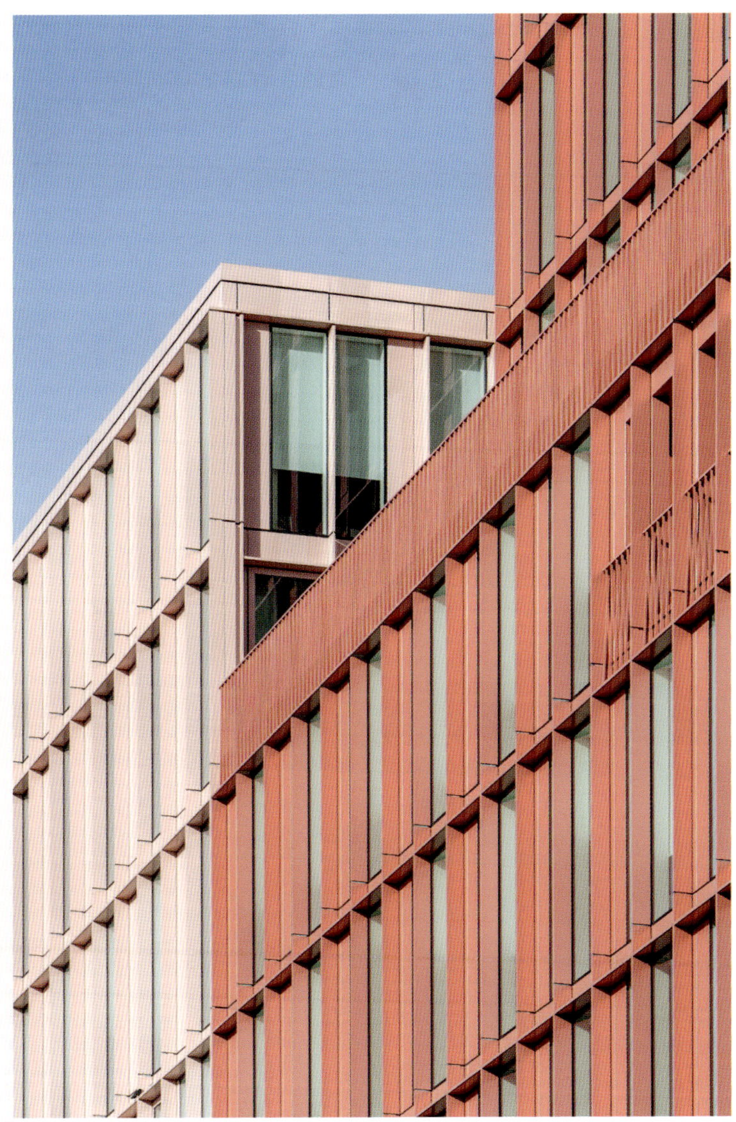

R7, UK, by Duggan Morris Architects, 2017

 # Aubergine

## Then

The deep purple-brown shade known as aubergine was
first classified as a colour in 1915. During the first part
of the 20th century, a mood of post-war austerity and
functionalism saw a movement towards standardized
colours and a set limit for manufacture, particularly
in paint and industrial coatings, famously promoted
by Henry Ford. This left many designers exasperated,
including Charles and Ray Eames. Upon creating
new furniture pieces for Herman Miller, Ray was
left uninspired by the basic shades of resin coatings
available to her. Influenced instead by a Japanese
eggplant, Ray fine-tuned a lustrous aubergine lacquer
shade for the legs of the 1968 Eames chaise longue and
the leather covers of the earlier lounge chair, instantly
lifting the distinctive shade to style highs.

## Now

Today aubergine is used as a sophisticated alternative
to plain black. Brothers Ronan and Erwan Bouroullec
have created furniture pieces for Vitra such as the
Vegetal chair, using the deep hue on structural parts to
neutralize the stark industrial plastics. In doing so they
created an approachable aesthetic that has the ability
to harmonize with different interior environments and
within a product line up.

## Use

Warm gold accents balance rich dark aubergines and
black to create an overall cosy and harmonious feel to
interior design schemes.

**Colour Values**
Hex code: #503c47
RGB: 80, 60, 71
CMYK: 61, 68, 47, 49
HSB: 327°, 25%, 31%

**Also Known As**
- Eggplant

**Common Connotations**
- Distinctive
- Sophisticated
- Approachable

**Aubergine in Art,
Design & Culture**
- 670 lounge chair by
  Charles and Ray Eames
  for Herman Miller, 1958
- Vegetal chair by Ronan
  and Erwan Bouroullec
  for Vitra, *furniture*, 2009

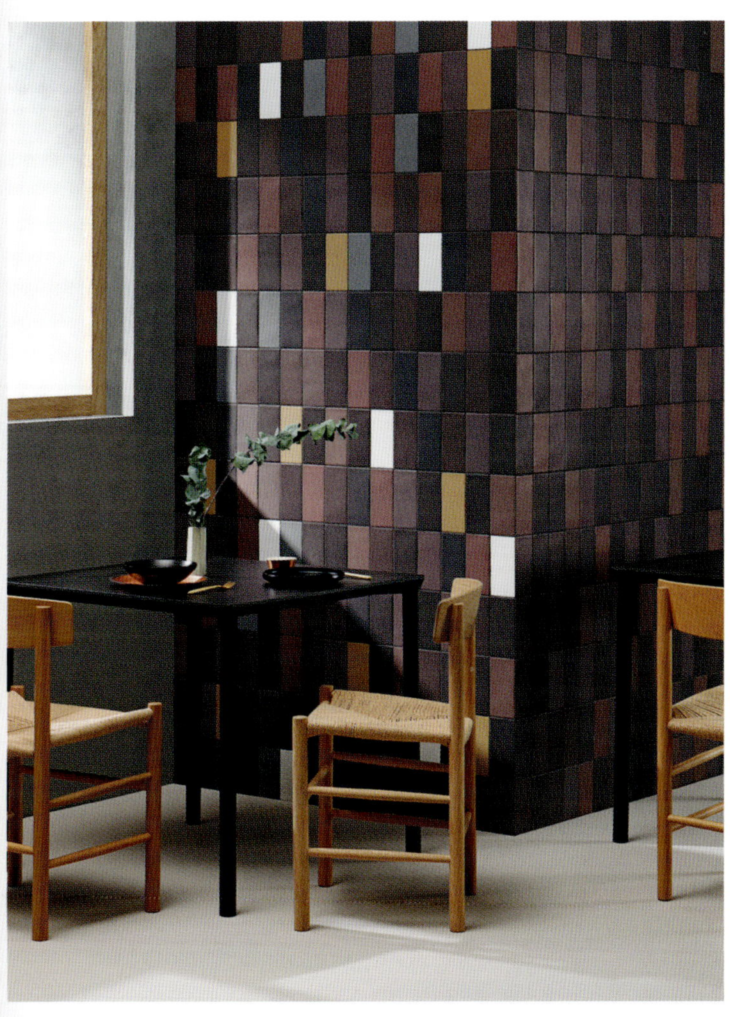

Lane tiles by Barber & Osgerby for Mutina, 2018

## Beetroot

**Then**

Anyone who's ever cooked with this root vegetable
will know how hard it is to remove a beetroot stain
from clothes. In fact, beetroot juice has been used
as a vegetable dye since at least the 16th century. In
Victorian Britain, it was deployed to tint all manner of
foodstuffs – it was even used as a coloured hair rinse
and served as a nifty lip and cheek stain. Beetroot's
pink tint comes from a mixture of betalain pigments.
Up until 1856, almost all textile dyes were made from
natural sources, but with the invention of synthetic
dyes and the ensuing vogue for vivid hues, natural
colours like beetroot were all but forgotten.

**Now**

Natural pigments are making a comeback, in part
due to health and environmental concerns about the
toxic and non-biodegradable nature of artificial dyes.
Bio-derived pigments can make recycling consumer
products simpler and, in turn, help them to become
more sustainable too. Many plants and fruits we eat
every day, such as avocados, onions and oranges, have
valuable colours within their skins and peels. Normally
these are left to rot in landfills, but material innovation
startup Kaiku Living Color, founded by Nicole
Stjernswärd, transforms this waste into a high value
resource for artists and designers.

**Use**

Take inspiration for an all-natural palette based on the
different parts of the beet plant, from the muddy roots
to the red-purple heart and the tender green leaves.

**Colour Values**

Hex code: #d31448
RGB: 344, 90, 83
CMYK: 10, 99, 59, 2
HSB: 214°, 90%, 83%

**Common Connotations**

- Vibrant
- Earthy
- Natural

**Beetroot in Art,
Design & Culture**

- 'Dyed by Nature'
  by G-Star Raw with
  Archroma, *fashion*, 2019
- *From a Mezzanine
  Window* by Jane Bustin,
  *mixed-media painting*,
  2019

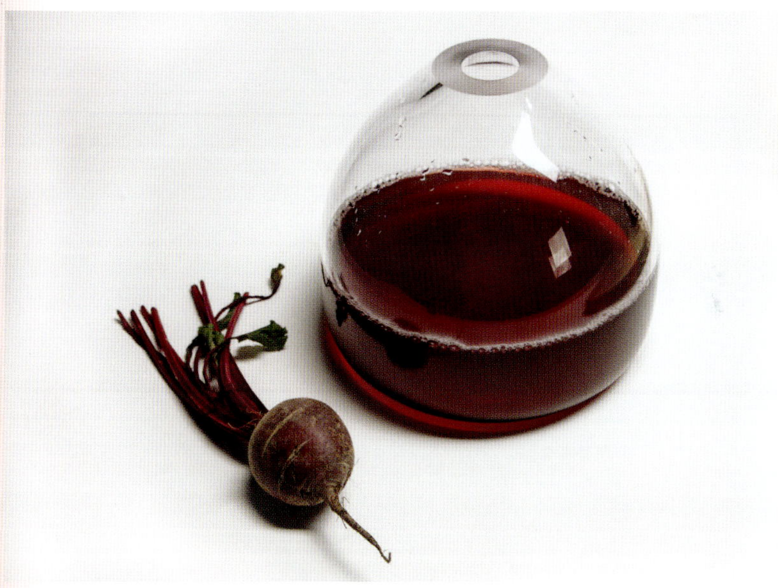

Beetroot dye extracted using Kaiku's machinery

 # Living Lilac

**Then**

Tiny violet dots scatter to create an intriguing surface effect. This intricate detailing is not the work of human hands but made by growing bacteria. Microbes are revealing a new frontier of hue and shade. This new addition to the Forbes Pigment Collection by Faber Futures in 2018 isn't just a dye or pigment but a set of instructions for creating colour from bacteria.

For the past seven years, Natsai Audrey Chieza, the bio-design pioneer and founder of biotech consultancy Faber Futures, has been exploring the ability of microbes to generate pigment. The *S. coelicolor* bacteria pigment molecule (actinorhodin) holds the key to a range of blue-purple hues. When these soil-dwelling organisms interact with protein fibres, they produce a living, biodegradable pigment, dyeing the textiles without the use of chemicals and requiring substantially less water than conventional processes. What emerges is colour that is organic in its nature, and which gracefully fades in the light: a new aesthetic and zero-waste concept for consumers and brands alike.

**Colour Values**
Hex code: #9e9af7
RGB: 158, 154, 247
CMYK: 39, 39, 0, 0
HSB: 243°, 38%, 97%

**Also Known As**
- Living Lividum

**Common Connotations**
- Innovative
- Sustainable
- Intelligent

**Living Lilac in Art, Design & Culture**
- Living Colour project by Laura Luchtman & Ilfa Siebenhaar, *textiles*, 2017
- Bio-dye for textiles by Colorifix, *dyes*, 2018

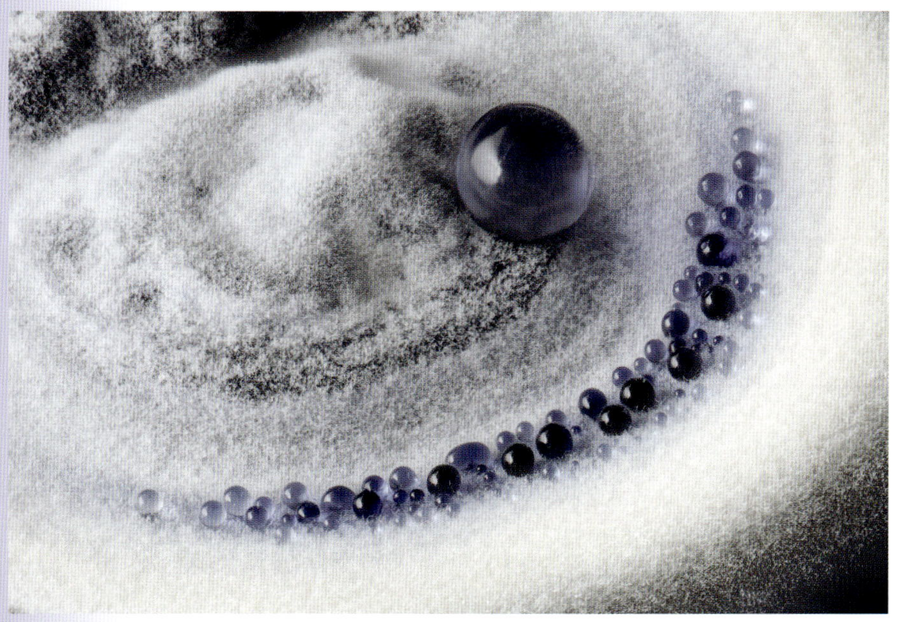

Colony of *Streptomyces coelicolor* bacteria

**Now**

This incredible innovation is a massive technological shift in colour, and it presents game-changing possibilities for a waste-free textile industry. In 2020, bio-design company Living Colour Collective exposed the bacteria strain *J. lividum* and its deep violet pigment molecule (violacein) to pH levels, temperature and even sound to produce an organic tonal colour range for sportswear giant Puma. Their joint Design To Fade concept reinvents the predictable activewear palette while minimizing the adverse effects on the environment.

The expectation is that this field of scientific research will continue to evolve, even forming pre-designed palettes that react to different base materials and environments.

**Use**

Take inspiration from the range of bio-organic blue-violet shades generated by this organic substance, and combine with complementary coral accents to create an advanced and intelligent palette.

'This incredible innovation is a massive technological shift in colour, and it presents game-changing possibilities for a waste-free textile industry.'

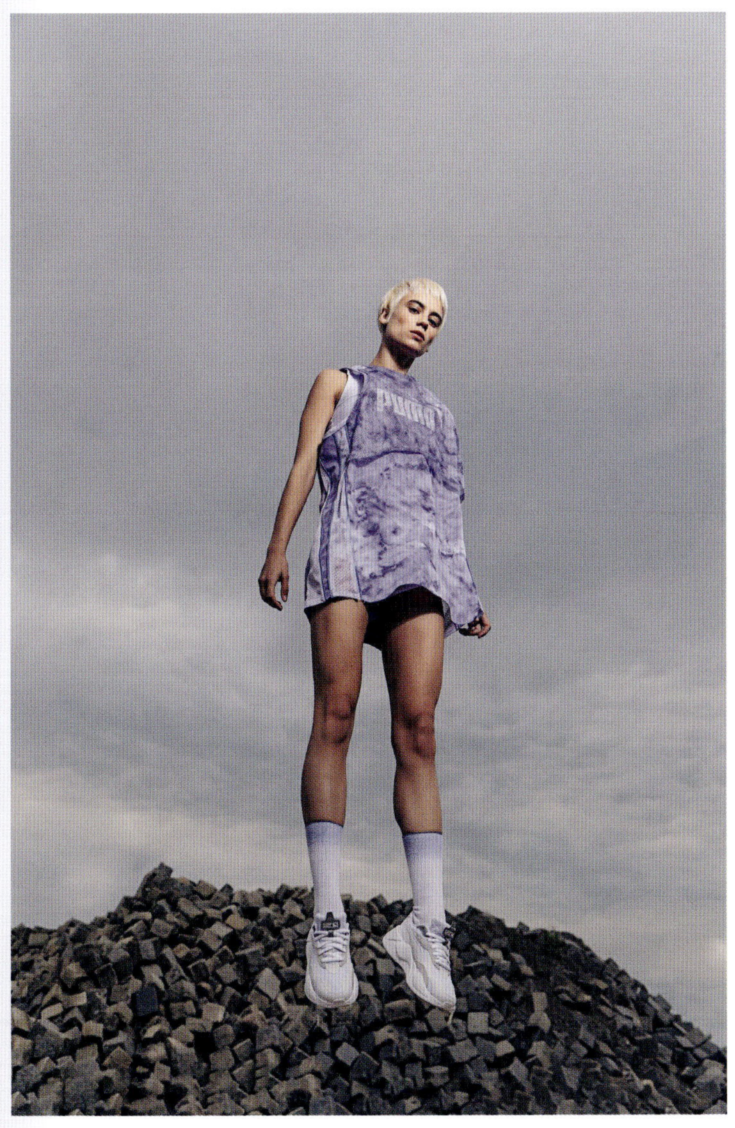



'Design to Fade' by Puma x Living Colour Collective, 2020

# White & Pale

Blink and you could miss these unassuming shades. But learn to tune your eye to the subtlety of the white family, and you will find that white isn't always what it seems; as with all colour, there is depth and duality to be found once you scratch the surface. The eye sees variations in pale tones well due to the colour's affinity with light: the whiter the hue, the more light is reflected into our eyes.

Context and culture can sway and affect the emotional responses of any given shade, and it's arguably easier to observe these nuances in the pale family than in any other colour group. A perfect pale pebble held in the palm of your hand can feel special, pure, untarnished; but when the same shade is applied to an entire room, it can bring the temperature down and feel harsh and clinical.

The earliest natural white pigments – chalk and burned bone – conjure up evocative traditions. In Japanese, the character for 'white', 白 (*shiro*) – appears with the compound for 'emptiness', while in China, white is transformational, signalling death and sadness, but also rebirth. A blank page, a clean slate, a new life in a pale eggshell, white can be an empty void to be filled.

Alongside these varying hues, there is also the ultimate brilliant white. This pigment, titanium white, did not become available until the early 20th century; now it seems to be omnipresent. Dazzling white is taken for granted, used everywhere from eye-catching road markings to kitchen appliances and medical products, creating a 'safe and clean' signal that consumers trust.

The minimalist art movement of the late 1950s saw achromaticity raised to new heights, idealizing empty white space to play with the perception and experience of light, and aesthetically we've never looked back. Today, tech brands such as Google and Facebook use white extensively for their typography and backgrounds. Apple uses tinted whites and light metals as a core brand palette, making their products feel essential and modern, and provoking minimal distraction from the quality of the product.

In recent years, contemporary designers and scientists are also exploring the phenomenon of iridescence that occurs naturally in pearls and certain other materials. The amazing colours we see in iridescent substances are created by the interactions of light with material structure rather than pigment, inspiring a new way of thinking about colour itself.

**Colours in this chapter:**

 # Chalk White

## Then

Millions of years ago, while Earth's landscape was still forming into the continents we know today, the flourishing oceans left huge deposits of microscopic phytoplankton that over time turned into calcium carbonate, or chalk. The famous white cliffs of England's coastline are an ode to this fossilized remnant.

A soft white substance that disintegrates easily into powder, chalk is mineral and colour combined, its materiality highly linked to its use. In early cave drawings, it was used to shade the illustrations of red ochre bison. 'Chalking' was an ancient ritual in England that involved communities or 'chalkers' smashing chalk to a paste to create the oldest form of English art, including the Uffington White Horse in Oxfordshire, as well as several other figures of men and horses carved into hillsides. Chalk has also been used for millennia as a filler and aid in painting to allow the mixing of pale hues, and it remains a popular artists' medium today.

## Now

Scrawled on the body, a blackboard or tarmac, chalk is an instant communication tool. Ethiopia's Kara people traditionally paint their faces and bodies with chalk to boost the chances of finding love and scare off rivals. The act of decoration is a unifying experience and a means of identity and rite of passage.

## Use

Chalk white can counterbalance saturation well. Fuse with hot pink and yellow ochre to express a confident visual identity.

**Colour Values**
Hex code: #f5ede4
RGB: 245, 237, 228
CMYK: 0, 3, 7, 4
HSB: 32°, 7%, 96%

**Also Known As**
- English Whiting
- *Creta*

**Common Connotations**
- Tactile
- Tranquil
- Expressive

**Chalk White in Art, Design & Culture**
- The Uffington White Horse, UK, *land art*, late Bronze Age
- *Chalk Paths* by Eric Ravilious, *painting*, 1935
- *The Erratics* by Darren Harvey-Regan, *photo book*, 2019

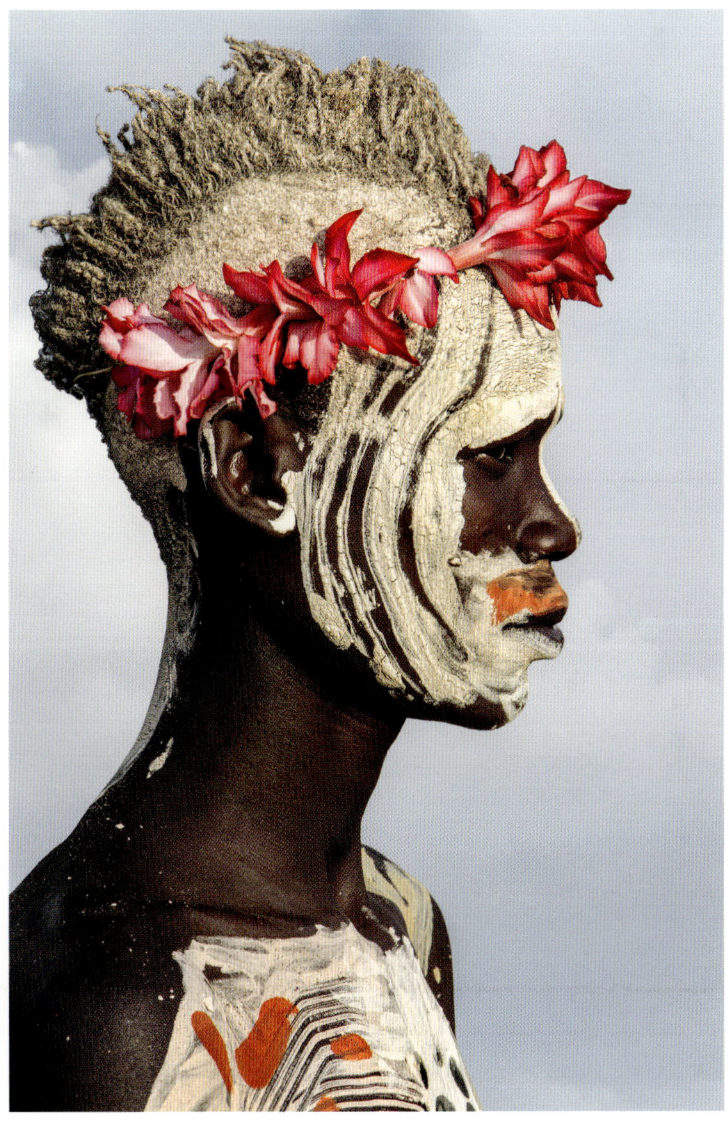

Young Kara man with chalk paint, Omo River, Ethiopia, by Carol
Beckwith and Angela Fisher, 2013

 # Lead White

### Then

Also known as flake white, this was the predominant white used by artists until the synthetic pigments of the 19th century replaced this dangerous colour.

First records indicate use of lead white started in Anatolia from the 4th century, where earthenware pots were lined with lead and vinegar and sealed with potent animal dung. Noxious fermenting vapours cooked up a flaky layer of lead carbonate, which was scraped, powdered and sold. Painters such as Titian, Vermeer and Rembrandt daubed with these lead-based pigments to bring a lucid quality to folds on elegant attire, ceramic jugs and skin tone. In Elizabethan England, lead white was used as a cosmetic to hide age and disguise skin imperfection. Rapidly absorbed into the human body, lead poisoning caused physical and neurological afflictions; the whiter the faces, the more damage done.

### Now

This toxic pigment remained in household paints, ceramic enamelware and cosmetics until the 1970s when it was banned. We can see its legacy in modern cosmetics, and while the concealers of today are thankfully not toxic, we might still remember lead white's ode to a perfectionism that was ultimately unobtainable, and even deadly.

### Use

Create an unusual off-beat palette with a similar solid white opaque base. The original lead white pigment had a subtle warm undertone that will pair well with muted mustard yellows for a rich yet weighty duotone palette ideal for luxury branding.

**Colour Values**
Hex code: #f2f9e7
RGB: 242, 249, 231
CMYK: 3, 0, 7, 2
HSB: 83°, 7%, 98%

**Also Known As**
- Flake White
- Cosmetic White
- Cremnitz White

**Common Connotations**
- Purity
- Concealment
- Sombre

**Lead White in Art, Design & Culture**
- *Portrait of a Lady ('La Schiavona')* by Titian, painting, c.1510–12
- *Lucy* by Marlene Dumas, painting, 2004

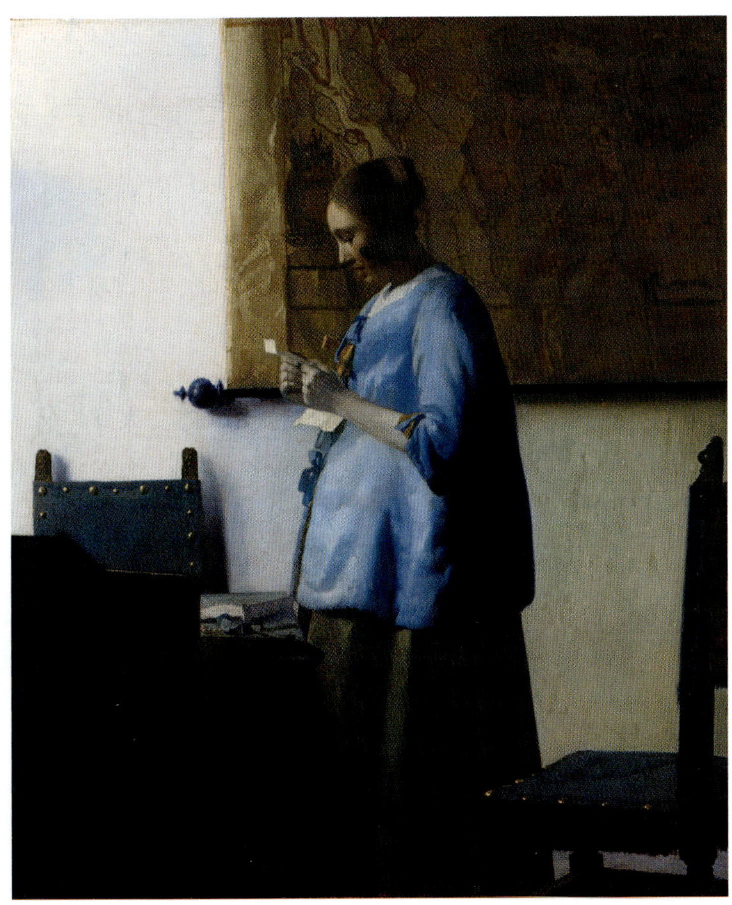

*Woman in Blue Reading a Letter* by Johannes Vermeer, 1663–4

# Plaster

**Then**

The perfect base, plaster is a warm, mellow pale with a tinge of pink. Traditionally made with lime or gypsum, water, ash – even hair – it was first used by early civilizations to protect reed shelters. Ancient hieroglyphics were often painted on smooth gypsum surfaces, and the Romans poured and cast in plaster many thousands of copies of Greek statues and developed frescos, painting directly onto the plaster on the walls of the wealthy, such as the House of the Vettii in Pompeii.

**Now**

Modern design has developed a nostalgia for the setting plaster and chalky patinas often found in interiors in places with warm climates. A pale plaster wall evokes tactility, colour and even a sense of place in our psyche. This is combined with a renewed desire to enjoy raw surface finishes in interiors.

We also have our awakening eco-conscience to thank for plaster's renewed popularity in a material sense, with greater use of limewash and chalk-based paints the result of increased knowledge of the damage of chemicals found in other base paints.

**Use**

This delicate tone has its roots in the past but can still deliver an inviting, contemporary mood. Create a calm, natural interior by combining with deep browns and burnt caramels.

**Colour Values**

Hex code: #dbcabf
RGB: 219, 202, 191
CMYK: 16, 21, 24, 1
HSB: 23°, 13%, 86%

**Also Known As**

- Limewash
- Lime White

**Common Connotations**

- Protective
- Honest
- Raw

**Plaster in Art, Design & Culture**

- Woman Holding a Sistrum, Egypt, *painting*, 1250-1200 BCE
- 'The Death of Pentheus', the House of the Vettii, Pompeii, Italy, *fresco*, 62 CE
- *Model III* by Rachel Whiteread, *sculpture*, 2006

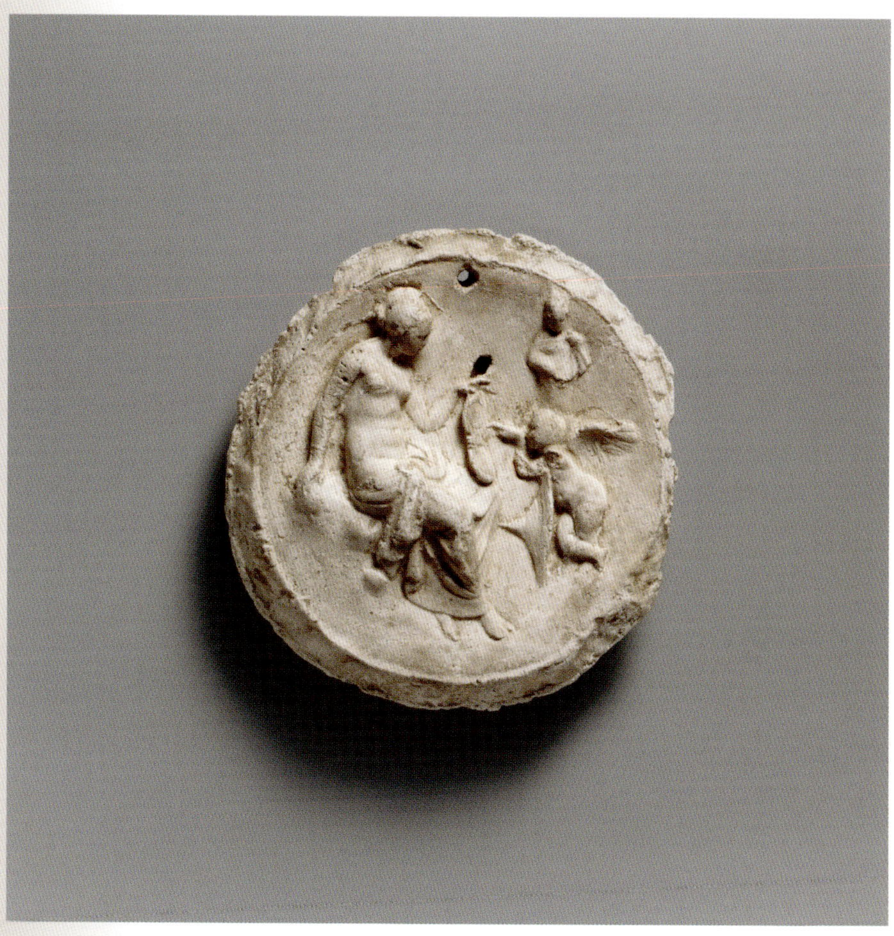

Plaster emblema with Aphrodite and Eros, Mediterranean,
c.1st–2nd century CE

# Bone

**Then**

Ancient humans created one of the earliest pigments by roasting animal skeletons in fire pits. The gritty, whitish mineral substance has a warm and soft undertone due to its calcified state. As an artist's pigment, with less gruesome alternatives available, it became obsolete quickly, but bones have a longstanding relationship with art history – from Leonardo da Vinci, who dissected cadavers to improve his figure drawing, to the 17th-century Dutch artists who included a faded skull in still life paintings as a memento mori, a symbol of mankind's mortality.

**Now**

Death is an archetypal theme, usually represented as a white skeleton or cloaked reaper. In traditional practices such as tarot, however, death is not menacing but a herald of rebirth. Either way, the traces that we leave after death have been an enduring fascination and a source of inspiration to artists up to the present day. A 2002 installation, for example, saw Swiss artist Olaf Breuning arranging skeletons in gardens or rooms as a piercing reminder of our barest, authentic selves.

In *Cumbrian Bone Marble*, artist Yesenia Thibault-Picazo imagines future bone material to be unearthed in hundreds of thousands of years at the site of the mass burial of a million cattle slaughtered in response to the foot-and-mouth epidemic in 2001. Exploring this thought-provoking project, we might also be reminded of the millions of tonnes of food waste that we produce annually.

**Colour Values**

Hex code: #d9cfc6
RGB: 217, 207, 198
CMYK: 17, 18, 22, 1
HSB: 28º, 9%, 85%

**Common Connotations**

- Corporeal
- Grounding
- Soft

**Bone in Art,
Design & Culture**
- *Still Life with a Skull
  (Vanitas)* by Philippe de
  Champaigne, *painting*,
  c.1660s
- *Skeletons* by Olaf
  Breuning, *installation*, 2002
- *Remember You Must
  Die* series by Emma
  Witter, *sculptures*, 2019

**Use**
Pair this grounding tone with unbleached, soft
neutrals, ideal for modern spaces or environments
where a dialogue with the past is critical.

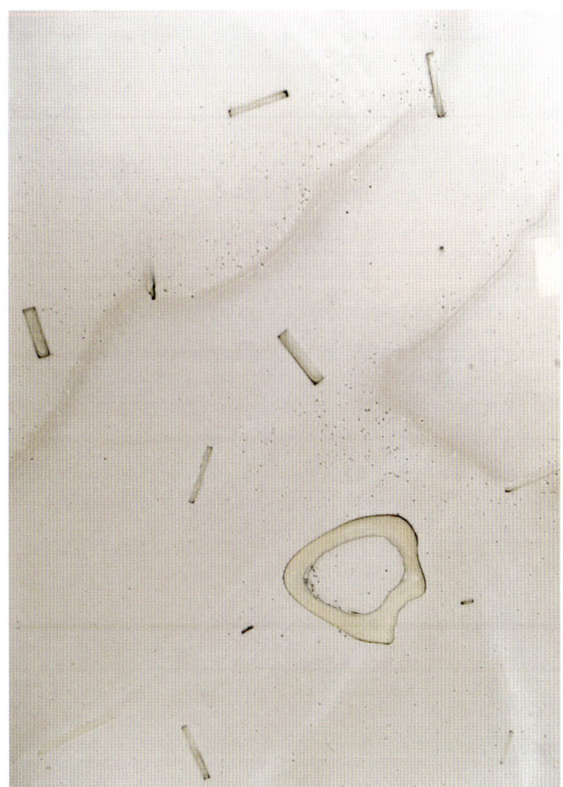

From the series *Cumbrian
Bone Marble* by Yesenia
Thibault-Picazo, 2013

# Titanium White

## Then

Elusive for millennia, the whitest of all whites eventually arrived in pigment form with the invention of titanium white in the early part of the 20th century. The formula was twice as opaque as lead white (see page 246) and reflected considerably more light than its predecessors, making it appear much brighter when used in paint. This transformed the use of white in art and design, giving birth to the bright tone we are now used to seeing.

Conceptually, brilliant white can be used to represent a resolute start point: the aftermath of a big bang; white light; a clean escape; a new beginning.

## Now

Ubiquitous today, brilliant white has come to be a symbol of quality. Apple uses pure white paired with bright anodized metals as a core palette for its main product range, minimizing distraction and optimizing the design language. Strict monochrome palettes of white, black and cream have created many commercial successes and are deployed by luxury brands as a universal signifier of modernism. Chanel's creative director Karl Lagerfeld once said, 'Black and white always looks modern, whatever that word means'.*

## Use

Titanium's luminous, clean quality perfectly balances jet black. Use this timeless combination to create a smart and sophisticated brand identity.

**Colour Values**
Hex code: #fbfaf6
RGB: 251, 250, 246
CMYK: 2, 1, 4, 0
HSB: 48°, 2%, 98%

**Also Known As**
- Brilliant White
- Bright White

**Common Connotations**
- Purity
- Divine
- Iconic

**Titanium White in Art, Design & Culture**
- *White on White* by Kazimir Malevich, *painting*, 1918
- *Broadway Boogie Woogie* by Piet Mondrian, 1942–3
- iBook in White by Apple, *product design*, 2001

*Lagerfeld, Karl and Roitfeld, Carine, *The Little Black Jacket: Chanel's Classic Revisited*, Göttingen: Steidl, 2014

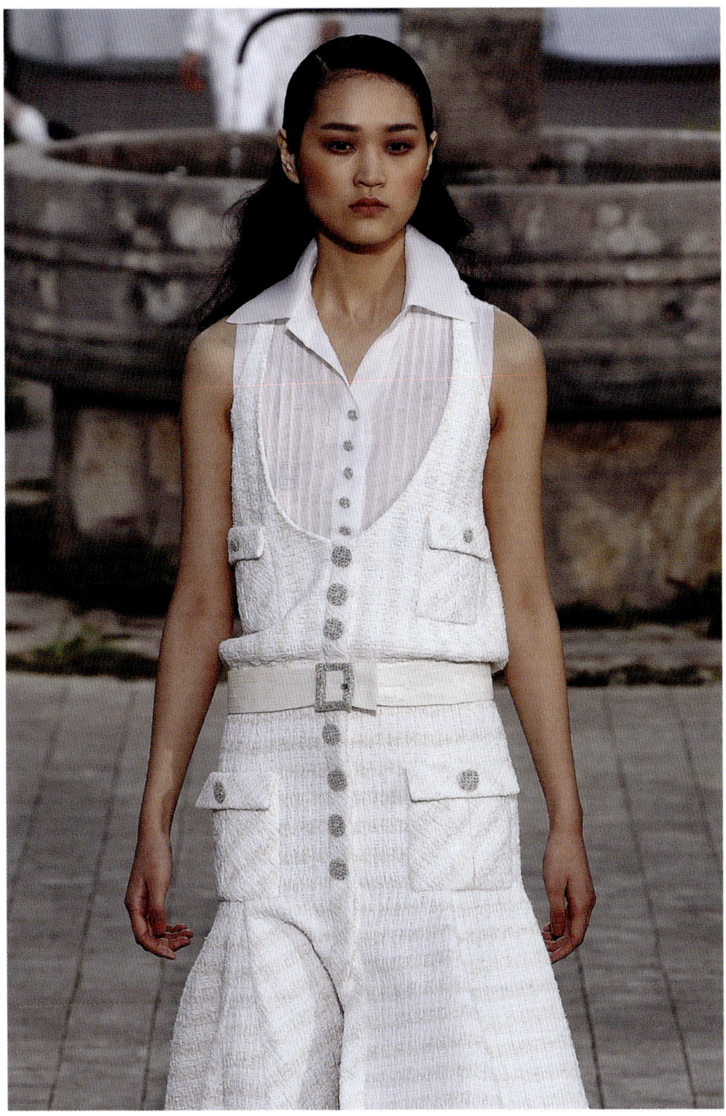

Chanel Haute Couture, Spring/Summer 2020, Paris

 # Lunar White

**Then**

The mystery of the moon has long captivated artists and scientists. Romantic painter Francisco Goya represented it as the guiding white light of 'the other' in his 1789 painting *Witches' Sabbath*. Similarly, the pearly, ethereal light of the thin crescent moon in *The Fighting Temeraire* by J.M.W. Turner is an immediate mood-setter. In 1969, during the first lunar landing, a blurry image of a flat, whitish-grey moonscape beamed onto TV screens around the world, presenting an entirely new view and mythology of the moon for the modern age.

**Now**

The moon continues to be an inspiration in art and design. In 2007, Habitat teamed up with Buzz Aldrin to create the Moonbuzz lamp – a perfect miniature replica of the surface Aldrin walked on in 1969. James Turrell's 2019 *Aquarius, Medium Circle Glass* presented luminous, lunar-inspired sculptures that when viewed alter perceptions and persuade us to pause for a moment of tranquillity. Addressing the growing desire for technology that blends in with the home, audio technology company Sonos selected a lunar white shade for its Move speaker, offering a quieter alternative to the harsh brilliant whites and severe blacks that dominate the industry.

**Use**

Ethereal, violet-grey-tinged lunar white can help create a sense of contemplation and peace, much needed in our over-stimulated world. Pair soft lunar white with delicate purple-blues on products for a mood-enhancing effect.

**Colour Values**
Hex code: #ced5dc
RGB: 206, 213, 220
CMYK: 23, 13, 11, 0
HSB: 210°, 6%, 86%

**Also Known As**
- Moon White

**Common Connotations**
- Introspective
- Alluring
- Tranquil

**Lunar White in Art, Design & Culture**
- *Le Monde* by Man Ray, *photography*, 1931
- *Earthrise* by William Anders, *photography*, 1968
- *Totality*, by Katie Paterson, *installation art*, 2016

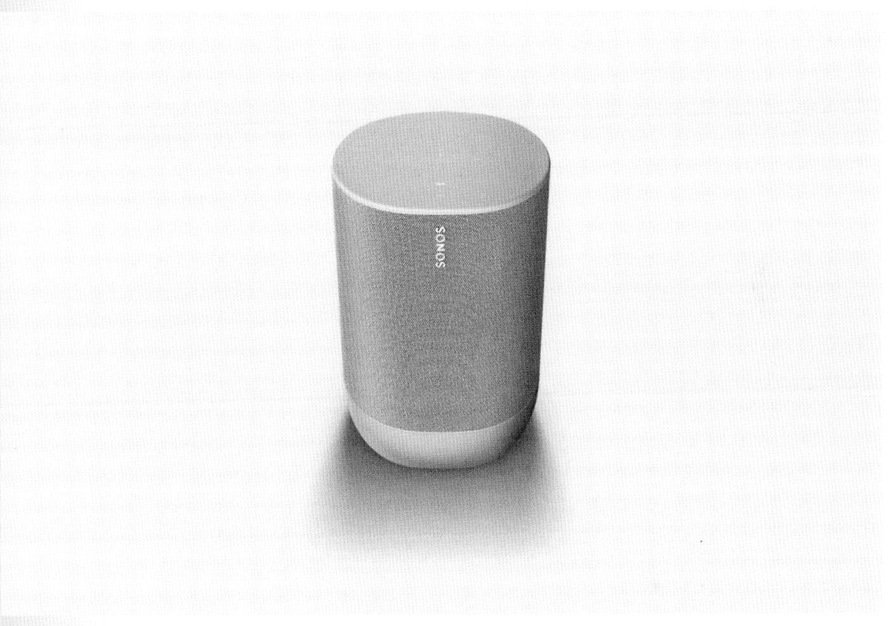

Sonos Move in Lunar White

# Glacial Ice

**Then**

In 1893, while freezing in the Arctic ice, Norwegian explorer Fridtjof Nansen reflected, 'Nothing more wonderfully beautiful can exist than the Arctic night. It is dreamland painted in the imagination's most delicate tints; it is colour etherealized. One shade melts into the other'.* Humans have a powerful fascination with this wilderness of brilliant white, reflecting a cool undertone of azure blue. In the 19th century, American artist Frederic Edwin Church explored the receding nature of the white horizon against the frozen permanence of glacial formations in his paintings.

**Now**

Twenty-eight trillion tons of ice in Antarctica has melted in the past thirty years, with more predicted loss to come. In a bid to show the impact of global temperature rises on the Arctic circle, Olafur Eliasson observed the shifts in glacial movement and its effects on the landscape. Using frozen water and colour, his work shows the delicate fragility of the glaciers that support life. Travelling to the North Pole in 1989, Andy Goldsworthy learned traditional Inuit techniques of snow-cutting and packing to erect four huge rings around the remote, northernmost point of the planet.

As we continue to realize the impact of man-made climate change and the importance of what we stand to lose, this hue has gained new and urgent relevance.

**Use**

This soft yet fresh ice tone represents a crucial supportive element for planetary survival. Use a palette of algae green, bright cyan and glacial ice white to bring a fresh yet sharp focus on ecological messaging.

**Colour Values**
Hex code: #c7d9e7
RGB: 199, 217, 231
CMYK: 26, 9, 7, 0
HSB: 206°, 14%, 91%

**Common Connotations**
- Otherworldly
- Cold
- Calm

**Glacial Ice in Art, Design & Culture**
- *The Icebergs* by Frederic Edwin Church, *painting*, 1861
- *Axing Ice to Cross the Sea* by Hu Xiaoyuan, *video installation*, 2014
- Ice Island from 'Altered States' installation by Snarkitecture and Caesarstone, *kitchen design concept*, 2018

* Nansen, Fridtjof, *Farthest North*, New York: Modern Library, 1999 (1897)

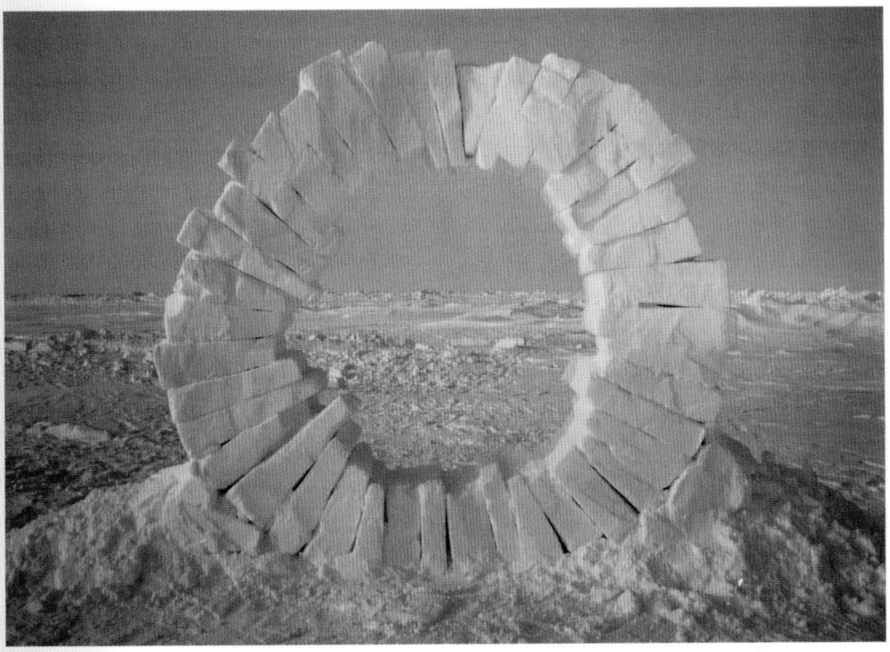

*Touching North* by Andy Goldsworthy, 1989

 # Architectural White

**Then**

There has often been a sense of space, openness and
spirituality associated with white. It's no wonder that
a clean, soft white with a slight neutral tone such as
architectural white is so highly valued in the design
world. According to coatings brand Sherwin-Williams,
it is the bestselling colour of all time.

In the early-to-mid-20th century, Swiss master Le
Corbusier used white to underscore purity in newly
stripped-back modern architecture. The image of an
all-white interior, clean, empty and pristine, has since
come to be worshipped in contemporary design for
its representation of simplicity and order in terms of
lifestyle as well as aesthetic.

**Now**

Architecture's love of white continues right up to
the present day, where it offers a clean, white canvas
quietly upholding all it contains. In the 1980s, British
architect John Pawson made architectural white his
signature, using the shade to elevate the sense of space
in a building by pairing it with peaceful and decluttered
minimalist environments. He said, 'The challenge lies
in bringing together mass, proportion, and light in the
most harmonious ways possible.'* Pawson gave Calvin
Klein's stores their signature sparseness and put Ian
Schrager's boutique hotels on the map by stripping away
any flashiness from the idea of luxury.

**Use**

Try pairing this simple tone with well-measured
proportions of grass green or sky blue to complement
a natural environment.

* Pawson, John, 'White on White', *John Pawson Journal*, January 2016
http://www.johnpawson.com/journal/white-on-white

**Colour Values**
Hex code: #e3e3e3
RGB: 227, 227, 227
CMYK: 13, 9, 11, 0
HSB: 0°, 0%, 89%

**Common Connotations**
- Modern
- Peaceful
- Light

**Architectural White in
Art, Design & Culture**
- Villa Savoye, Paris,
  France by Le
  Corbusier, *architecture*,
  1928–31
- Abbey of Our Lady of
  Nový Dvůr, Bohemia,
  Czech Republic, by John
  Pawson, *architecture*,
  1999–2004
- Louvre-Lens Museum,
  France, by SANAA,
  *architecture*, 2006

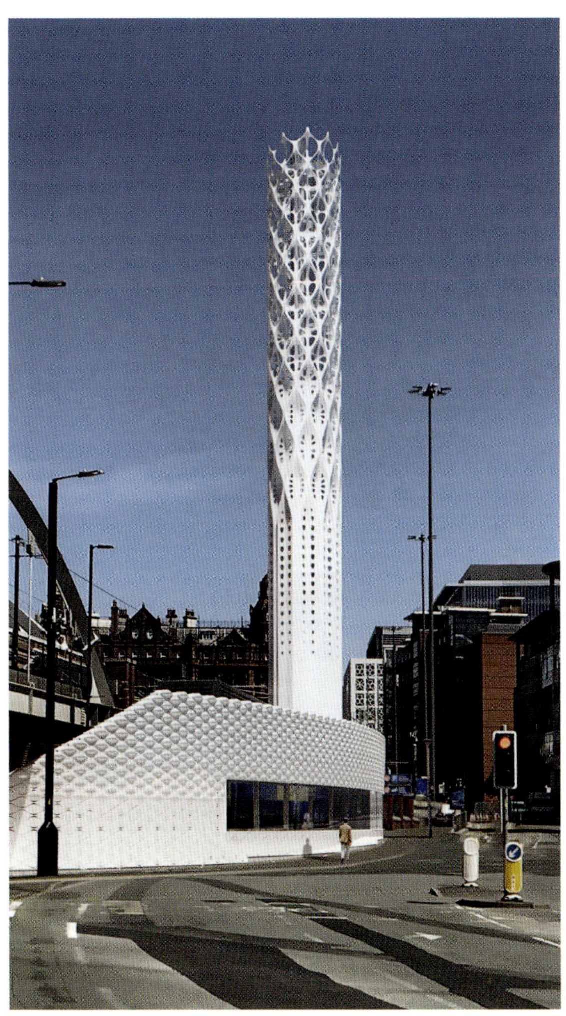

Tower of Light by Tonkin Liu, Manchester, 2021

# Pearl

**Then**

If you've ever seen light catch the wings of a dragonfly, a bubble of soap or the lustre of pearls and their shells, you'll have seen how they shimmer with pale-to-vivid colours. Pearl white, a creamy tone that glows with sunset hues, has a beautifully subtle sheen. This phenomenon, known as iridescence, is a natural expression of 'structural colour'. Minuscule, naturally occurring ridges are invisible to the naked eye, but they interfere with the way lightwaves reflect, producing colour effects that alter depending on the angle of view. This is not limited to pale surfaces; the same effect can be seen in dark materials such as the feathers of a magpie, oil and rare black (as well as white and grey) opals. The remarkable thing about iridescent colour is that it is immaterial – a quality of light not pigment – and so it will only fade with the degradation of the material substrate.

In the 19th century, Western artists attempted to record this phenomenon, for instance in John James Audubon's colourful illustrations of exotic birds, but success was limited by a lack of mediums capable of capturing the wonder of iridescence.

**Also Known As**
- Pearlescence
- Iridescence

**Common Connotations**
- Captivating
- Magical
- Exotic

**Pearl in Art, Design & Culture**
- Jardinière by Clément Massier, *lustreware*, 1893–5
- *Untitled* by Matti Braun, *textiles painting*, 2014
- 'Inkjet Colour Printing by Interference Nanostructures' by Aleksandr V. Yakovlev et al, ACS Publication, *nanoink research*, 2016

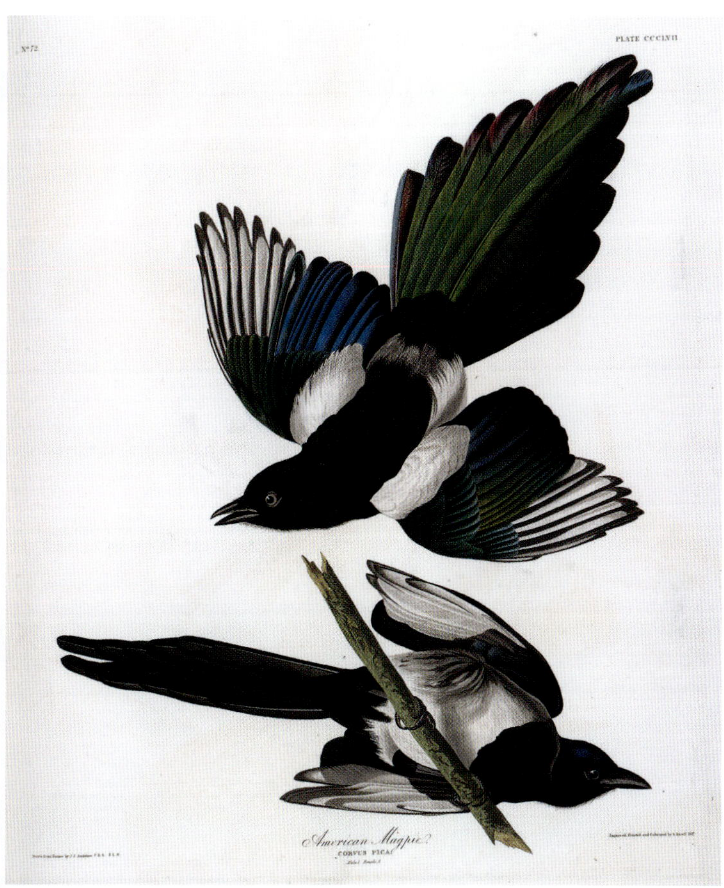

'American Magpie' from *The Birds of America* by
John James Audubon, 1827–38

**Now**

Since the mid-20th century, sustained research into natural iridescence has led to the invention of an increasing number of artificial materials that mimic the effect. These have found wide application, from automotive coatings and cosmetics to printed security features on banknotes. More recently, responding to increased awareness around plastic waste, designer Elissa Brunato has harnessed cellulose's light-interfering qualities to create a colour-shifting and compostable alternative to plastic sequins.

This fascinating area of science and design research is still only beginning to realize the full potential of structural colour. As we look closer at naturally iridescent surfaces, their fluid, shimmering hues reveal a world of optical colour we are still yet to discover fully.

**Use**

Explore a primary palette of black and white, with waves of bright gradients. The perfect brand identity for a pioneering technology company, for instance.

'As we look closer at naturally iridescent surfaces, their fluid, shimmering hues reveal a world of optical colour we are still yet to discover fully.'

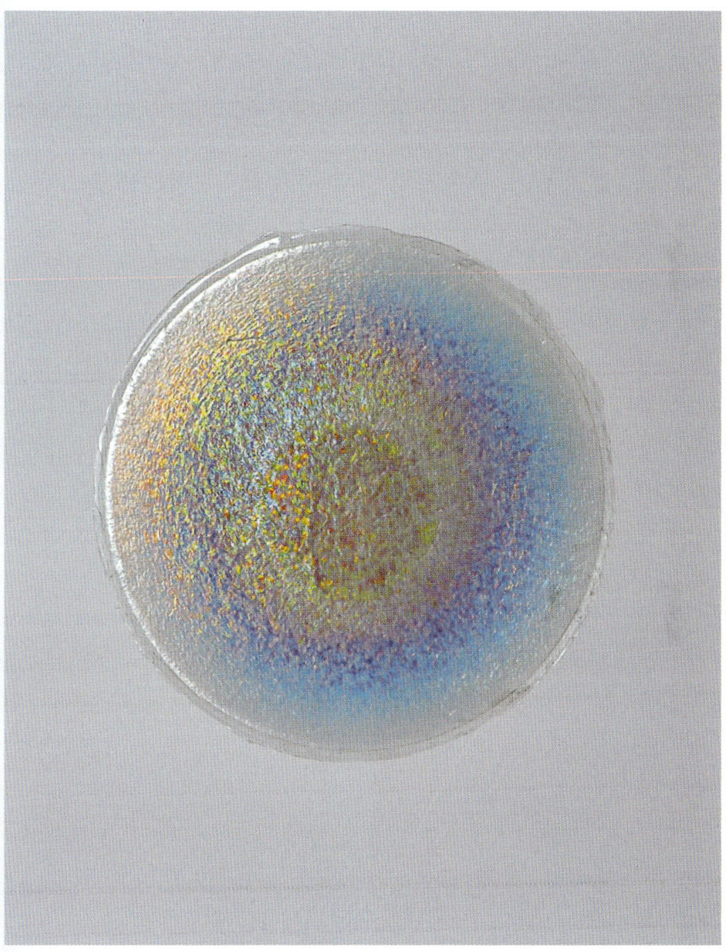



*Bio Iridescent Sequin* by Elissa Brunato, 2018

# Grey & Black

Grey and black may have a dark and dour reputation, but the reality is that this category is made up of a subtle range of tones with different histories and personalities. The journey from white to black is not one simple monochrome line, but contains innumerable nuances of blue and green, purple and brown. The tension between light and dark, and what lies between in the shadows, has long been a preoccupation of fine art. Italian Renaissance painters developed the technique of chiaroscuro, using dramatic contrasts to emphasize subject and atmosphere, like a spotlight on a dark stage.

Many of our greys and blacks like silver, concrete and obsidian are materials first and foremost, celebrated for the quality of their colour as well as their physical characteristics. The first black pigments are still in use today – the burnt remains of ancient fires produced the charcoal that our ancestors used to mark the walls of caves. Beloved by artists for the velvety rich black mark it makes, today this modest medium is making waves in design for its absorbent qualities. On the other end of the technological scale, we come to the cutting edge of colour development with the creation of surreal and uncanny Vantablack. This substance is so black that it absorbs 99.965 percent of light, making it almost impossible to perceive the shape of objects coated in it, and it has been adopted for use in deep-space imaging and optics as well as by artists and designers.

From brooding shadows to airy shades, greys are the support; they give depth and nuance to form. Many of the grey shades included here have a grubby industrial heritage and, love them or hate them, they often form part of the palette of everyday life, from an aluminium staircase to a brutalist concrete flyover. A particularly interesting area of contemporary colour use and theory is how these materials can now be part of a post-industrial, more ecologically friendly palette.

This spectrum of grey manifests in a multidimensional space instead of a linear one. We should see it as an incredibly malleable and multifaceted palette for the modern designer or contemporary artist.

## Colours in this chapter:

 # Silver

**Then**

As gold is associated with the sun and masculine energy,
silver is linked to the moon and femininity, and like the
moon, this bright, reflective metal's associations are often
complex and contrary. An elemental metal, it is associated
with purity – but it tarnishes easily: the phrase 'silver-
tongued' describes one whose persuasive words hide
corruption. A malleable metal, it has been mined for and
made into jewellery and other objects since prehistoric
times, but its softness makes it liable to wear and break.

One of the most precious metals in the world, silver
has seen wars fought for it, countries named after it and
currencies made from it, so for most of history it has been
tied to wealth and status. However, it gained new meaning
in the 1960s. Pop artist Andy Warhol painted his hair
silver, celebrated it in his artworks and even declared that
the '60s were 'the perfect time for silver'.* The Space Race-
inspired fashion movement of the same era saw metallic
eyeshadow matched with shimmering silver body paints,
and designers such as André Courrèges dressing models
in futuristic silver costumes.

**Now**

Connotations aside, silver is a versatile and timeless
shade. Its neutral tonality means that, unlike gold, it
doesn't clash with other tones, and it complements a
wide range of the spectrum. From the red carpet to the
silver screen, when we see this hue, we most commonly
associate it with elegant sophistication. As a material,
silver has antimicrobial qualities, which has led to the
medical industry embedding the metal into surgical
gowns and wound dressings.

**Colour Values**
Hex code: #d5d5d5
RGB: 213, 213, 213
CMYK: 19, 14, 15, 0
HSB: 0°, 0%, 84%

**Common Connotations**
- Prosperity
- Sophistication
- Futurity

* Atelier Éditions (Ed.), *An Atlas of Rare and Familiar Colour: The
Harvard Art Museums' Forbes Pigment Collection*, Los Angeles:
Atelier Éditions, 2019

**Silver in Art,
Design & Culture**
- *Silver Clouds* by Andy Warhol, *installation art*, 1966
- Silver and black dress from Twelve Unwearable Dresses in Contemporary Materials by Paco Rabanne, 1966
- Ready-to-Wear collection by MM6 Maison Margiela, *fashion*, A/W 2018

**Use**
Consider the use of bright silver as more than just adornment. Embed the shade with pale cream and nude shades for a neo-futuristic style statement.

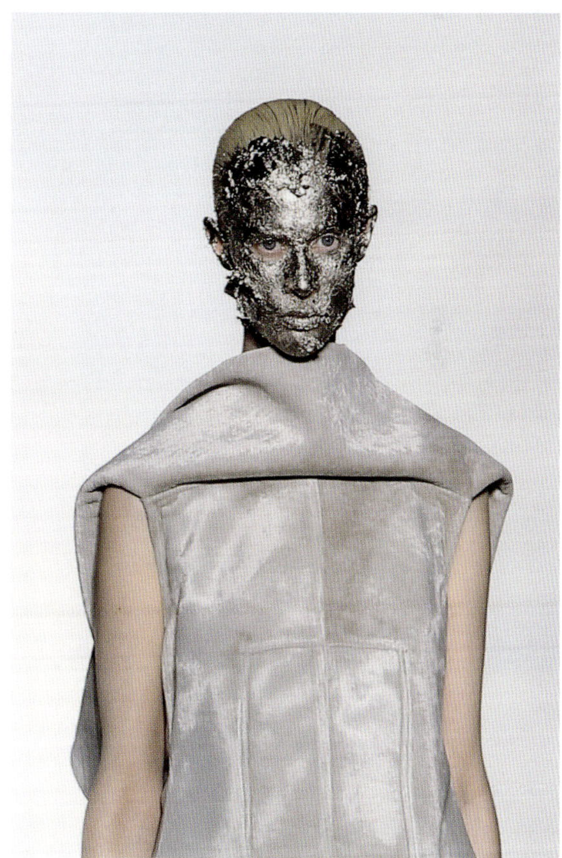

Womenswear by Rick Owens Fall/Winter 2015–16

# Aluminium

**Then**

This bright grey elemental metal with a relatively modern industrial past is one of the world's most common materials. Though it has been used in its compound form for thousands of years, pure aluminium wasn't industrially produced until the late 19th century. Its lightweight nature helped the Wright Brothers to achieve flight at the turn of the 20th century; later, the Adolph Coors Company used it to create the now ubiquitous aluminium can.

Cheap, abundant and relatively easy to work with, the metal was quickly adopted by a wide range of industries and products, including aeronautics and car engines, but also household products, architecture and the decorative arts. It can be cast, cut, spun, extruded, rolled, crumpled, cut and machined into a wide range of states. Due to its widespread use in mechanical engineering, it is often used to give a deliberately industrial look. The utilitarian Emeco Navy Chair 1006, for example, was designed for the US Navy, with strategically placed bolt holes to tie the seats to the hold to brace for rough seas. These iconic chairs were later adopted in high-end interior design.

**Colour Values**
Hex code: #adacab
RGB: 173, 172, 171
CMYK: 35, 27, 28, 6
HSB: 30°, 1%, 68%

**Common Connotations**
- Industrial
- Cold
- Sleek

**Aluminium in Art, Design & Culture**
- Shaftesbury Memorial Fountain, Piccadilly Circus, London, by Sir Alfred Gilbert, *sculpture*, 1892–3
- *Winged Figure* by Barbara Hepworth, *sculpture*, 1963
- Daily Paper flagship store, New York City, by Heather Faulding of 4plus Design, *interior/ exterior design*, 2020

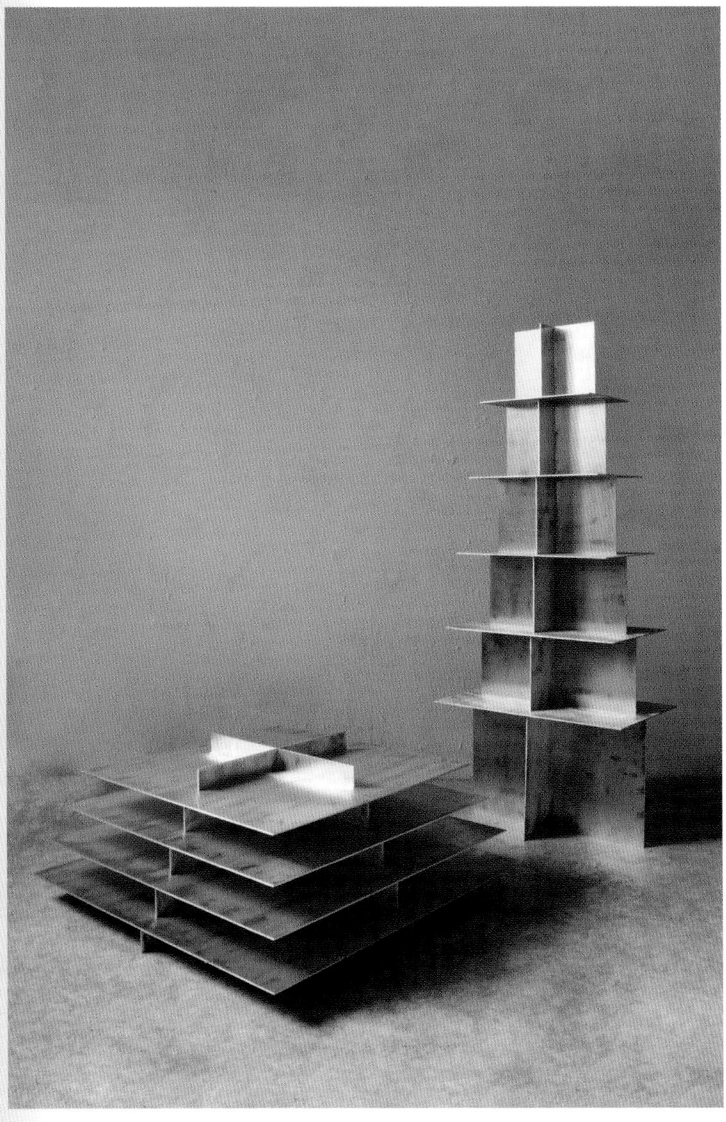

The Pyramid Shelves by Bram Vanderbeke and
Wendy Andreu, 2019

**Now**

In design, aluminium is synonymous with sleek, mass-produced objects, but a new generation of designers and brands are reinventing aluminium for the present day, taking it out of factories and back into foundries. Once used to brand Formula One cars, transparent colouring techniques such as anodizing are now being applied by artists who have taken the surface treatment to levels of high craft, with subtle patinas showcasing the true beauty of the metal.

Aluminium can be recycled again and again with no loss of quality, making it a sustainable choice in product design. In 2018, Apple announced that new models of its MacBook Air would use 100 percent recycled aluminium.

**Use**

Aluminium invites you to embrace the raw industrial look and feel. Paired with radiant, fully saturated colours, the tones will work together to increase the vibrancy of the whole palette.

'Due to its widespread use in mechanical engineering, aluminium is often used to give a deliberately industrial look.'

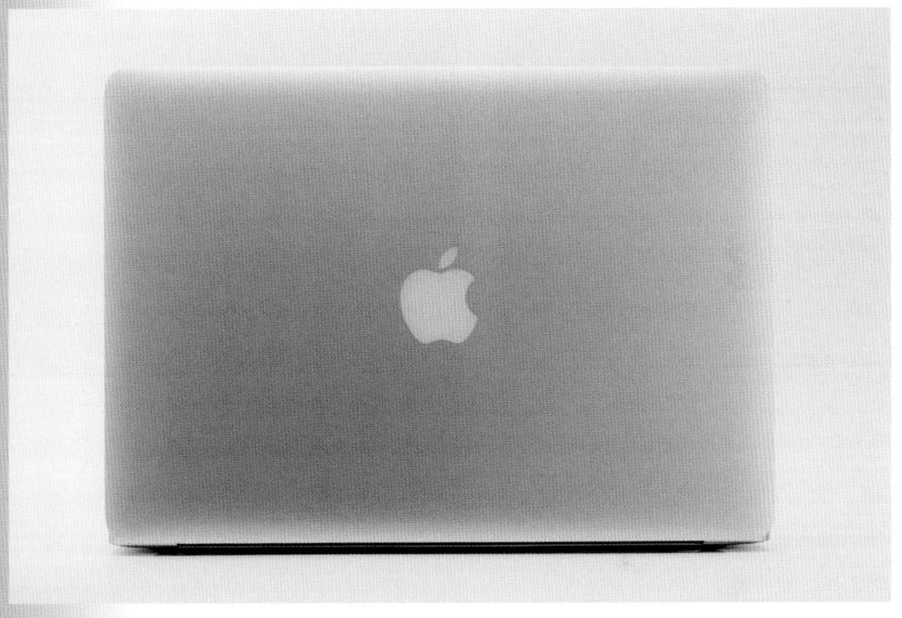

MacBook Air in Aluminium by Apple, 2018

 # Altostratus

**Then**

Altostratus is the name for the grey-blue mid-altitude
sheet layer of cloud. The wonderfully variable nature
of clouds has inspired artists and writers of all kinds to
attempt to describe them. J.M.W. Turner captured their
luminous qualities at sunrise and sunset, and the sublime
menace of dark storm clouds rolling in over shipwrecks.

The Japanese language has a remarkably diverse
vocabulary to describe each permutation, with some
terms that are descriptive, such as the 'sardine sky',
similar to the scale-like 'mackerel sky' in English; some
spiritual, such as 'novice monk clouds', a cumulus
whose name refers to the bald pates of Buddhist initiate
monks; and some seasonal, such as 'autumn sky',
a high, thin sheet on a pleasant blue sky that might
refer to altostratus. The fantastic range of these cloud
types can be seen in Hokusai's most famous set of
works, *Thirty-six Views of Mount Fuji* (1830–2), which
demonstrate how a shift in cloud cover, from a blue-
spotted sky to an overcast afternoon, can change the
whole mood of the day.

**Now**

In the wide range of cloud-based hues used in design
and art, altostratus has a sense of translucence and
light. The colour's poetic and lightweight nature is
captured beautifully by Japanese design studio Nendo
in its homeware. Overlapping glass discs tinted with
warm and cool greys imbue a beautiful vista of subtlety
to their bespoke shelving design.

**Colour Values**
Hex code: #a9abb1
RGB: 169, 171, 177
CMYK: 42, 28, 25, 6
HSB: 225°, 5%, 69%

**Also Known As**
• Cloud Grey

**Common Connotations**
• Ethereal
• Solitude
• Gentle

Right: *Ejiri in Suruga
Province (Sunshū Ejiri)*,
from the series *Thirty-six
Views of Mount Fuji (Fugaku
sanjūrokkei)* by Katsushika
Hokusai, c. 1830–2

**Altostratus in Art,
Design & Culture**
- *Seascape Study: Boat
  and Stormy Sky*, John
  Constable, *painting*, 1828
- *Abstract Painting (Grey)
  (880-3)* by Gerhard
  Richter, *painting*, 2002
- Rotating glass shelf
  by Nendo for Lasvit,
  *furniture*, 2013

**Use**
Soothing, not dull, soft cloud-like greys can have
a meditative effect. Take inspiration from the pale
horizon fading from salmon peach to grey-blue to
create a calming interior palette.

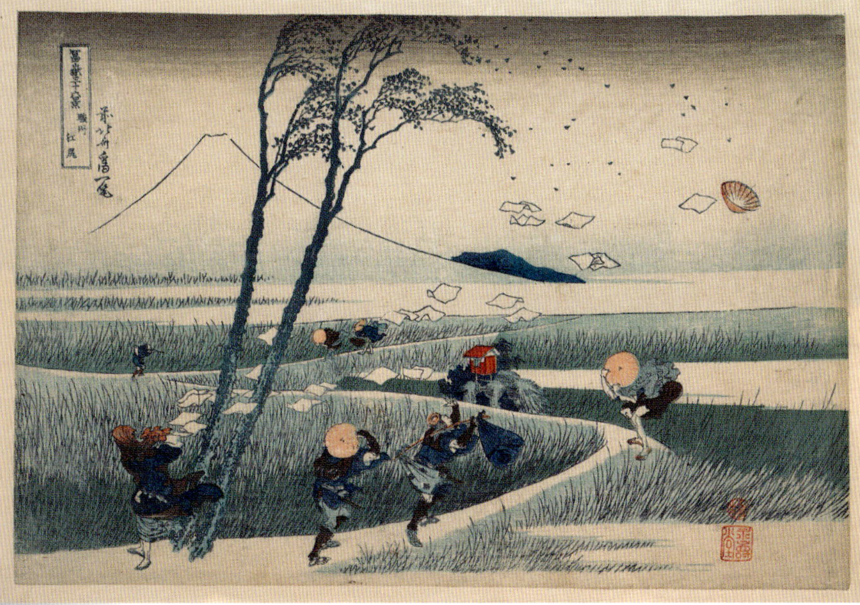

 # Concrete

**Then**

Love it or hate it, concrete is omnipresent in the architecture and infrastructure of most modern cities. The synthetic material comprising aggregate (such as brick or sand) and lime, mixed with water, creates a semi-fluid, workable substance that sets as hard as stone. Allowing infinite possibilities for sculptural and tactile effects, it can be polished or ground, shuttered or etched, poured like cake mix, or roughly squashed with terrazzo chips.

The material is usually associated with the functionalist and brutalist social architecture of the mid-20th century, but early forms of lime-based concrete in use in the Middle East as long ago as 1300 BCE were already demonstrating its potential. Nabataeans used it to build houses, but more significantly also waterproof underground cisterns. The ability to collect and store water allowed the Nabataeans to establish a powerful kingdom, with the extraordinary city of Petra as its capital built out of the rock in the heart of the desert.

**Now**

Today, the material has crossed over from functional use to lifestyle products with plant pots, polished concrete worktops and even a perfume by Comme des Garçons. Exposed concrete has been a source of inspiration for many designers and architects, with some connecting to the raw aesthetic to communicate a restrained luxury, and others to the sleek potential of the polished material.

**Colour Values**

Hex code: #a6a2a0
RGB: 166, 162, 160
CMYK: 36, 30, 31, 9
HSB: 20°, 4%, 65%

**Common Connotations**

- Robust
- Tactile
- Minimal

However, the material's environmental impact is high, both in its creation – which generates large quantities of $CO_2$ and requires vast amounts of beach sand; desert sand not being of a suitable consistency – and in its disposal – which is invariably in landfill. British architectural collective Assemble is rethinking the urban environment by creating temporary buildings with hand-coloured concrete tiles, made directly on site, and designed for disassembly, to be rebuilt as needed elsewhere.

**Use**
Offset concrete's sombre tones with warm, revitalizing earthy hues, and be mindful of the environmental impact of your design.

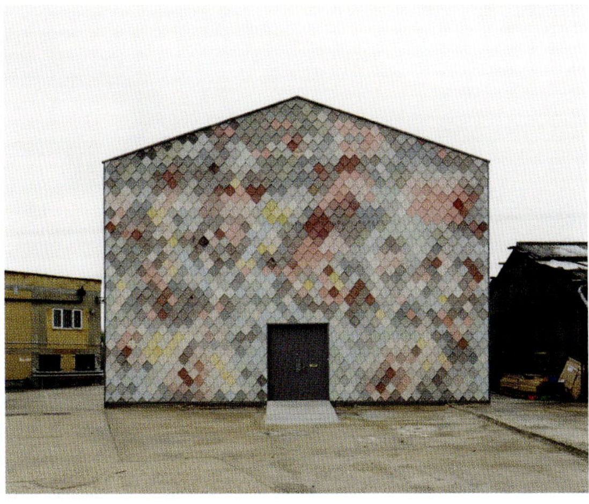

Yardhouse by Assemble
Architects, London, 2014

# Slag

## Then

Slag is a brown-grey, semi-lustrous residue material made up of the leftover impurities from smelting metal. Slag traces have been found in ancient Mesopotamian glassware, where it was ground down and fired to create black, glassy vessels. The Industrial Revolution saw the beginning of the widespread commercial refining of steel, and by the early 20th century, huge slag piles were being dumped in the natural landscape – a sight that left an impression on many artists working at the time. British artist Prunella Clough observed the raw heaps of residue against the pastoral countryside: a haunting image of ecological damage that is yet to be undone.

## Now

The primary use for slag in the modern day is in the creation of cement, another functional grey. Studio ThusThat repurposed this residue, giving it a new value while simultaneously cleaning up its carbon footprint. Using geopolymerization, they created a new black cement directly from slag, saving energy and making furniture as a byproduct.

## Use

With a gritty industrial heritage, this warm grey can still be a grounding asset. Pair with charcoal black and pale blue to create surfaces and textures that work with a modern, eco-driven palette.

**Colour Values**
Hex code: #736f6c
RGB: 115, 111, 108
CMYK: 51, 43, 44, 29
HSB: 26°, 6%, 45%

**Common Connotations**
- Dirty
- Waste
- Revalue

**Slag in Art, Design & Culture**
- *Tipping the Slag* by Edwin Butler Bayliss, *painting*, c.1940–5
- *Slag Heap II* by Prunella Clough, *painting*, 1959
- *Slag Studies* by Jamie North, *sculpture*, 2019

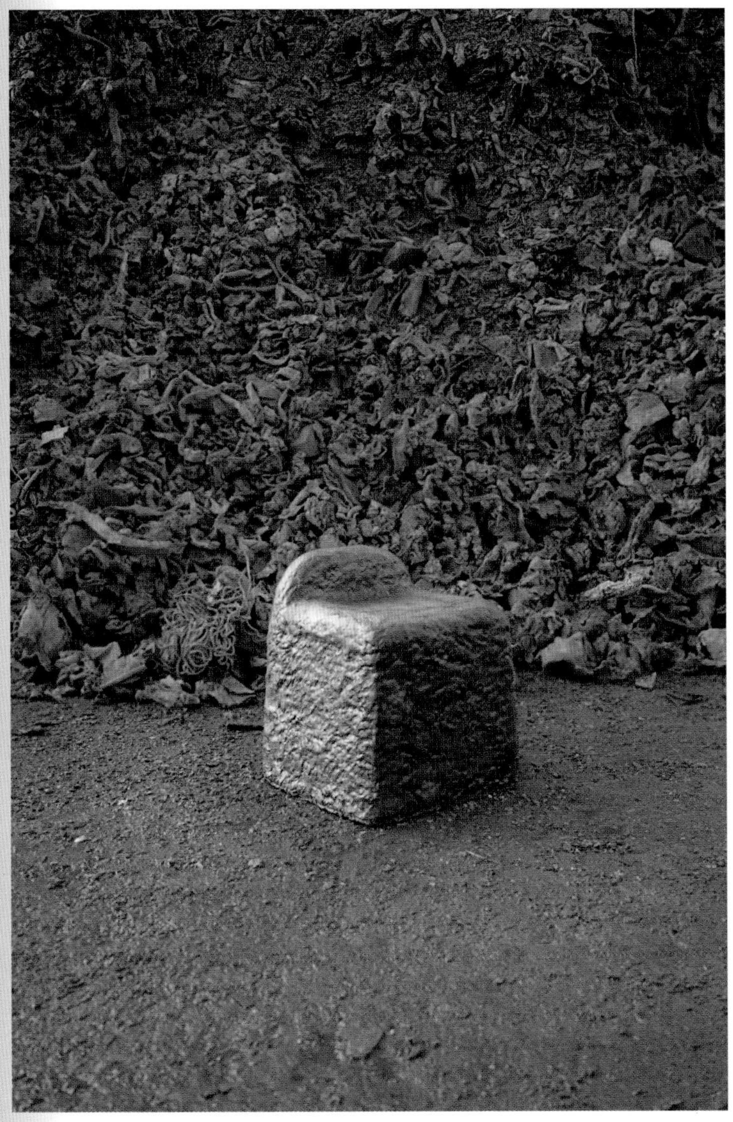



From the 'This is Copper' collection by Studio ThusThat, 2019

 # Charcoal

**Then**

A naturally black material made from burning wood slowly with little oxygen, this humble residue was our first drawing implement, and it has had an incredible number of applications through history. Charcoal has been used in medicine since the ancient Egyptians, in water filtration as far back as the Phoenicians, and in the 9th century CE, a Chinese alchemist combined it with saltpeter and sulphur to invent gunpowder.

In art, a charcoal stick is a fluid, expressive and versatile medium that leaves a rich black mark. Edgar Degas used it delicately to sketch the female form, while 20th-century British artist David Bomberg reduced his industrial subjects and settings to graphic geometric shapes, with charcoal's rich shading underscoring tension and energy in compositions.

**Now**

Charcoal is back in the public eye today for its ability to extract impurities, but, as we've seen, charcoal filtration is hardly new. In Japan, the use of charcoal to purify drinking water has been common practice since the 17th century, while in the US, Jack Daniel's filters its whiskey through maple charcoal to achieve clarity and a smoky flavour.

**Colour Values**
Hex code: #2a271f
RGB: 42, 39, 31
CMYK: 61, 55, 63, 80
HSB: 43°, 26%, 16%

**Common Connotations**
- Timeless
- Primal
- Expressive

In design, Amsterdam clothing brand Senscommon partnered with Japanese textile designer Uchino to create a 'self-purifying' line of clothing using activated charcoal to eliminate body odours and protect the wearer from environmental pollution. Italian design duo Formafantasma, based in the Netherlands, reference the traditional craft of charcoal making, as well as the material itself, in a series of filters, ladles and vessels.

## Use

A deep, smoky black, charred with a long history, is an innately grounding shade. Use it to create a serene yet moving monochromatic palette of soft blacks and greys.

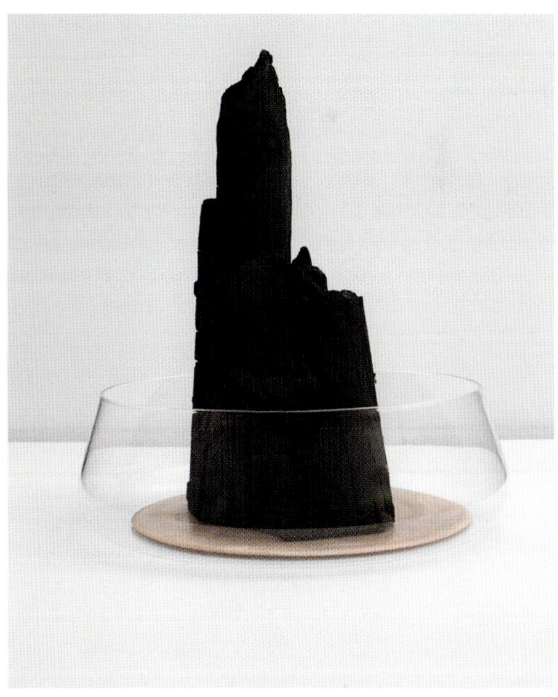

From the Charcoal project by Formafantasma for The Vitra Design Museum, 2012

# Ink Black

## Then

The earliest known carbon-based black ink to be used as a writing medium was lampblack, the sooty residue of burning oil or wood. In 3200 BCE, the ancient Egyptians were already setting the rules of typography, using black ink for main text, with other colours, particularly an iron-based red, used for accents and headings. When the mechanical printing press was first developed in Europe in the mid-15th century, lampblack was the first ink to pioneer this new realm.

Writing with ink and a sharp-pointed needle was common in early civilizations in China, Japan and Southeast Asia. Various other cultures were also developing natural inks from charring fruit stones or boiling plants and tree bark, each producing different nuances and symbolic meanings. Ink made from carbonizing oak galls was the preferred drawing fluid of Leonardo da Vinci.

However, the best-known ink today is Indian ink: an opaque, velvety black initially made in China, with the English term India(n) ink evolving due to ink trade deals. Made from finely ground soot and a binding agent such as shellac, it produced a distinctive and permanent colour to be used in art, writing and calligraphy.

## Now

Messy, visceral and hands-on in a way that digital technology can never be, the allure of ink has hardly faltered in the digital world. Calligraphy has found a new lease of life in recent years as a mindful activity, and the annual online event Inktober sees artists around the world creating works in ink and posting them on social media. Ink continues to be a popular fine art material, and calligrapher Keiko Shimoda explores its material qualities and heritage, using the same sumi ink her grandmother once used.

**Colour Values**
Hex code: #3b3e41
RGB: 59, 62, 65
CMYK: 70, 58, 52, 56
HSB: 210°, 9%, 25%

**Also Known As**
- Inkwell
- Indian Ink

**Common Connotations**
- Formal
- Prestigious
- Authentic

Right: *Creation* by Keiko Shimoda

**Black Ink in Art,
Design & Culture**
- The DermalAbyss
  Project by MIT's Media
  Lab, *wearable ink* 2017
- *somebody-010* by Kim
  Joon, *digital print*, 2014
- Ichimura Kakyo as
  Shirataki Sakichi, by
  Utagawa Toyokuni
  III, *Japanese woodblock
  print*, 1861

## Use
A palette of soft greens and pinks with ink black and
gold can create an evocative palette for spaces that wish
to nurture contemplation and learning.

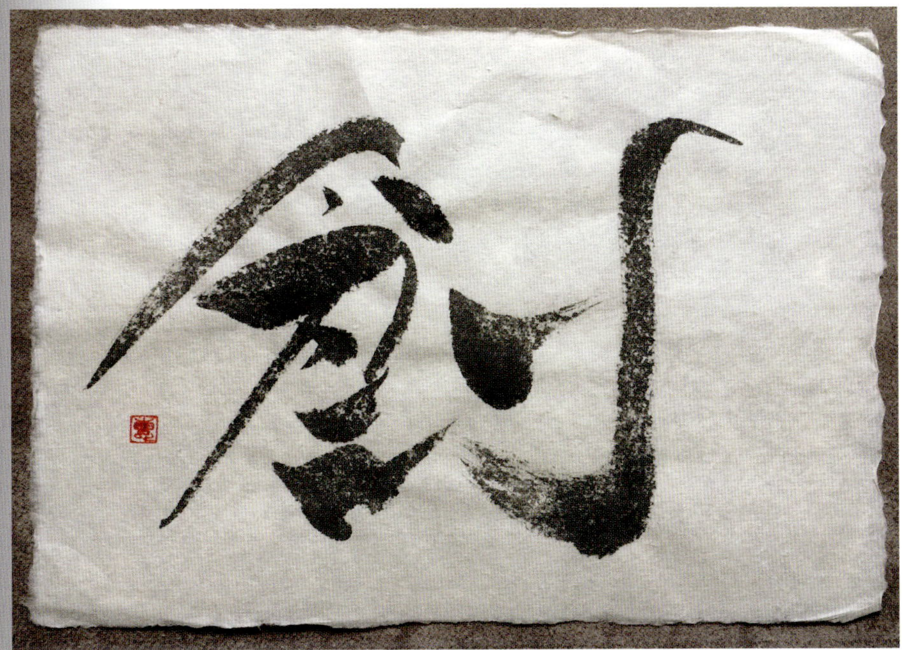

# Payne's Grey

**Then**

The ultimate brooding colour, Payne's grey was invented and first used in the early 19th century. It was originally made from a combination of Prussian blue, yellow ochre and crimson lake, resulting in a shade that appears midnight blue or slate grey depending on how much it is watered down. William Payne, the watercolour artist credited with creating it, used the hue to depict shadows, cloudscapes and distant mountains. A wash of the hue can give a landscape an emotionally charged air of foreboding or melancholy.

Artist Georgia O'Keeffe proved an expert at conveying emotion with this hue, as can be seen in her work *Storm Cloud, Lake George*. The smoky shade gives depth to the far-off mountains, and her darker use of the hue has been said to express the oppression she felt while staying with her husband's family at Lake George.

**Now**

Sober, naturalistic hues tend to remain relevant and often outperform brighter colours over time. The rise of the *Fifty Shades of Grey* franchise in the 2010s appears to have had a surprising impact on interior design, inspiring a renewed interest in this distinctly moody grey. Indeed, from the opening scene, interiors in the film sequel, *Fifty Shades Darker*, are painted with Payne's grey and other cool, neutral tones to create a dark and sensuous mood.

**Use**

Draw on various shades of Payne's grey to create a nuanced palette, and enliven it with brighter, naturalistic hues such as botanical greens and indigo blue.

**Colour Values**

Hex code: #395266
RGB: 57, 82, 102
CMYK: 76, 51, 33, 40
HSB: 207°, 44%, 40%

**Common Connotations**

- Gloomy
- Thoughtful
- Gender-neutral

**Payne's Grey in Art, Design & Culture**

- *Landscape with Donkeys* by William Payne, *painting*, 1798
- *Fifty Shades Darker* set by Nelson Coates, *production design*, 2017
- Ready-to-Wear collection by Hussein Chalayan, *fashion*, S/S 2018

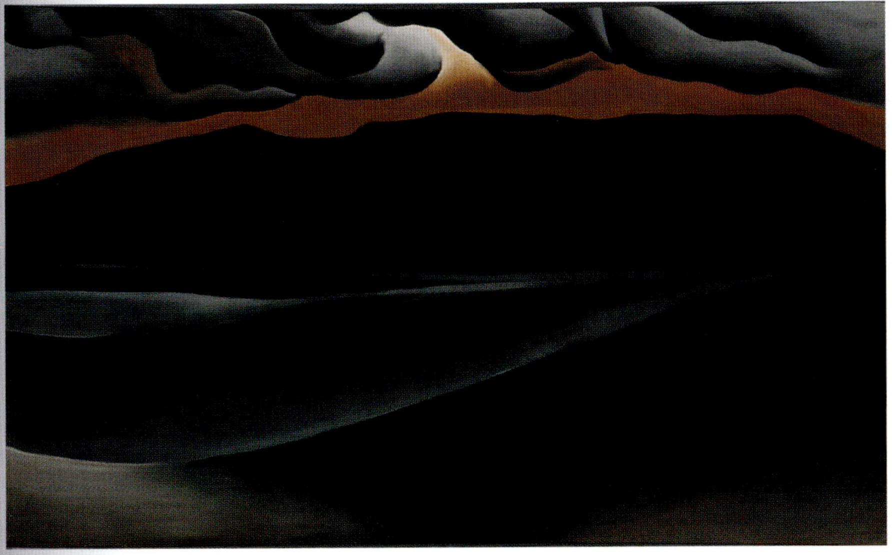

*Storm Cloud, Lake George* by Georgia O'Keeffe, 1923

# Obsidian

**Then**

Obsidian is a form of volcanic glass, with a captivating black shade and a blue-green undertone. People have used sharp obsidian as cutting tools since the Stone Age, and *macuahuitl*, a paddle-shaped weapon with blades of obsidian embedded in its sides, were used in Mesoamerica from 900 CE. The Aztecs also created obsidian mirrors in honour of their god Tezcatlipoca, whose name translates literally as 'smoking mirror'; these luminous black mirrors were prized for their use in divination.

The material has been adopted by artists including the 17th-century Spanish painter Bartolomé Esteban Murillo, who used it as a surface with oil paints. Obsidian's natural lustre creates a mesmerizing interplay of dark and light, elevating the sense of wonder in his religious scenes.

**Now**

Performance design industries have adopted obsidian's light-bending effects to create a streamlined, liquid effect. In 2020, Hyundai presented its new 'Prophecy' concept car, with its sleek obsidian finish. However, it's the substance's mind-bending quality that has captured the eye of contemporary creatives. Korean designer Seungjoon Song's 'Obsidian' mirror recalls the Aztecs' ancient use of the substance, with a small obsidian hemisphere that becomes a complete sphere; a surreal, meditative pinpoint floating in the centre of our daily vanity.

**Use**

Bring a sense of curiosity to technology products with dominant, glossy obsidian; ramp up the intensity with fiery red touches to communicate performance and power.

**Colour Values**
Hex code: #011a22
RGB: 1, 26, 34
CMYK: 99, 66, 56, 70
HSB: 195°, 94%, 7%

**Common Connotations**
- Mystical
- Revered
- Amorphous

**Obsidian in Art, Design & Culture**
- *Sacred and Profane Love* by Giovanni Baglione, *painting*, 1602–3
- *The Nativity*, Bartolomé Esteban Murillo, *painting*, 1665–70
- 'Prophecy' electric concept car by Hyundai, *automotive*, 2020

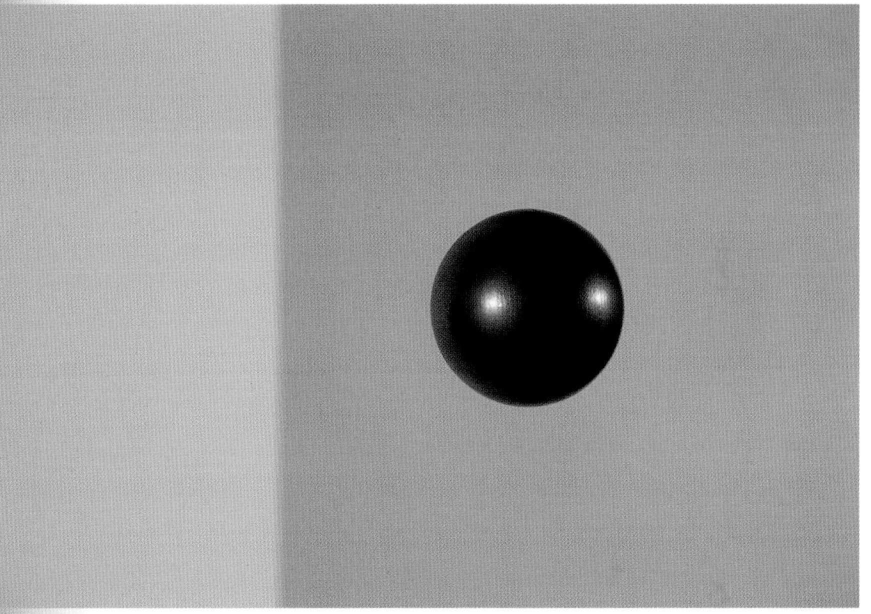

Obsidian by Seungjoon Song, 2020

# Vantablack

**Then**

Colour performance pulls its biggest magic trick to date with Vantablack. Like something out of a science fiction movie, this is a black that evades perception and is able to absorb 99.965 percent of visible light, which makes it almost impossible for the human eye to decipher the shape of an object it coats. There is no Pantone number, as it's not really a colour in the strictest sense; rather, it's the total absence of reflection of all colours. The substance is packed full of vertically aligned nanotubes, microscopic filaments of super carbon called 'forests', that stand to attention when stimulated.

Since its invention in 2014 by Surrey NanoSystems, this unique substance has gained traction within NASA's deep space imaging work, smart optics and also in the art world. Artist Anish Kapoor controversially licensed the pigment's exclusive rights for use in his art and developed a series of world-exclusive art projects using it.

**Now**

Outraged by Kapoor's monopoly of Vantablack, in 2019, artist Stuart Semple launched Black 3.0, described as the 'flattest, mattest, black acrylic paint in the world'. The paint, which absorbs 98–99 percent of visible light, is now available for anyone to buy via the project's Kickstarter page – on the condition that 'To the best of your knowledge, information and belief this material will not make its way into the hands of Anish Kapoor'.*

MIT researchers and others have since developed more commercially available nanoblack substances. BMW enveloped the X6 model with Vantablack, while architect Asif Khan bent spatial perception with angular, hypnotizing Vantablack walls for the South Korean Winter Olympics Pavilion in 2018.

* https://www.kickstarter.com/projects/culturehustle/the-blackest-black-paint-in-the-world-black-30

**Also Known As**
- Nanoblack

**Common Connotations**
- Futuristic
- Absorbing
- Stealthy

Right: Hyundai Pavilion designed by Asif Khan at PyeongChang Winter Olympics, South Korea, 2018

**Vantablack in Art,
Design & Culture**
- *Descent into Limbo* by
Anish Kapoor, *installation
artwork*, 1992
- *The Redemption of Vanity*
by Diemut Strebe and
Brian Wadle, *installation*,
2019
- BMW X6 Vantablack,
*automotive*, 2019

**Use**
Applied to objects or details, nanoblacks create a
dramatic aesthetic illusion ideal for gallery installations
or experiences. The shade's functional properties,
such as thermal control, can be applied to surfaces
that reach sub-zero temperatures, with far-reaching
applications that are still being explored.

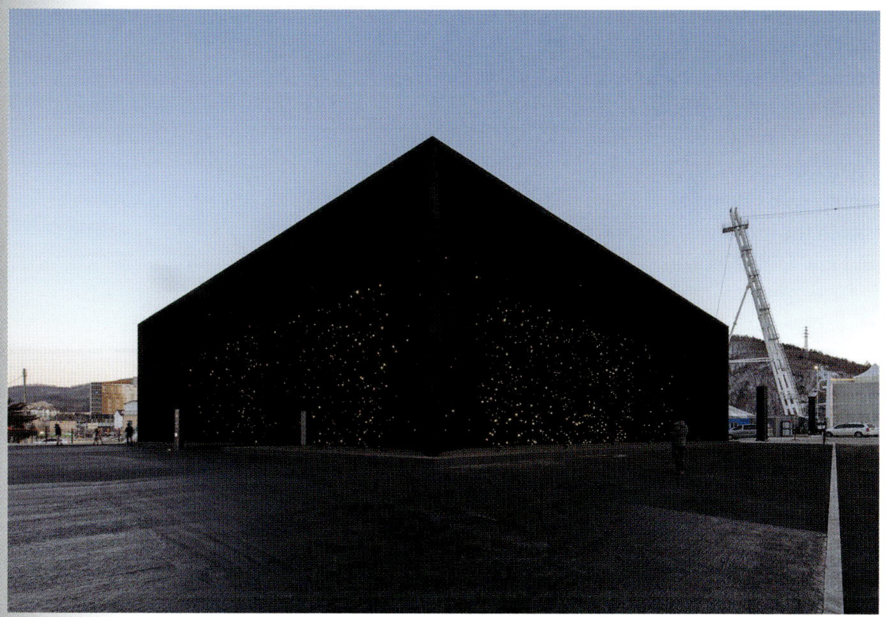

 # Brown

There is something undeniably levelling and grounding about brown. It is fundamentally regenerative in its origins – as soil rich with nutrients sustains life itself. The prehistoric drawings on cave walls at Altamira and Lascaux were created with still-extant earth pigments, and clay and pottery were used as a primary vessel of communication, decoration and art in early cultures around the world. Today, a revival in ceramics and working with natural clays speaks of heritage and the value of craft (see Tenmoku).

Throughout history, when it came to dyeing cloth, brown was often the colour left for the poor, who were unable to afford the price tags attached to brighter hues. The monks of the Franciscan order wore it as a sign of poverty and humility. The term for the plebeians, or urban poor, in Classical Latin was *pullati*, literally meaning 'those dressed in dark garments', demonstrating the extent to which different shades defined class and identity in eras past.

In spectral definition, brown is not a hue but a low yellow or orange shade; the perception is generated when low-intensity light of these wavelengths reaches our eyes. In art and design, brown remains a critical tool in the artisan's arsenal. Without rich burnt sienna and raw umber as artistic pigments, the drama of chiaroscuro and tone would be lost. In the work of artists from Van Dyck to Rothko, brown brings a mesmerizing depth to painted shadows like nothing else.

In recent years, plain, honest brown has taken on a very contemporary symbolism as the colour of wholesome eco-friendliness. Brown paper bags and brown boxes can allow brands and establishments to give a coded nod to environmentalism (without necessarily following through in practice, of course). Coupled with brown's innate natural and soft qualities, earth shades are once again emerging to gift us a set of grounded and supportive tones to keep things rooted and temper the chaotic world around us.

**Colours in this chapter:**

# Sepia

**Then**

Sepia is the colour of the dark brown pigment produced by cuttlefish. This natural substance has been used as a drawing ink and watercolour wash for millennia. Sepia wash drawings became particularly popular among expedition illustrators recording anthropological discoveries in the 18th and 19th centuries. Fine artists and craftspeople have also deployed sepia to create delicate background washes before gestural brushmarks build up tone and depth, such as in the draft work of William Morris's fabric designs.

However, sepia is perhaps best known in the modern world for its use in early photography. In the 19th century it was discovered that dipping or washing cyanotype photographs in sepia naturally protected the images from light damage, at the same time as giving them a distinctive brown colouring.

**Now**

Though cuttlefish ink is no longer widely in use, taste for sepia's natural colour expression has not faded in the contemporary world. A nostalgia for vintage photographs and curiosities means sepia tinting is still on trend; whether that's in an Instagram filter or with chemicals in a darkroom.

**Use**

Create a sense of natural richness with two softly muted complementary shades. Muted sepia and washed-out indigo blue contrast in a beautiful yet unimposing way. Add a delicate outline or graphic accent in a darker nutty brown to make a naturalistic palette that will draw the eye to crucial details.

**Colour Values**
Hex code: #bf9f64
RGB: 191, 159, 100
CMYK: 24, 33, 64, 10
HSB: 39°, 48%, 75%

**Common Connotations**
- Nostalgic
- Delicate
- Authentic

**Sepia in Art, Design & Culture**
- *Crystal Palace Transept* by Benjamin Brecknell Turner, *photography*, c.1852
- *Large Melbourne Sepia or Cuttlefish, Sepia Apama* by John James Wild, *lithographic print*, c.1889–90

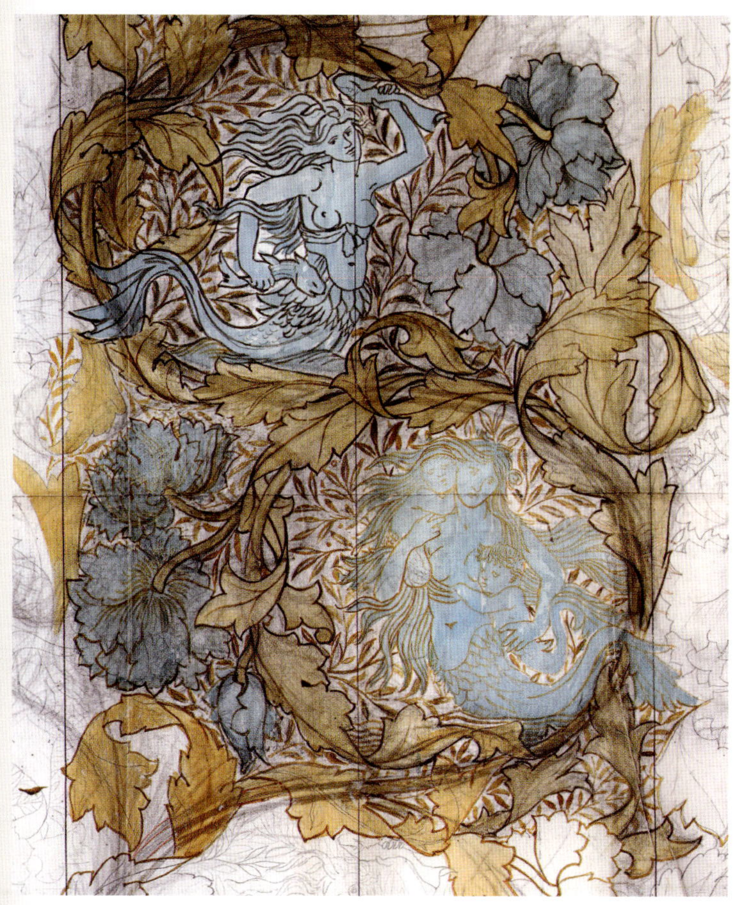

Cartoon for 'Mermaid' woven fabric by Edward Burne-Jones, c.1880

# Van Dyke Brown

## Then

Upon the shelf of renowned artists' supplies shop L. Cornelissen & Son in London, a bottle of the organic pigment Van Dyke brown is marked 'Unstable in all media. Dries poorly in oil, can turn grey'. Not the most glamorous advert for a shade that at one time created some of the most dramatic and profound shadows in painting history.

Somewhere between black soot and earthy peat lies this brooding shade made from natural earth. By packing oil carriers with freshly dug soil, lignite (a brown coal substance) and other earthy ochres including Cassel earth, Flemish Baroque artist Anthony van Dyck made a tarry glaze that he most famously used to paint King Charles I. Van Dyck's masterworks are characteristically theatrical and sombre, which we now know is in part as a result of fugitive pigments.

## Now

Naturally fluctuating, as with all earth pigments, Van Dyck's brown became grey with UV exposure. Still available today in artists' tubes and with a new, less unstable formula, this shadowy brown is a reminder that colour can be derived from the very earth beneath us.

## Use

Embrace the natural aspect of Van Dyke brown by crafting a palette based on varying natural earth shades found close to your locality. Rustic nuances work well with red earth and pale clay accents to create authentic hue contrasts that speak of longevity and environmental history.

**Colour Values**
Hex code: #28171a
RGB: 40, 23, 46
CMYK: 63, 75, 57, 82
HSB: 349º, 43%, 16%

**Also Known As**
- Cassel Earth
- Cologne Umber

**Common Connotations**
- Pensive
- Conservative
- Authentic

**Van Dyke Brown in Art, Design & Culture**
- *Marchesa Geronima Spinola* by Anthony van Dyck, *painting*, c.1624
- 'De Straat Makers: Colours of the City' project by Atelier NL, *research project*, 2019

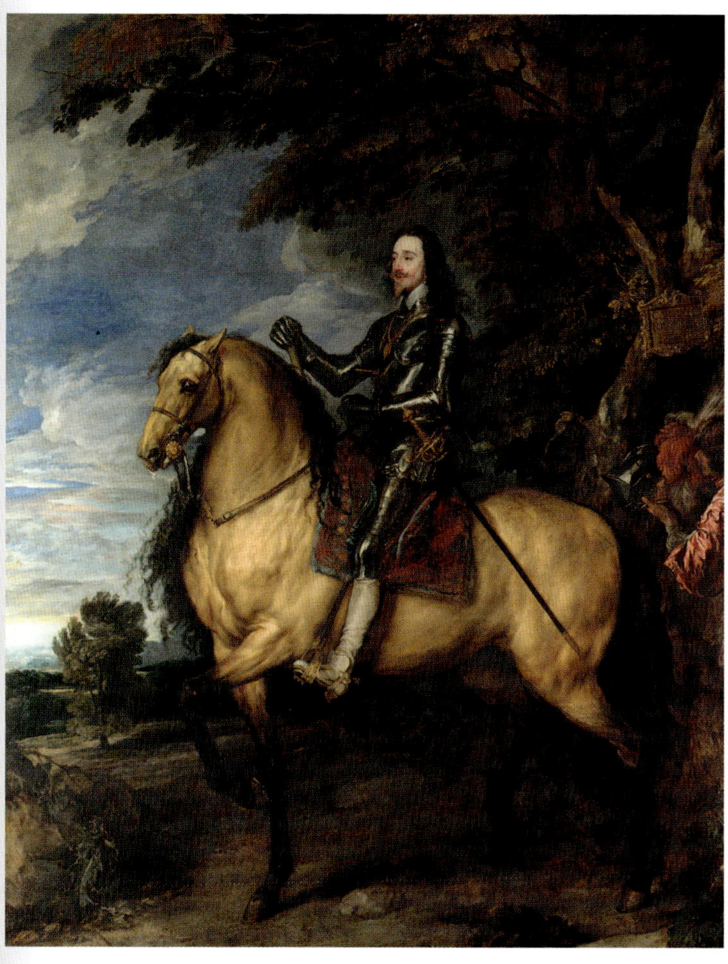

*Equestrian Portrait of Charles I* by Anthony van Dyck, 1637–8

# Umber

**Then**

Natural umber is one of the oldest pigments known to have been used by humans, and due to its robust make-up of manganese and iron oxide, it can still be seen in paintings on cave walls at Altamira in Spain that date back to the Palaeolithic age. In more recent history, Rembrandt was known for his technique of layering, scumbling and brushing back umber ochres with lampblack to create chocolate hues.

As colour theory and terminology developed, umber, with its yellow-brown undertone, came to be described as a warm, chromatic dark. In his 1923 painting *Static-Dynamic Gradation*, Bauhaus artist and teacher Paul Klee explored colour relationships through a harmonized progression from chromatic darkness to lightness, drawing your eye into the middle of the painting. Darker outer squares are made with rich umber, while the heart of the piece has cool blue blocks offset by contrasting hot orange.

**Now**

A neutral and supportive tone, umber allows more saturated colours to sing, and has featured widely in fine art, from atmospheric Rothkos to the dark, contemporary vistas of Peter Doig. Indeed, Mark Rothko is known to have requested, upon the hanging of the Mark Rothko room at Tate Modern in 1970, that the ideal gallery wall tone be an 'off-white with umber and warmed by a little red'.*

**Use**

Explore Klee's principles and play with warm chromatic shades to bring weight or attention to certain functions or features. To contrast or highlight, add an accent of soft, cool blue.

**Colour Values**

Hex code: #534024
RGB: 83, 64, 36
CMYK: 49, 57, 80, 59
HSB: 36º, 56%, 33%

**Common Connotations**

- Timeless
- Sombre
- Supportive

**Umber in Art, Design & Culture**

- *The Night Watch* by Rembrandt, *painting*, 1642
- *Untitled (Umber, Blue, Umber, Brown)* by Mark Rothko, *painting*, 1962
- *Moruga* by Peter Doig, *painting*, 2002–8

* Quoted in Banville, John, 'Temple of Mysteries: Mark Rothko', *Tate Etc.*, Issue 7, 1 May 2006

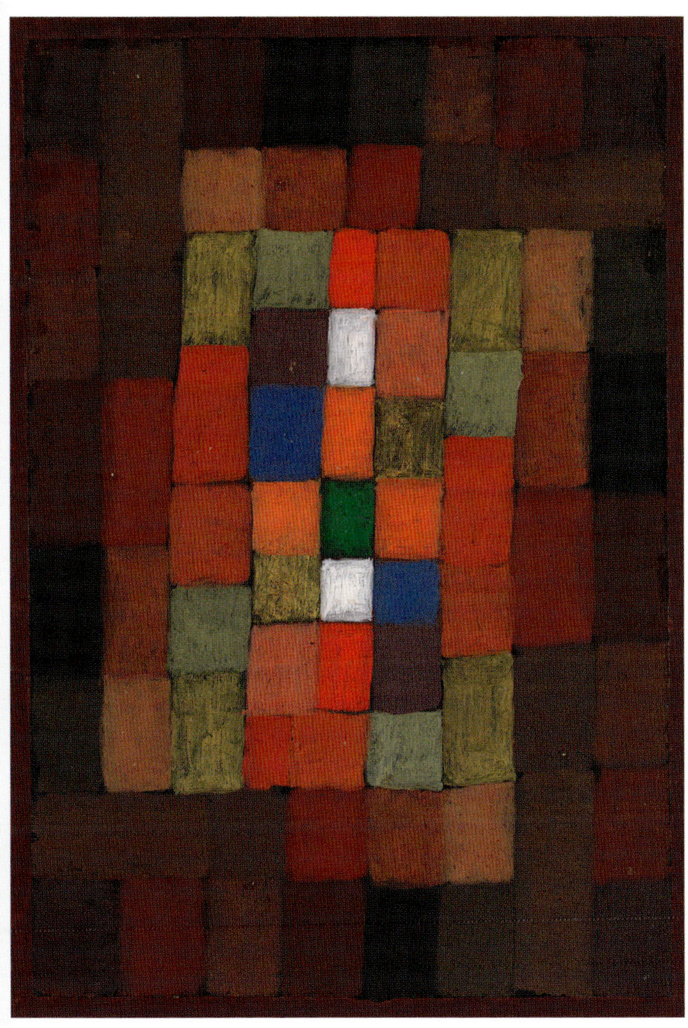

*Static-Dynamic Gradation* by Paul Klee, 1923

# Tenmoku

**Then**

*Tenmoku* pottery began life as a Chinese art in Buddhist temples on Mount Tianmu (known as Mount Tenmoku by the Japanese), which entailed finishing tea bowls with an iron-rich dark ceramic glaze, made of the ashes of burnt plants or potash, and iron oxide. Japanese Zen monks made pilgrimages to the mountain to study the ritual process of tea-making and brought the practice back with them.

    *Tenmoku* glazes are traditionally intensely warm black, but are further characterized by how the glaze breaks or spots to a beautiful rust colour, with a natural beauty that speaks of hand-craft and uniqueness.

**Now**

There has been a revival in *tenmoku*, though there are still very few artisans able to reproduce the exacting historical process. Contemporary Japanese ceramicist Kyosuke Hayashi is one such artist, and his hypnotic work, which is held in galleries around the world, demonstrates the ongoing appeal of this ancient craft.

**Use**

Let the traditional *tenmoku* glaze inspire a palette of burnt bark to warm chocolate brown nuances to make a perfect scheme for a profoundly nourishing interior space.

**Colour Values**
Hex code: #341601
RGB: 52, 22, 1
CMYK: 54, 76, 78, 80
HSB: 25°, 98%, 20%

**Also Known As**
- Hare's Fur

**Common Connotations**
- Unique
- Timeless
- Rarity

**Tenmoku in Art, Design & Culture**
- 'Flat-Sided Bottle' by Bernard Leach, *ceramics*, 1957
- 'Yōhen Tenmoku Chawan' by Kyosuke Hayashi, *ceramics*, 2001
- 'Galaxy' by Kondō Takahiro, *ceramics*, 2001

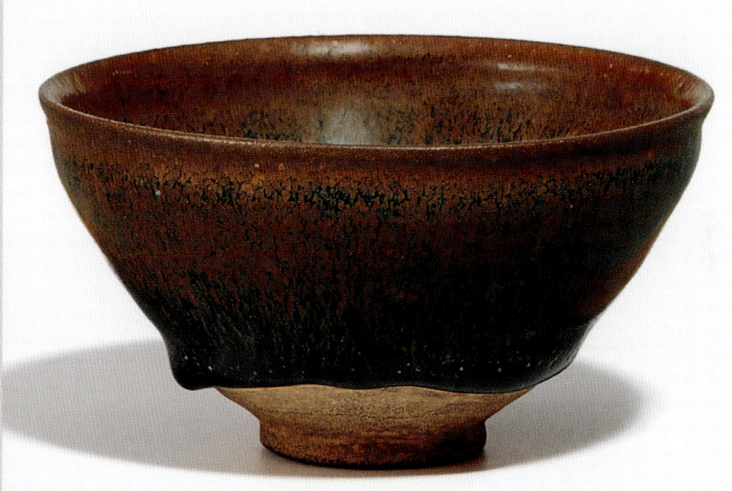

*Tenmoku* tea bowl, China, Song period, 10th–13th century

# Burnt Sienna

### Then

Raw sienna is one of the planet's naturally occurring ochres or earth colours. Burnt sienna, a warm brownish red shade, is created by heating the naturally yellow ochre until the heat partially converts the iron oxide into hematite. The name comes from the Tuscan city of Siena that produced the colour in large quantities during the Renaissance. European artists such as Caravaggio and Rembrandt brought out the beauty of burnt sienna by diluting it to bring forward undertones of subdued pinks and chromatic brown tints. The colour was later employed in the energetic, abstract paint marks of 20th-century artists Pierre Soulages and Howard Hodgkin, the latter juxtaposing the colour's primal earthiness with powerful synthetic hues such as chrome green.

### Now

With reserves of ochre in Tuscan mines much depleted by the end of the 20th century, the commercial colour market began to use chemically made iron oxides. However, contemporary artists are reverting back to making colour in traditional ways: Colombian designer and artist Laura Daza creates coloured sienna tones from locally sourced soils, creating a range of shades from yellow to reddish brown.

### Use

This rich and natural brownish red tone may suit brands and companies that are nature-focused at heart. Pair yellow ochres with small accents of leaf green to create colour harmonies that are naturally warm and evocative of a natural landscape.

**Colour Values**
Hex code: #8d3715
RGB: 141, 55, 21
CMYK: 29, 83, 99, 32
HSB: 17°, 85%, 55%

**Common Connotations**
- Earthy
- Natural
- Transformative

**Burnt Sienna in Art, Design & Culture**
- *Sacrifice of Isaac* by Caravaggio, *painting*, 1602
- *36* by Pierre Soulages, *painting*, 1965
- *Two Figures Lying on a Bed with Attendants* by Francis Bacon, *painting*, 1968

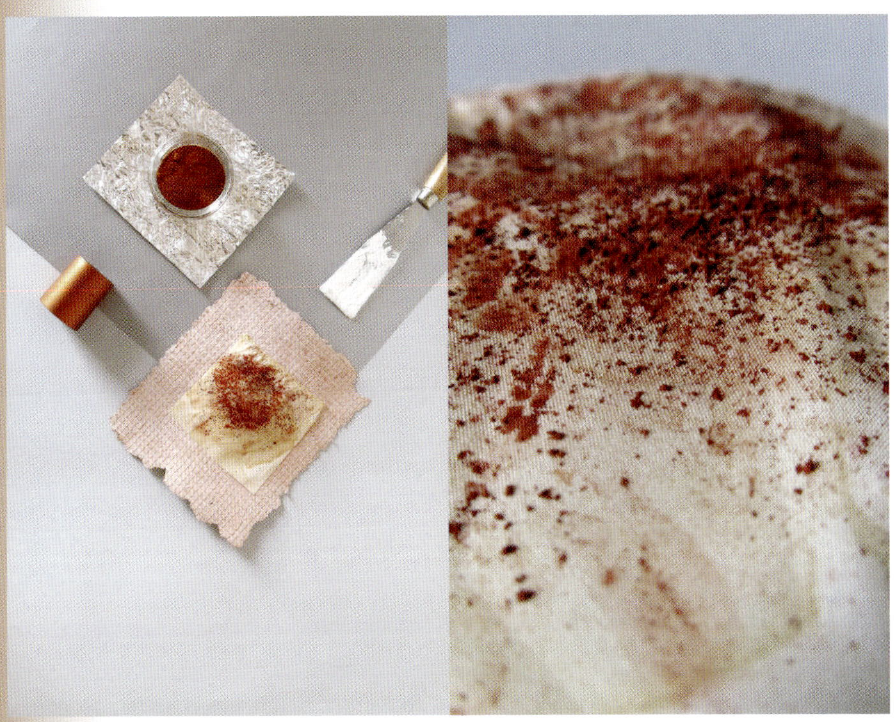



From the Burnt Sienna collection by Laura Daza, 2015

# Taupe

## Then

Not an easy colour to define, the name taupe comes from the French word for 'mole', and throughout history the term has defined a series of warm, mousy greys, sometimes tinged with dusky purple or ruddy brown undertones. At the turn of the 20th century, this shade range became associated with a sophisticated neutrality, and it appeared in both home décor and wearable pieces. Décor schemes of the period, influenced by the Arts and Crafts movement, were defined by muted shades of blue, green, taupe brown and softened whites. Taupe became fashionable again during the 1970s, accompanied by burnt oranges and harvest golds in a wholesome palette used on everything from kitchen appliances to injection-moulded chairs.

## Now

Muted taupes enjoyed a resurgence in the 2000s and are still a popular choice for interiors and fashion, when creating a soft and safe sanctuary is vital. From a colour psychology standpoint, the colour's grounding effect married with a soft, desaturated neutrality is not only easy on the eyes, but also restful for the mind.

## Use

Taupe can be used to form a naturalistic, neutral scheme with clay, muted avocado, soil brown and sand shades.

**Colour Values**
Hex code: #a59089
RGB: 165, 144, 137
CMYK: 35, 39, 39, 12
HSB: 16°, 17%, 65%

**Common Connotations**
- Restrained
- Restful
- Nurturing

**Taupe in Art, Design & Culture**
- Robie House by Frank Lloyd Wright, *architcture*, 1909–10
- *Still Life* by Giorgio Morandi, *painting*, 1960
- Menswear collection by Rick Owens, *fashion*, S/S 2017

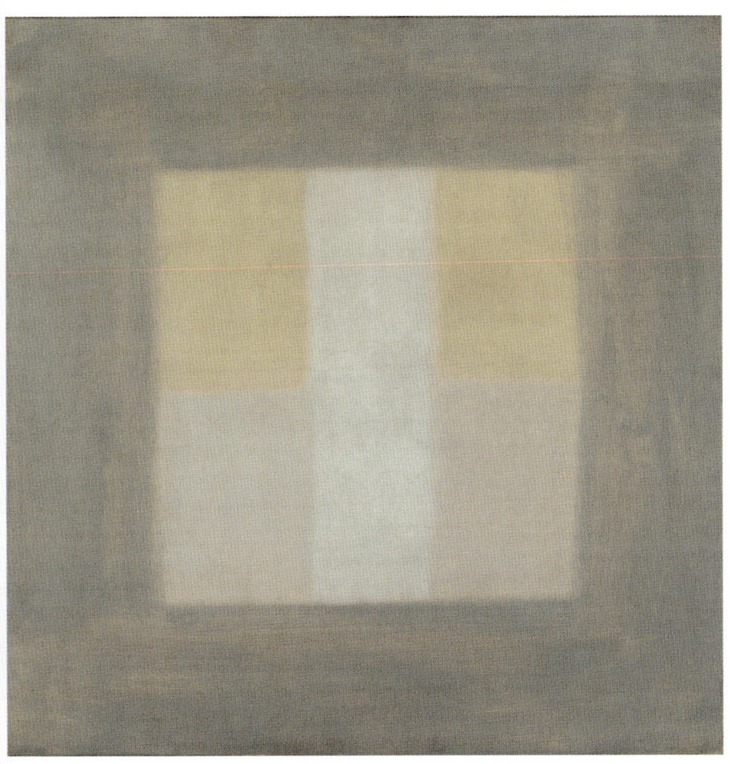

*Desert Rain*, by Agnes Martin, 1957

# Khaki

## Then

The colour name 'khaki' is borrowed from the Urdu word meaning the colour of earth, ashes or dust. The yellowy-brown fabric it refers to in English was first issued as a camouflage uniform to soldiers in the 19th century on the north-west frontier of India by Lieutenant-General Harry Burnett Lumsden. The pigment used was from a dye called cutch, extracted from the bark of the *Senegalia catechu* tree, which had long been used in India to colour calico fabric.

The scale of khaki cloth manufacturing would later escalate in response to the high demand for uniforms for those enlisting during the First World War. Through variations in dyers' baths, khaki lost its sandiness and took on a more olive nuance. By 1917, approximately 45 million separate woollen articles had been recovered from the trenches. In an act of mass salvage, khaki garments were broken down, rewoven, recut and redistributed.

## Now

Later in the 20th century, khaki garments became a ubiquitous item of utilitarian casual wear, but also fashion rebellion. Skinheads became emblematic of British youth culture in basic khaki army trousers, and at Stella McCartney's Central Saint Martin graduate collection in 1995, Kate Moss famously walked in a green camisole dress, pink stockings and a khaki army hat, taking the shade from lowly uniform to fashion statement.

## Use

Pair khaki with other warm and cool neutrals to create a modern palette that works with active outdoor brands to express a kinship with natural settings.

**Colour Values**
Hex code: #857856
RGB: 133, 120, 86
CMYK: 43, 40, 64, 27
HSB: 43º, 35%, 52%

**Common Connotations**
- Utility
- Salvaged
- Rebellious

**Khaki in Art, Design & Culture**
- *The Arrival of a Leave Train, Victoria Station* by Bernard Meninsky, *painting*, 1918
- Survival Jacket by Franco Moschino, *fashion*, S/S 1991

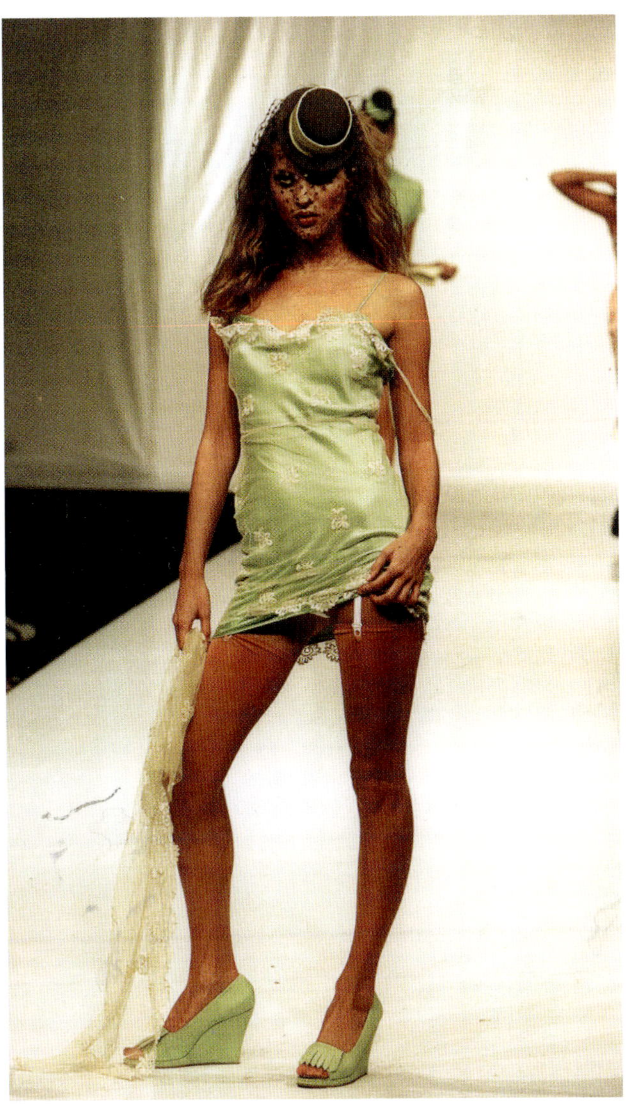

Kate Moss models at Stella McCartney's
degree show, 1995

# Cardboard

**Then**

A warm yellow-brown, cardboard is similar in shade
to other brown neutrals such as tan, biscuit and camel.
What differentiates it is that unlike these other, descriptive
colour names, cardboard is first and foremost a ubiquitous
and useful material that happens to have a distinctive hue.
Today, most industrial cardboard is made from virgin
and recycled wood pulp sourced from managed forests,
resulting in a natural, organic appearance.

The cardboard box's cheapness and availability has
made it fair game to swathes of modern creatives. In 1919,
German artist Kurt Schwitters famously began constructing
collaged artworks made of discarded debris and cardboard,
which he called Merz art – a nonsense word akin to Dada.
Later in the century, Canadian-American architect and
designer Frank Gehry was inspired by corrugated sheets
of cardboard to create his corrugated furniture forms,
including the iconic Wiggle Side Chair, as a cheap and
lightweight alternative to traditional furniture in the 1960s.

**Now**

Today, in marketing terms, cardboard brown is a signifier
of eco-friendliness. Boxes and products shipped to
consumers in this basic tone boast a stripped-back
aesthetic and fewer superfluous details, suggesting a
low-waste approach. The reality, however, is that over
850 million tonnes of paper and cardboard – equating to
approximately a billion trees – is thrown away every year
in the USA alone.

**Use**

Embrace the simple and straightforward nature of
cardboard brown. In print, pair eye-catching contrasts
of yellow ochre and bold teal blue while still allowing
the material's natural colour to come through.

**Colour Values**
Hex code: #d7a77c
RGB: 215, 167, 124
CMYK: 15, 37, 53, 4
HSB: 28°, 42%, 84%

**Common Connotations**
- Basic
- Neutral
- Thrifty

**Cardboard in Art, Design & Culture**
- *Picture of Spatial Growths – Picture with Two Small Dogs* by Kurt Schwitters, *assemblage*, 1920–39
- *Cake Lift* by Michael Johansson, *sculpture*, 2009
- Cardboard Stool by Luisa Kahlfeldt, *furniture*, 2016

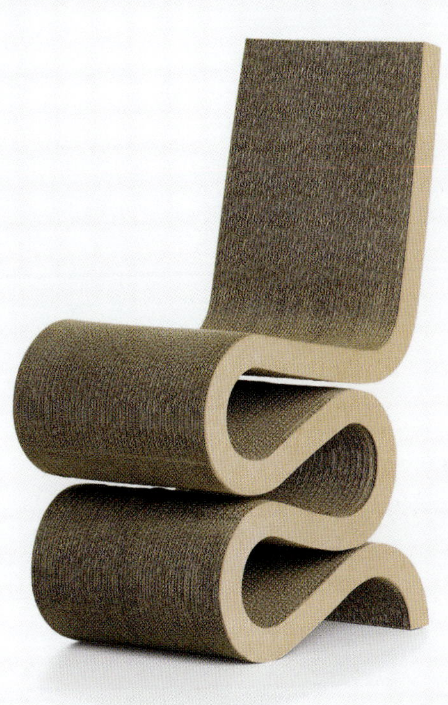

Wiggle Side Chair, designed by Frank Gehry c.1970.
Vitra Edition, 1998

# Melanin

**Then**

Melanin is one of the world's most ancient and powerful colours. This natural pigment is responsible for the vast spectrum of animal fur, bird plumage and human skin tones, and has been found in the fossils of dinosaurs and earlier, primitive organisms. When we gain a freckle, it is caused by our skin increasing localized melanin production to offer protection against UV damage.

Today, it is believed that when our early ancestors were covered with fur, our skin was probably pale underneath. When we developed more sophisticated mechanisms for regulating body temperature and shed most of our body hair, the early homo sapiens evolved with darker skin with higher concentrations of melanin to help protect them from the equatorial sun's intense radiation. Later, descendants of the groups that migrated to regions with less natural sunlight progressively developed paler skin, as it is essential to absorb some UV radiation for the body to make vitamin D, which is needed for strong and healthy bones.

**Now**

The Mediated Matter Group at MIT is a research group working with melanin as a material for design and architecture. Having extracted melanin from bird feathers, the group chemically synthesizes it with modern lab techniques and can replicate the pigment on large scales to give sun protection to materials such as architectural glass. The results have yielded an environmentally responsive, melanin-infused glass structure, which displays pigments that naturally darken in response to sunlight.

**Colour Values**
Hex code: #996e43
RGB: 153, 110, 67
CMYK: 30, 50, 73, 27
HSB: 30º, 56%, 60%

**Common Connotations**
- Natural
- Evolutionary
- Powerful

Right: 'Totems' by Neri Oxman and The Mediated Matter Group, 2019

**Use**

The performative potential of responsive melanin opens up new opportunities for the design world. Along with other powerful natural pigments such as chlorophyll, it suggests we look to colours for more than aesthetics or symbolic associations, and follow the function with innovative uses.

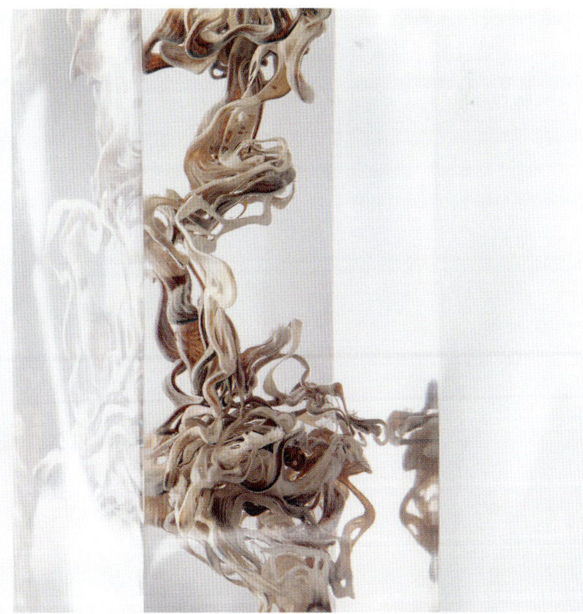

# Select Bibliography

**Introduction**

Albers, Josef *The Interaction of Color: 50th Anniversary Edition*, New Haven and London: Yale University Press, 2013 (1963)

Cheung, Vien, Mahyar, Forough, Westland, Stephen, 'Complementary Colour Harmony in Different Colour Spaces', *International Colour Association (AIC) Conference*, July 2013 *https://www.researchgate.net/publication/263334546* (accessed October 2020)

Chu, Alice and Rahman, Osmud, 'What Color is Sustainable? Examining the Eco-friendliness of Color', *International Foundation of Fashion Technology Institutes Conference*, March 2010 *https://www.researchgate.net/publication/332401739_What_color_is_sustainable_Examining_the_eco-friendliness_of_color* (accessed October 2020)

Eastlake, Charles L., '*The Theory of Colours by Johann Wolfgang von Goethe*', first published 1810

Franklin, Anna, 'Origins of Color Preference – Prof. Anna Franklin, Ph.D.', *Internationalen Konferenz Farbe im Kopf, Universität Tübingen*, September 2016 *https://www.youtube.com/watch?v=XM3eZDg6xwg* (accessed January 2021)

Haller, Karen, *The Little Book of Colour*, London: Penguin, 2019

Harrison, Sara, 'A New Study About Color Tries to Decode 'The Brain's Pantone', *Wired*, 24 November 2020 *https://www.wired.com/story/a-new-study-about-color-tries-to-decode-the-brains-pantone* (accessed 10 December 2020)

Itten, Johannes, *The Art of Color: The Subjective Experience and Objective Rationale of Color*, New York: John Wiley & Sons, 2001 (1961)

Jongerius, Hella, '*I Don't Have a Favourite Colour*', Berlin: Gestalten, 2006

Loske, Alexandra, *Colour: A Visual History*, London: Ilex, 2017

Klee, Paul, 'On Modern Art' [lecture], Kunstverein, Jena, 26 January 1924, trans. Paul Findlay in *Paul Klee: On Modern Art*, London: Faber & Faber, 1948

Street, Ben, *Art Unfolded: A History of Art in Four Colours*, London: Ilex, 2018

Wohlfarth, Harry and Sam, Catherine, 'The Effect of Color Psychodynamic Environmental Modification upon Psychophysiological and Behavioral Reactions of Severely Handicapped children', *The International Journal of Biosocial Research*, Vol. 3, No. 1, 1982

Wright, Angela, *Beginner's guide to Colour Psychology*, London: Colour Affects, 1998

**Red**

Amar, Zohar, Gottlieb, Hugo, Iluz, David and Varshavsky, Lucy, 'The Scarlet Dye of the Holy Land', *BioScience*, Volume 55, Issue 12, December 2005 *https://academic.oup.com/bioscience/article/55/12/1080/407161* (accessed July 2020)

Coles, David, *Chromatopia: An Illustrated History of Colour*, London: Thames & Hudson, 2018

Geeraert, Amélie, 'Traditional Meanings of Colors in Japanese Culture', *Kokoro*, 15 June 2020 *https://kokoro-jp.com/culture/298* (accessed 1 August 2020)

'In Search of Forgotten Colours: Sachio Yoshioka and the Art of Natural Dyeing', Victoria & Albert Museum, 6 June 2018 *https://www.youtube.com/watch?v=7OiG-WjbCQA* (accessed August 2020)

Isean Honten, 'Beni: A Special Red Color Extracted from Safflower' *https://www.isehanhonten.co.jp/en/about* (accessed October 2020)

Kaukas-Havenhand, Lucinda, *Mid-Century Modern Interiors: The Ideas that Shaped Interior Design in America*, London: Bloomsbury, 2019

Larking, Matthew, 'Genta Ishizuka: Beneath and On the Surface', *Japan Times*, 13 August 2019 *https://www.japantimes.co.jp/culture/2019/08/13/arts/genta-ishizuka-beneath-surface* (accessed August 2020)

Liles, J.N, '*The Art and Craft of Natural Dyeing*, Knoxville: University of Tennessee Press, 1990

Nelson, Kate Megan, 'A Brief History of the Stoplight', *Smithsonian*, May 2018 *https://www.smithsonianmag.com/ innovation/brief-history-stoplight-180968734* (accessed September 2020)

Oxford Psychology Team, 'Seeing Red at the Olympics', *Oxford Education Blog*, 1 September 2016 *https://educationblog.oup.com/ secondary/psychology/seeing-red-at-the-olympics* (accessed August 2020)

Pastoureau, Michel, *Red: The History of a Color*, Princeton: Princeton University Press, 2016

Phipps, Elena, *Cochineal Red: The Art History of a Color*, New York: Metropolitan Museum of Art/Yale University Press, 2010

Spindler, Ellen, 'The Story of Cinnabar and Vermilion (HgS) at The Met', *Met Museum*, 28 February 2018 *https://www.metmuseum.org/blogs/ collection-insights/2018/cinna-bar-vermilion* (accessed July 2020)

Travis, Anthony S, 'Madder Red: A Revolutionary Colour', *Chemistry & Industry*, via Colorant History, 3 January 1994 *http://www.colorantshistory. org/MadderRed.html* (accessed November 2020)

Viegas, Jen, 'Why is the Colour Red so Powerful', *Seeker*, 2015 *https://www.seeker.com/why-is-the-color-red-so-powerful-photos-1769836764.html* (accessed August 2020)

Wininger, Aaron, 'China's Supreme Court Rules in Favor of Christian Louboutin's Red Sole Trademark', *The National Law Review*, 18 February 2020 *https://www.natlawreview.com/ article/china-s-supreme-court-rules-favor-christian-louboutin-s-red-sole-trademark* (accessed January 2021)

**Orange**
Atelier Éditions (Ed.), *An Atlas of Rare and Familiar Colour: The Harvard Art Museums' Forbes Pigment Collection*, Los Angeles: Atelier Éditions, 2019

Baker, Logan, 'Manipulating the Audience's Emotions with Color', *Premium Beat*, 2 August 2016 *https://www.premiumbeat.com/ blog/manipulate-emotions-with-color-in-film* (accessed October 2020)

Blumberg, Jess, 'A Brief History of the Amber Room', *Smithsonian*, 31 July 2007 *https://www.smithsonianmag. com/history/a-brief-history-of-the-amber-room-160940121* (accessed October 2020)

Chapman, John and Gaydarska, Bisserka, 'The Aesthetics of Colour and Brilliance', *Geoarchaeology and Archaeomineralogy Conference*, 2008 *http://citeseerx.ist.psu. edu/viewdoc/download?-doi=10.1.1.548.8669&rep=rep1&-type=pdf* (accessed October 2020)

Coles, David, *Chromatopia: An Illustrated History of Colour*, London: Thames & Hudson, 2018

'Conservators Struggle to Preserve True Original Colors of China's Terracotta Warriors', *Southern Weekly – Global Times*, 10 October 2017 *https://www.globaltimes.cn/ content/1069632.shtml* (accessed October 2020)

'Japanese Traditional Colors', Kidoraku Japan *http://kidoraku-japan.com/know/others_color. html* (accessed October 2020)

Maerz, Aloys John and M. Rea, *A Dictionary of Color'*, New York: McGraw-Hill, 1930

'Orange Light Helps Thinking' *Science Learning Hub*, 10 March 2014 *https://www.sciencelearn.org.nz/ resources/2290-orange-light-helps-thinking* (accessed October 2020)

Salamone, Lorenzo, 'The History of the Most Iconic Color of Luxury', *NSS Magazine*, 7 June 2020 *https://www.nssmag.com/en/fash-ion/22580/hermes-packaging-orange* (accessed October 2020)

Schüler, C. J, *Along the Amber Route: From St. Petersburg to Venice*, Inverness: Sandstone Press, 2020

Yates, Julian, 'Orange' in *Prismatic Ecology: Ecotheory Beyond Green*, ed. Jeffery Jerome Cohen, Minneapolis, University of Minnesota Press, 2013

**Yellow**
Atelier Éditions (Ed.), *An Atlas of Rare and Familiar Colour: The Harvard Art Museums' Forbes Pigment Collection*, Los Angeles: Atelier Éditions, 2019

Ball, Philip, *Bright Earth*, Kindle Edition: Vintage Digital, August 2012

Chatterjee, Meeta, 'Khadi: The Fabric of the Nation in Raja Rao's Kanthapura', *New Literatures Review*, Issue 36, June 2000

Griffith, Ralph T. H. (trans.), *The Rig Veda*, Santa Cruz: Evinity Publishing, March 2009

Han, Jing, 'Imperial Yellow: A Costume Colour at the Top of the Social Hierarchy', *The Asia Dialogue*, 22 July 2015 *https://theasiadialogue. com/2015/07/22/imperial-yellow-a-costume-colour-at-the-top-of-the-social-hierarchy* (accessed September 2020)

Harley, Rosamond D., *Artists' Pigments c.1600-1835*, London: Butterworth & Co., 1970

Hulsey, John and Trusty, Ann, 'Turner's Mysterious Yellow', *Artists Network* https://www.artistsnetwork.com/art-subjects/plein-air/turners-mysterious-yellow (accessed September 2020)

Indian Yellow', *Bulletin of Miscellaneous Information (Royal Botanic Gardens, Kew)*, No. 39, 1890 www.jstor.org/stable/4111404 (accessed September 2020)

Maerz, Aloys John and M. Rea, *A Dictionary of Color'*, New York: McGraw-Hill, 1930

Potts, Lauren and Rimmer, Monica, 'The Canary Girls: The Workers the War Turned Yellow', *BBC News*, 20 May 2017 https://www.bbc.co.uk/news/uk-england-39434504 (accessed September 2020)

Prance, Ghillean T. and Nesbitt, Mark, *The Cultural History of Plants*, New York: Routledge, 2005

Ravenscroft, Tom, 'Grey Brick and Yellow Polycarbonate Contrast to Create Striking Peckham Primary School', *Dezeen*, 27 July 2020 https://www.dezeen.com/2020/07/27/bellenden-primary-school-peckham-cottrell-vermeulen-architecture (accessed September 2020)

St Clair, Kassia, *The Secret Lives of Colour*, London: John Murray, 2016

Thorpe, Harriet, 'This Year's Dulwich Pavilion is Inspired by Nigerian Fabric Markets', *Wallpaper**, 3 June 2019 https://www.wallpaper.com/architecture/dulwich-pavilion-2019-pricegore-yinka-ilori-london (accessed September 2020)

Welbourne, Lauren, 'Human Colour Perception Changes Between Seasons', *Current Biology*, Volume 25, Issue 15, 3 August 2015 https://www.cell.com/current-biology/fulltext/S0960-9822(15)00724-1 (accessed September 2020)

Whybrow, Kayleigh, 'Influencing Learning with the Psychology of Colour', *Building 4 Education*, 26 August 2017 https://b4ed.com/Article/influencing-learning-with-the-psychology-of-colour (accessed September 2020)

Wilkinson, Tom, 'Gilt Complex: Buildings that Glitter', *Architectural Review*, 3 September 2019 https://www.architectural-review.com/essays/gilt-complex-buildings-that-glitter (accessed October 2020)

**Green**
Ball, Philip, '*Bright Earth*', Kindle Edition: Vintage Digital, August 2012

Barton, Chris, *The Day-Glo Brothers*, Watertown: Charlesbridge Publishing, 2009

Becker, Doreen, *Color Trends and Selection for Product Design*, Norwich: William Andrew, 2016

Berry, Jennifer, 'What Are the Benefits of Chlorophyll?', *Medical News Today*, 4 July 2018 https://www.medicalnewstoday.com/articles/322361 (accessed September 2020)

Coles, David, *Chromatopia: An Illustrated History of Colour*, London: Thames & Hudson, 2018

Ferro, Shaunacy, 'This Is the Most Visible Color in the World', *Mental Floss*, 10 May 2017 https://www.mentalfloss.com/article/500751/most-visible-color-world (accessed July 2020)

Finlay, Victoria, *Color: A Natural History of the Palette*, New York: Ballantine, 2002

Gerritsen, Anne and Riello, Giorgio, *The Global Lives of Things: The Material Culture of Connections in the Early Modern World*, New York: Routledge, 2015

Higham, James P., 'All the Colors That Human Vision Neglects', *The Atlantic*, 7 February 2018 https://www.theatlantic.com/science/archive/2018/02/seeing-red/552473 (accessed September 2020)

Lee, David, *Nature's Palette: The Science of Plant Color*, Chicago: University of Chicago Press, 2010

'Life Seacolors: Demonstration of New Natural Dyes from Algae as Substitution of Synthetic Dyes Actually Used by Textile Industries', *European Union Life Projects*, Third Newsletter, 1 July 2016 https://ec.europa.eu/environment/life/project/Projects/index.cfm?fuseaction=search.dspPage&n_proj_id=5017 (accessed September 2020)

Maerz, Aloys John and M. Rea, *A Dictionary of Color'*, New York: McGraw-Hill, 1930

Nierenberg, Cari 'A Green Scene Sparks our Creativity', *NBC News*, 28 March 2012 https://www.nbcnews.com/health/body-odd/green-scene-sparks-our-creativity-flna578364 (accessed July 2020)

Oakley, Howard, 'Pigment: The unusual green of Malachite', *The Eclectic Light Company*, 1 June 2018 https://eclecticlight.co/2018/06/01/pigment-the-unusual-green-of-malachite (accessed July 2020)

Pastoureau, Michel, *Green: The History of a Color*, Princeton: Princeton University Press, 2014

Pritchard, Emma-Louise, 'The Real Reason Wine and Beer Bottles are Only Ever Brown or Green', *Country Living*, March 9, 2017 *https://www.countryliving.com/ uk/create/food-and-drink/news/ a1465/reason-wine-beer-bottles-brown-green* (accessed July 2020)

'Textile Produced from Algae', *Sustainable Fashion*, 2 April 2020 *https://www.sustainablefashion. earth/type/recycling/textile-produced-from-algae* (accessed September 2020)

'Urban Algae Folly', ecoLogicStudio at Expo Milan 2015, 23 May 2015 *https://www.youtube.com/ watch?v=os2ZznTTIYA* (accessed September 2020)

Ziegler, Chris, 'Toyota's Weird, Bright Green Prius Uses Science to Stay Cooler in the Sun', *The Verge*, 12 February 2016 *https://www.theverge. com/2016/2/12/10979166/toyota-thermo-tect-lime-green-prius-sun-heat* (accessed August 2020)

**Blue**
Ball, Philip, *'Bright Earth'*, Kindle Edition: Vintage Digital, August 2012

'Blue Light Has a Dark Side', *Harvard Health Publishing*, May 2012; updated 7 July 2020 *https://www.health.harvard.edu/ staying-healthy/blue-light-has-a-dark-side* (accessed August 2020)

Brown, D., Barton, J. & Gladwell, V., 'Viewing Nature Scenes Positively Affects Recovery of Autonomic Function Following Acute-Mental Stress', *Environmental Science & Technology*, 4 June 2013 *https://www.ncbi.nlm.nih.gov/ pmc/articles/PMC3699874* (accessed February and June 2020)

Cascone, Sarah, 'The Chemist Who Discovered the World's Newest Blue Explains Its Miraculous Properties', *Artnetnews*, 20 June 2016 *https://news.artnet.com/art-world/ yinmn-blue-to-be-sold-commercially-520433* (accessed February 2020)

Cifuentes, Beatriz and Vignelli, Massimo, *Design: Vignelli: Graphics, Packaging, Architecture, Interiors, Furniture, Products*, New York: Rizzoli International Publications, 2018

Coles, David, *Chromatopia: An Illustrated History of Colour*, London: Thames & Hudson, 2018

Geldof, Muriel and Steyn, Lise, 'Van Gogh's Cobalt Blue: Van Gogh's Studio Practice', *Mercatorfonds*, July 2013 *https://www.researchgate.net/publication/304626297_Van_Gogh's_Cobalt_Blue* (accessed July 2020)

Koddenberg, Matthias, *Yves Klein: In/Out Studio*, Dortmund: Verlag Kettler, 2016

Loske, Alexandra, *Colour: A Visual History*, London: Ilex, 2017

Maerz, Aloys John and M. Rea, *A Dictionary of Color'*, New York: McGraw-Hill, 1930

McCouat, Philip, 'Prussian Blue and Its Partner in Crime', *Journal of Art in Society*, 2014 *http://www.artinsociety.com/ prussian-blue-and-its-partner-in-crime.html* (accessed July 2020)

McKinley, Catherine, *Indigo*, London: Bloomsbury, 2011

Meier, Allison, 'Lapis Lazuli: A Blue More Precious than Gold', *Hyperallergic*, 5 August 2016 *https://hyperallergic.com/315564/ lapis-lazuli-a-blue-more-precious-than-gold* (accessed February 2020)

Morris, William, *The Collected Letters of William Morris, Volume I: 1848-1880*, ed. Norman Kelvin, Princeton: Princeton University Press, 2014

Pappas, Stephanie, 'Oldest Indigo-Dyed Fabric Ever Is Discovered in Peru', *Live Science*, 14 September 2016 *https://www.livescience.com/ 56099-oldest-indigo-dyed-fabric-discovered-peru.html* (accessed March 2020)

Penrose, Nancy L., 'Curious Blue', *Hand and Eye Magazine*, 19 September 2012 *http://handeyemagazine.com/ content/curious-blue* (accessed February 2020)

Roy, Ashok, 'Monet's Palette in the Twentieth Century: "Water-Lilies" and "Irises"', *The National Gallery Technical Bulletin*, Volume 28, 2007 *https://www.nationalgallery. org.uk/upload/pdf/roy2007.pdf* (accessed March 2020)

St Clair, Kassia, *The Secret Lives of Colour*, London: John Murray, 2016

Street, Ben, *Art Unfolded: A History of Art in Four Colours*, London: Ilex, 2018

Taggart, Emma, 'The History of the Color Blue: From Ancient Egypt to the Latest Scientific Discoveries', *My Modern Met*, 12 February 2018 *https://mymodernmet.com/shades-of-blue-color-history* (accessed 22 February 2020)

**Pink & Purple**
Atkinson, Diane, *The Purple, White & Green: Suffragettes in London 1906-14*, London: Museum of London, 1992

Becker, Doreen, *Color Trends and Selection for Product Design*, Norwich: William Andrew, 2016

‘Colour Coded’, *Faber Futures*, 2018 *https://faberfutures.com/projects/project-coelicolor/colour-coded* (accessed 12 February 2020)

Garfield, Simon, *‘Mauve: How One Man Invented a Colour that Changed the World*, London: W. W. Norton & Company, 2002

Gilliam, James E. and Unruh, David, ‘The Effects of Baker-Miller Pink on Biological, Physical and Cognitive Behaviour,’ *Journal of Orthomolecular Medicine*, Volume 3, Number 4, 1988 *http://www.orthomolecular.org/library/jom/1988/pdf/1988-v03n04-p202.pdf* (accessed February 2020)

Hofmeister, Sandra, ‘What Colour Was the Bauhaus?’ *Kvadrat Interwoven* *http://kvadratinterwoven.com/colours-at-bauhaus* (accessed March 2020)

Jongerius, Hella, *‘I Don’t Have a Favourite Colour’*, Berlin: Gestalten, 2006

Kandinsky, Nina, *Kandinsky und Ich*, Kindle version: München, 1976

Liffreing, Ilyse, ‘Millennial Pink: A Timeline for the Color that Refuses to Fade’, *DigiDay*, 31 July 2017 *https://digiday.com/marketing/millennial-pink-timeline-color-refuses-fade* (accessed February 2020)

Maerz, Aloys John and M. Rea, *A Dictionary of Color’*, New York: McGraw-Hill, 1930

Rizzo, Alice, ‘Coronavirus: The Posters Spreading Kindness Across London’, *BBC News*, 17 April 2020 *https://www.bbc.co.uk/news/uk-england-london-52315966* (accessed June 2020)

Schauss, A.G., ‘Tranquilising Effect of Colour Reduces Aggressive Behaviour and Potential Violence, in Orthomolecular Psychiartry’, *International Journal of Biosocial and Medical Research*, Vol. 8, No. 4, 25 May 1985 *https://www.researchgate.net/publication/242777200_Tranquilizing_Effect_of_Color_Reduces_Aggressive_Behavior_and_Potential_Violence* (accessed February 2020)

St Clair, Kassia, *The Secret Lives of Colour*, London: John Murray, 2016

Stavely-Wadham, Rose, ‘Beetroot, Barley and Brilliantine: Historic Makeup Tips and Tricks from the British Newspaper Archive’, *British Newspaper Archive*, 7 September 2020 *https://blog.britishnewspaperarchive.co.uk/2020/09/07/historic-makeup-tips-and-tricks* (accessed September 2020)

Steele, Valerie (ed.), *Pink: The History of a Punk, Pretty, Powerful Color*, London: Thames & Hudson, 2018

Thavapalan, Shiyanthi and Warburton, David A. (eds), *The Value of Colour: Material and Economic Aspects in the Ancient World*, Berlin: Edition Topoi, 2020

Uffindell, Andrew, ‘Austro-Sardinian War: Battle of Magenta’, *Military History*, June 1996 *https://www.historynet.com/austro-sardinian-war-battle-of-magenta.htm* (accessed February 2020)

‘UNESCO World Heritage Bauhaus Houses with Balcony Access in Dessau’, *Bauhaus Dessau* *https://www.bauhaus-dessau.de/en/talks/houses-with-balcony-access.html* (accessed June 2020)

**White & Pale**

Atelier Éditions (Ed.), *An Atlas of Rare and Familiar Colour: The Harvard Art Museums’ Forbes Pigment Collection*, Los Angeles: Atelier Éditions, 2019

Buckley-Jones, Kiera, ‘All Your Questions about Eco-Friendly Paints Answered’, *Elle Decoration*, 10 June 2020 *https://www.elledecoration.co.uk/decorating/a32767488/all-your-questions-about-eco-friendly-paints-answered* (accessed September 2020)

Cleaver, Emily, ‘Against All Odds, England’s Massive Chalk Horse Has Survived 3,000 Years’, *Smithsonian*, 6 July 2017 *https://www.smithsonianmag.com/history/3000-year-old-uffington-horse-looms-over-english-countryside-180963968* (accessed September 2020)

Coles, David, *Chromatopia: An Illustrated History of Colour*, London: Thames & Hudson, 2018

Eisler, Maryam and Pawson, John, ‘At Home with the Master of Minimalism: John Pawson’, *Lux Magazine*, 2018 *https://www.lux-mag.com/john-pawson* (accessed September 2020)

Hara, Kenya, *White*, Baden: Lars Müller, 2009

Hutchings, Freya, ‘Next Generation: Elissa Brunato’s Bio Iridescent Sequin Shimmers with Nature’, *Next Nature*, 29 January 2020 *https://nextnature.net/2020/01/interview-elissa-brunato* (accessed September 2020)

Kinoshita, Shuichi and Yoshioka, Shinya, *Structural Colors in Biological Systems*, Osaka: Osaka University Press, 2005

Logan, Jason, *Make Ink: A Forager's Guide to Natural Inkmaking*, New York: Abrams, 2018

McGrath, Katherine, 'These Are the Best-Selling Sherwin-Williams Paint Colors', *Architectural Digest*, 6 July 2017 *https://www.architecturaldigest.com/story/best-sherwin-williams-paint-colors* (accessed October 2020)

McKie, Robin, 'Earth has Lost 28 Trillion Tonnes of Ice in Less Than 30 Years', *The Guardian*, 23 August 2020 *https://www.theguardian.com/environment/2020/aug/23/earth-lost-28-trillion-tonnes-ice-30-years-global-warming* (accessed September 2020)

Nansen, Fridtjof, *Farthest North*, New York: Modern Library, 1999 (1897)

Pawson, John, 'White on White', *John Pawson Journal*, January 2016 *http://www.johnpawson.com/journal/white-on-white* (accessed September 2020)

Saftig, Steven, 'Lunar White Move: A Conversation with Sonos's Design Director of Color, Material, Finish', Sonos, 2020 *https://blog.sonos.com/en-gb/move-lunar-white* (accessed November 2020)

**Grey & Dark**
Atelier Éditions (Ed.), *An Atlas of Rare and Familiar Colour: The Harvard Art Museums' Forbes Pigment Collection*, Los Angeles: Atelier Éditions, 2019

Brill, Robert H, 'The Chemical Interpretation of the Texts', *Glass and Glassmaking in Ancient Mesopotamia*, ed. Leo Oppenheimer, via The Corning Museum of Glass, 1970 *https://www.cmog.org/sites/default/files/collections/EE/*

*EECF0FB5-8390-48EA-8B17-0050D4AADB3F.pdf* (accessed July 2020)

Coles, David, *Chromatopia: An Illustrated History of Colour*, London: Thames & Hudson, 2018

Hitti, Natashah, 'Hyundai Unveils Electric Vehicle Concept that Looks like a "Perfectly Weathered Stone"', *Dezeen*, 5 March 2020 *https://www.dezeen.com/2020/03/05/hyundai-prophecy-electric-vehicle-concept* (accessed September 2020)

Imbabi, Mohammed S., Carrigan, Collette and McKenna, Sean, 'Trends and Developments in Green Cement and Concrete Technology', *International Journal of Sustainable Built Environment*, Volume 1, Issue 2, December 2012 *https://www.sciencedirect.com/science/article/pii/S2212609013000071* (accessed July 2020)

Katona, Brian G., Siegel, Earl G and Cluxton Jr, Robert J., 'The New Black Magic: Activated Charcoal and New Therapeutic Uses', *The Journal of Emergency Medicine*, Volume 5, Issue 1, 1987 *https://www.sciencedirect.com/science/article/abs/pii/0736467987900047* (accessed October 2020)

Logan, Jason, *Make Ink: A Forager's Guide to Natural Inkmaking*, New York: Abrams, 2018

Maerz, Aloys John and M. Rea, *A Dictionary of Color'*, New York: McGraw-Hill, 1930

'"Modern Nature" Exhibit Explores Georgia O'Keeffe's Love Affair With The Adirondacks', *HuffPost*, [updated] 6 December 2017 *https://www.huffpost.com/entry/modern-nature-georgia-oke_n_4044942* (accessed January 2021)

Saunders, Nicholas J., 'A Dark Light: Reflections on Obsidian in Mesoamerica' in *World Archaeology Vol. 33*, New York: Routledge, 2001 *https://www.academia.edu/2424264/A_Dark_Light_Reflections_on_Obsidian_in_Mesoamerica* (accessed 17 September)

Sharma, Nisha, Agarwal, Anuja, Negi, Y. S., Bhardwaj, Hemant and Jaiswal, Jatin, 'History and Chemistry of Ink: A Review', *World Journal of Pharmaceutical Research*, Volume 3, Issue 4, 2014 *https://wjpr.net/admin/assets/article_issue/1404208081.pdf* (accessed September 2020)

Stathaki, Ellie, 'Step Inside Asif Khan's Dark Pavilion for the Winter Olympics', *Wallpaper**, 7 February 2018 *https://www.wallpaper.com/architecture/asif-khan-pavilion-winter-olympics-south-korea-2018* (accessed September 2020)

Stengel, Jim, 'Jack Daniel's Secret: The History of the World's Most Famous Whiskey', *The Atlantic*, 9 January 2012 *https://www.theatlantic.com/business/archive/2012/01/jack-daniels-secret-the-history-of-the-worlds-most-famous-whiskey/250966* (accessed September 2020)

Webb, Marcus, 'Shifting Sands', *Delayed Gratification*, Issue 36, 2019

Winston, Anna, 'Young Designers Are Making Aluminium "More Desirable" for Collectors' *Dezeen*, 16 May 2019 *https://www.dezeen.com/2019/05/16/aluminium-furniture-design-collectors* (accessed July 2020)

**Brown**
Atelier Éditions (Ed.), *An Atlas of Rare and Familiar Colour: The Harvard Art Museums' Forbes*

*Pigment Collection*, Los Angeles: Atelier Éditions, 2019

Ball, Philip, *Bright Earth*, Kindle Edition: Vintage Digital, August 2012

Becker, Doreen, *Color Trends and Selection for Product Design*, Norwich: William Andrew, 2016

'Benjamin Brecknell Turner – Working Methods', Victoria & Albert Museum *https://www.vam.ac.uk/articles/benjamin-brecknell-turner-working-methods* (accessed October 2020)

Coles, David, *Chromatopia: An Illustrated History of Colour*, London: Thames & Hudson, 2018

Dejoie, C., Sciau, P., Li, W. *et al.*, 'Learning from the Past: Rare $\varepsilon$-Fe$_2$O$_3$ in the Ancient, Black-Glazed Jian (*Tenmoku*) Wares', *Nature Briefing, Scientific Reports*, Volume 4, 13 May 2014 *https://www.nature.com/articles/srep04941* (accessed October 2020)

Grovier, Kelly 'Umber: The Colour of Debauchery' *BBC News*, 19 September 2018 *https://www.bbc.com/culture/article/20180919-umber-the-colour-of-debauchery* (accessed October 2020)

Karagiannidou, Evrykleia G. 'Colors in the Prehistoric and Archaic Era', Chemica Chronica/ Association of Greek Chemists (EEX) via *Chemistry Views*, 6 March 2018 *https://www.chemistryviews.org/details/ezine/10872110/Colors_in_the_Prehistoric_and_Archaic_Era.html* (accessed October 2020)

Klee, Paul, *The Thinking Eye*, Notebooks Volume 1, London: Percy Lund, Humphries & Co., Ltd, 1961

Loske, Alexandra, *Colour: A Visual History*, London: Ilex, 2017

Moriarty, Catherine, 'Dust to Dust: A Particular History of Khaki', *Textile The Journal of Cloth and Culture*, November 2010 *https://www.researchgate.net/publication/233680235_Dust_to_Dust_A_Particular_History_of_Khaki* (accessed October 2020)

Plank, Melanie, 'How Sustainable Is Paper And Cardboard Packaging?', *Common Objective*, January 2020 *https://www.commonobjective.co/article/how-sustainable-is-paper-and-cardboard-packaging* (accessed October 2020)

St Clair, Kassia, *The Secret Lives of Colour*, London: John Murray, 2016

West FitzHugh, Elisabeth (ed.), *Artists' Pigments: A Handbook of Their History and Characteristics*, Volume 3, Washington: National Gallery of Art, 199

# Quotes

**8**
Eastlake, Charles L., '*Goethe's Theory of Colours*', London: John Murray, 1840

**12**
Jongerius, Hella, '*I Don't Have a Favourite Colour*', Berlin: Gestalten, 2006

**29**
Albers, Josef *The Interaction of Color: 50th Anniversary Edition*, New Haven and London: Yale University Press, 2013 (1963)

**34**
Kerouac, Jack, *On The Road*, London: Penguin Classics, 2000 (1957)

**41**
Itten, Johannes, *The Art of Color: The Subjective Experience and Objective Rationale of Color*, New York: John Wiley & Sons, 2001 (1961)

**76–7**
Stein, Gertrude, *Picasso*, New York: Dover Publications, 2000 (1938)

**194–5**
Koddenberg, Matthias, *Yves Klein: In/Out Studio*, Dortmund: Verlag Kettler, 2016

**212–3**
Ball, Philip, *Bright Earth*, Kindle Edition: Vintage Digital, August 2012

**222**
Schiaparelli, Elsa, *Shocking Life: The Autobiography of Elsa Schiaparelli*, London: V&A, 2007

# Index

# Picture Credits



Ilex would like to acknowledge and thank the following for providing images for use in this book:

13 Courtesy Galerie kreo. Photo © Sylvie Chan-Liat; 16 Studio Olafur Eliasson Boros Collection, Germany. Photo: María del Pilar García Ayensa; 18 Karl Gaff/Science Photo Library; 27 © The Josef and Anni Albers Foundation/DACS 2021. Image: Yale University Press; 31 Mint Images Ltd/Alamy Stock Photo; 43 Wikimedia/Creative Commons Attribution-Share Alike 3.0 © 2007 Jacob Rus, 2007; 45 Mika Baumeister/Unsplash; 55 Courtesy Agnė Kučerenkaitė; 56 Photo: Cyrille Wiener; 59 Library of Congress, Department of Prints and Drawings; 61 album/Alamy Stock Photo; 63 Illustration courtesy of Shepard Fairey/Obeygiant.com; 65 Metropolitan Museum of Art, New York, Gift of George D. Pratt, 1930; 67 akg-images; 69 Courtesy of ARTCOURT Gallery. Photo: Takeru Koroda; 71 Robert Harding/Alamy Stock Photo; 73 © Banco de México Diego Rivera Frida Kahlo Museums Trust, Mexico, D.F./DACS 2021. Photo: Archivart/Alamy Stock Photo; 75 Victoria and Albert Museum, London; 79 Courtesy Ward Wijnant. Photo: Ronald Smits; 81 Beatie Wolfe; 83 Courtesy Marco Menghi and Mandalaki; 87 © The Barnett Newman Foundation, New York/DACS, London 2021. Photo: World History Archive/ akg-images; 89 Ashmolean Museum, Oxford/ Bridgeman Images; 91 Russ Images/Alamy Stock Photo; 93 Brionvega is a brand of BV2 srl Milano: the Brionvega Art Products Company, www.brionvega.it. Photo: Giorgio Serinelli; 95 Robert Morris/Alamy Stock Photo; 97 Artokoloro/Alamy Stock Photo; 99 Galit Seligmann/Alamy Stock Photo; 101 Jimlop Collection/Alamy Stock Photo; 103 © Keith Haring Foundation; 105 Victor Virgile/Gamma-Rapho via Getty Images; 109 Metropolitan Museum of Art, New York, Cynthia Hazen Polsky and Leon B. Polsky Fund, 2006; 111 Fabric dyed by Joanna Fowles. Stylist: Megan Morton, photo: Pablo Viega; 113 © Succession H. Matisse/DACS 2021. Photo: Museum of Fine Arts, Houston. Museum purchase funded by Audrey Jones Beck/Bridgeman Images; 115 Photo: Anthony Coleman; 116 Nathaniel Noir/Alamy Stock Photo: 119 incamerastock/Alamy Stock Photo; 121 Metropolitan Museum of Art, New York, Rogers Fund, 1949; 123 Pascal Le Segretain/Getty Images; 125 PAINTING/Alamy Stock Photo; 127 Marco Montalti/ Alamy Stock Photo; 129 Courtesy Studio RENS. Photo Ronald Smits; 131 Merrill Images/Getty Image; 132 Giacomo Pasqua/ Shutterstock; 137 Matteo Omied/Alamy Stock Photo; 139 Styling by Yenchen & Yawen Studio. Photo: Anna Pors (annaslichter. com); 141 Courtesy of Fornasetti; 143 Photo © Christie's Images/Bridgeman Images; 145 National Gallery of Art, Washington, Chester Dale Collection; 147 Courtesy Ptolemy Mann; 149 Vitra UK © Studio Bouroullec; 151 Courtesy Parley for the Oceans; 153 Little Greene; 155 Illustration by Oleksandr Khoma/Dreamstime.com; 156 Rob Kim/Getty Images; 159 Virgile/Gamma-Rapho via Getty Images; 161 Timothy A Clary/Getty Images; 163 Courtesy Delft School of Microbiology Archives at Delft University of Technology, The Netherlaands; 165 Marion Carniel/Alamy Stock Photo; 169 IItajime airvase, designed by Torafu Architects and manufactured by Fukunaga Print Co. Photo Kyoko Nishimoto/Buaisou; 171 incamerastock/Alamy Stock Photo; 173 Francois Guillot/AFP via Getty Images; 175 Heritage Image Partnership Ltd/Alamy Stock Photo; 177 Photo © Christie's Images/Bridgeman Images; 179 © Succession Picasso/DACS, London 2021. Photo National Galleries of Scotland, Edinburgh/Bridgeman Images; 181 Metropolitan Museum of Art, New York, Rogers Fund, 1926; 183 © Estate of William Scott 2021. Photo © Tate; 185 Alfredo Dagli Orti/Shutterstock; 187 Courtesy Dulux; 189 © Olivetti SpA. Photo Bahadir Yeniceri/Dreamstime.com; 191 © MTA. Used with permission; 193 © Succession Yves Klein c/o ADAGP, Paris and DACS, London 2021. Photo © Phillips Auctioneers Ltd; 197 Photo: Mercedes-Benz AG; 199 Courtesy Kremer Pigmente; 203 Raffaello Bencini/Bridgeman Images; 205 Victor Boyko/Getty Images; 207 Archives Charmet/Bridgeman Images; 209 © Jeff Koons. Photo © 2017 Fredrik Nilsen. Courtesy Gagosian; 211 Neil Juggins/Stockimo/ Alamy Stock Photo; 215 Peter White/Getty Images; 217 WBC Art/Alamy Stock Photo; 218 Courtesy JACK ARTS; 221 Philadelphia Museum of Art. Gift of Mme Elsa Schiaparelli, 1969/Bridgeman Images; 223 Robert van Hoenderdaal/ Alamy Stock Photo; 225 Courtesy Vollebak. Photo Andy Lo Po; 227 © Stephen Flavin/Artists Rights Society (ARS), New York 2021. Photo: Bridgeman Images; 229 Photo © Thomas Rusch; 231 Victor Boyko/Getty Images; 233 Arcaid Images/Alamy Stock Photo; 235 Courtesy Mutina. Photo Gerhardt Kellermann; 237 © 2020 Nicole Stjernswärd, Kaiku Living Color; 239 Wim Van Egmond/Science Photo Library; 241 Courtesy Puma; 245 Photo by Carol Beckwith and Angela Fisher. Courtesy THK Gallery; 247 Rijksmuseum, Amsterdam. On loan from the City of Amsterdam (A. van der Hoop Bequest); 249 Metropolitan Museum of Art, New York, Gift of Alexander Götz, in honor of Samuel Eilenberg, 1996; 251 © Yesenia Thibault-Picazo; 253 Pixelformula/ SIPA/Shutterstock; 255 Courtesy Sonos; 257 © Andy Goldsworthy. Courtesy Galerie Lelong & Co; 259 © Tonkin Liu; 261 © British Library Board. All Rights Reserved/Bridgeman Images; 263 © Elissa Brunato; 267 Richard Bord/WireImage/Getty Images; 269 Courtesy Wendy Andreu & Bram Vanderbeke; 271 Patrik Slezak/ Shutterstock; 273 Metropolitan Museum of Art, New York, The Howard Mansfield Collection, Purchase, Rogers Fund, 1936; 275 © Assemble; 277 Courtesy Studio ThusThat; 279 Photo: Luisa Zanzani, Formafantasma; 281 Courtesy Keiko Shimoda, www.kcalligraphy.com; 283 © Georgia O'Keeffe Museum/DACS 2021. Photo: Art Resource/Scala, Florence; 285 Courtesy Seungjoon Song; 287 Luke Hayes/Asif Khan via Getty Images; 291 William Morris Gallery, London Borough of Waltham Forest; 293 Niday Picture Library/Alamy Stock Photo; 295 agefotostock/Alamy Stock Photo; 297 Saša Fuis/Van Ham, Cologne/akg images; 299 Photo: Studio Laura Daza; 301 © Agnes Martin Foundation, New York/DACS 2021. Photo © Christie's Images/Bridgeman Images; 303 Mike Floyd/Daily Mail/Shutterstock; 305 Courtesy Vitra; 307 Courtesy Neri Oxman and the Mediated Matter Group. Produced by Stratasys Ltd.

# Acknowledgements

Many thanks to all the designers and colour makers
I was able to interview and garner individual and
unique colour stories from, which informed much of
the raw research material, especially during lockdown
restrictions. Particular mentions go to Laura Luchtman
and Ilfa Siebenhaar from Living Colour Collective, and
to Agnė Kučerenkaitė for introducing me to a world of
fascinating and game-changing nuances.

Many thanks to Ellie Corbett for seeking me out
and supporting the bandwidth of colour this book
covers. To the editorial, picture, and design team,
including Rachel Silverlight, Ben Gardiner and Giulia
Hetherington, whose expertise brought it all together.

Special thanks to Sarah Conway – writer and
friend – for lending the time to discuss colour's endless
possibilities and the importance of the narrative, and
to Laura Salter for assisting on the research just at
the right moment. An extra special mention to my
husband Daniel for supporting me always, reading
many drafts and making shrewd comments and
suggestions, and building me a beautiful garden studio
to write in. This book is also dedicated to my late
grandmother Kitty, who always loved to read. It was
one of her life pleasures to sit with a book and get
lost, if only just for a few hours.